Liberal Democracy and Political Science

Liberal Democracy and Political Science

JAMES W. CEASER

JOHNS HOPKINS UNIVERSITY PRESS
Baltimore and London

Printed in the United States of America on acid-free paper

Originally published, 1990
Johns Hopkins Paperbacks edition, 1992

The Johns Hopkins University Press, 701 West 40th Street, Baltimore,
Maryland 21211-2190
The Johns Hopkins Press Ltd., London

LIBRARY OF CONGRESS CATALOGING-IN-PUBLICATION DATA

Ceaser, James W.
Liberal democracy and political science / James W. Ceaser.
p. cm.
Includes bibliographical references (p.).
ISBN 0-8018-3985-8 (alk. paper) ISBN 0-8018-4511-4 (pbk.)
1. Political science—United States—History. 2. Political scientists—United States—History. 3. Democracy—History. 4. Liberalism—United States—History. 5. Representative government and representation—United States—History. 6. Political culture—United States—History. I. Title.
JA84.U5C43 1990
320′.0973—dc20 89-27310
CIP

To Blaire

Contents

Acknowledgments ix
Introduction 1
1. What Is Liberal Democracy? 5
2. How Liberal Is Liberal Democracy? 26
3. Traditional Political Science 41
4. Modern Political Science 70
5. Reconstructing Political Science 94
6. The New Normativism 114
7. Political Science and the Political Culture of Liberal Democracy 143
8. The Constitution and Its Critics 177
Notes 211
Index 235

Acknowledgments

I WOULD LIKE TO THANK the Bradley Institute for Democracy at Marquette University and the Center for Advanced Studies at the University of Virginia for their kind support while writing this book. I am also greatly indebted to friends and colleagues who commented on parts of the manuscript: Harvey Mansfield, Jr., Randall Strahan, Jeffery Tulis, Steven Rhoads, Philippe Bénéton, Michael Brint, Michael Joseph Smith, Gary Marks, David Nichols, and Stephen Elkin. A number of graduate students at the University of Virginia helped me by reading, criticizing, and editing different drafts: Andrew Busch, Cary Federman, William Aniskovich, John Frazier, and Margaret Brabant. Finally, I would like to thank the editors at the Johns Hopkins University Press, in particular, Jane Warth, for her patience and expert assistance in preparing this book for publication.

Liberal Democracy and Political Science

Introduction

Liberal democracy is home to most political scientists, and most political scientists make liberal democracy—or some aspect of it—the focus of their life's work. One might think, therefore, that the relationship between political science and liberal democracy would be one of the first questions political scientists consider. But this is not the case. Political scientists "do" political science, but they seldom examine the status of that activity as a part of the phenomena they study.

This omission is all the more curious in our times, when modern philosophy insists on an acute self-consciousness as the starting point for any kind of human inquiry. Philosophers remind social scientists that they are not only subjects engaged in the activity of studying reality but also that their activity itself is part of the reality they study. To acquire a full picture of society therefore involves both practicing social science and taking account of the implications and consequences of practicing it. An acknowledgment of the dual nature of social science represents the highest kind of awareness: thought taking cognizance of itself.

None, of course, but the most precocious in political science will be troubled by violating any of these speculative injunctions of modern philosophy. It is quite a different matter, however, for political scientists to disregard the practical maxims of their discipline. Can political science justify its inattention to its own activities, or does it stand condemned by its own standards?

Political science today is a powerful force in society. It educates thousands of students about political life and helps shape the intellectual environment in which discussions of public policy and institutional change occur. As a major activity or enterprise in society, political science clearly merits inclusion in the "power elite," however much political scientists may resist being put in a category they have reserved for Wall Street bankers and the heads of large corporations. Because political science aims to understand how liberal democracy works, it cannot legitimately exempt an important societal force such as itself from consideration.

This line of reasoning can be extended a bit further. Political science not only describes specific liberal democratic systems but also reflects on the properties of liberal democracy as a general type or model. Just as political scientists explore the potential effects on liberal democracy of alternative arrangements of general factors like the electoral system or the legal system, so they should consider the potential effects of alternative arrangements for the discipline of political science. Their own logic compels equal treatment.

It is only a short step from inquiring about what political science *could* do in society to asking what it *should* do. To be sure, the Is (or the Could Be) cannot resolve the Ought; questions of value are not reducible to questions of fact. But neither is it the case that an intelligent prescription for political science is a purely normative matter that can be determined by bold proclamations of one's values. Discovering the consequences for society of alternative ways of practicing political science is an inquiry that is in principle analytic or empirical, not normative. It is difficult to see how any responsible choice about the character of the discipline could entirely ignore these consequences.

In this book, I have made the relationship between liberal democracy and political science an object of conscious examination. Although this kind of inquiry might seem to invite indulgence in abstract matters of epistemology or methodology, it points in quite the opposite direction. It leads to a consideration of the major practical concern of traditional political science: the factors that support and undermine different political systems. Only now, the discipline of political science itself is included among the factors to be examined.

My analysis of liberal democracy arrives at the conclusion, well known to the founders of this type of regime, that liberal democracy has a special need for political science. Liberal democracy depends on political science for its well-being to a greater extent than any other form of government. Not any kind of political science, however, can answer this need. It must be a political science that is conscious of the intellectual niche potentially open to it in modern society and that is willing to engage in a constructive enterprise on behalf of liberal democracy. Just because liberal democracy needs political science, of course, is no reason for those in political science to make any kind of commitment to it. However comforting it may be to feel needed, especially for those in a profession that suffers from such acute problems of self-esteem, political scientists must have their own grounds for devoting part of the profession's activity to the service of a given regime.

Whether such grounds exist is an open question. But in the profession today, it is unlikely to be treated as open, at least by those who set the discipline's intellectual agenda. Any suggestion that political science should in some sense be engaged in support of liberal democracy is certain to run into objections that reflect the prejudices of the two major establishments that dominate the discipline today.

The first objection, which comes from the positivist or behavioral school, is that a political science devoted in some way to helping liberal democracy will degrade the discipline, transforming it from a science into a form of civic education. According to this school, the true scientist cannot be engaged in promoting some part of his or her material, which is only so much data to be processed and analyzed. Some in the profession even go so far as to take a curious pride in spurning the needs of liberal democracy, as if an ascetic detachment constituted the surest proof of a genuine commitment to objective social science. I have never understood, however, why one should give a privileged position to this narrow understanding of social science, which incidentally is so manifestly asocial. If a body of knowledge can succeed in accounting for its own activity in the scheme of human affairs, including a certain kind of engagement for itself, there seems no valid reason to treat it as an inferior order of knowledge. Nor does a political science that assists liberal democracy necessarily lower itself to the status of routine civic education. If the enterprise on behalf of liberal democracy derives from a framework supplied by political science, not by liberal democracy, then even if the two should work along parallel lines, political science has not bowed to another master. Finally, to say that political science may assist liberal democracy in no way means that this task exhausts its purposes or constitutes its only or highest horizon.

The second objection, quite unlike the first, is not that political science is wrong to undertake an engagement on behalf of a political regime, but that it is wrong to undertake it on behalf of liberal democracy. This objection comes from a large number of those who today espouse a normative approach to political science. Political science, in this view, should put itself on the side of justice and right. But justice and right are not today on the side of liberal democracy. Liberal democracy is defective and retrograde. It does not realize the highest values or norms of which society is capable. The task of political science is to work for the achievement of these higher values or norms. If liberal democracy must be replaced in the process—which seems almost a certainty—then we can only welcome the new and more progressive options that lie before us. Taking up this objection would lead to an inquiry into the ultimate grounds for preferring one political system over another, which goes beyond my purpose in this book. At a different level, however, I have been struck by how many of the criticisms of liberal democracy made today in the name of justice have lost connection with a systematic treatment of political systems. The renaissance of the study of values and justice in the discipline—what I suppose should be called the new normativism—has drifted into an exercise of positing (or discovering) norms and then proposing policies to realize them—all without reference to the concrete forms of government in which these norms might be embedded. It is political philosophy without political science.

As the major establishments of political science have their own interests to protect, I am under no illusion that a proposal for a different role for political science can meet with a welcome reception. At the same time, there is a notable uneasiness in the discipline today in regard to both its proper focus and its methods. The moment may therefore be right to reconsider the function of political science, not just as an academic discipline in our universities, but as an important human enterprise in a free society.

1

What Is Liberal Democracy?

TO SPEAK NOWADAYS of a "crisis" of liberal democracy—or, more ominously, of "*the* crisis of liberal democracy"—is more than a commonplace; it is a cliché. For spokesmen of the Left, liberal democracy in the early 1980s was verging on economic collapse, a near-victim of its reliance on the outmoded system of capitalism. Today, these same writers are apt to deplore the excesses of capitalism, in particular the growth of selfish attitudes among the young and a reckless disregard for a looming environmental catastrophe. For spokesmen of the Right, liberal democracy a decade ago was likewise threatened with economic disaster, the cause being the cumulative effect of years of creeping statism. Even more important, liberal democracy suffered then—and continues to suffer today—from a breakdown of moral standards and a loss of will.

Whether talk of a crisis is meant to be taken literally, or is now just a literary device designed to indicate a seriousness of purpose, it is difficult to say. At least on the surface, liberal democracy—whatever crisis it may happen to be experiencing—seems today to be the envy of those who do not possess it and the model toward which more and more nations aspire. To avoid any possible confusion, therefore, I prefer to speak in this chapter not of a crisis of liberal democracy, but of a problem. Moreover, the problem I have in mind is of a different kind than the various crises identified by the Left and the Right. It is a problem that goes beyond substance to structure. Liberal democracy has need of an intellectual discipline or enterprise in society that is devoted to maintaining it. The absence of this enterprise today—indeed its improbability given the prevailing ideas of what the social sciences should be doing—puts liberal democracy at risk, if not immediately, then in the long run.

To speak of a structural problem for liberal democracy implies, of course, that liberal democracy has a certain structure. Describing that structure must be my first task.

The Structure of Liberal Democracy

The names that political analysts usually employ to identify the dominant form of government in the West, especially when striving for a degree of precision, are compounds. The list of these names, which is remarkably long, includes *liberal democracy, constitutional republic, democratic republic, constitutional democracy, representative democracy, and representative republic*.

Is this linguistic practice of using compounds an accident, or does it reflect something fundamental about the nature of this form of government? The unsatisfactory experience with simple terms, such as *republic, democracy*, or *polyarchy*, may help provide an answer. All simple terms have proven inadequate. James Madison was one of the first to propose a single term, when he attempted in *The Federalist* to appropriate the word *republic* for the form of government offered in the Constitution. Madison defined a *republic* as a popular government in a large sphere "in which the scheme of representation takes place" and in which the protection of the citizens' individual rights and liberties is paramount. Madison went on to contrast a *republic* with a *democracy*, which he defined as direct popular government in a small sphere. Democracies, he continued, had usually been unfriendly to individual liberty.[1]

Madison's use of *republic* in this new sense turned out to be too restrictive and never fully took hold. Even Madison's chief collaborator in *The Federalist*, Alexander Hamilton, broke with the new definition and continued to refer to ancient democracies as republics.[2] Thomas Jefferson, Madison's great ally in founding the Democratic-Republican party, later observed that "the term republic is of very vague application"; but he also defined it, in exactly the opposite way from Madison, as a "government by its citizens in mass, acting directly and personally."[3]

In popular speech today, the word *republic* maintains certain positive connotations that originally attracted Madison to it. Americans identify their regime as a *republic* in the Pledge of Allegiance, where the term has a quiet majesty that evokes notions of citizen duty and sacrifice. Yet this usage is more poetic than analytic, and few political scientists designate the contemporary regime by this term alone.

Among contemporary scholars, the term *republic* is used in two quite different ways. One group follows Madison and identifies a republic with a representative government operating under constitutional restraints. Yet these scholars are not content to use *republic* by itself, for they are aware of the great difference between representative governments such as that of nineteenth-century Great Britain, in which only a very small part of the populace possessed the vote, and modern representative regimes in the West, in which the great body of the adult population may vote. In order, therefore, to designate the *kind* of indirect government that exists in nations such as the United States or France, these analysts usually add an adjective that brings the popular element of these contemporary regimes to the forefront, giving us the compound *democratic republic*.[4]

Others—and this includes most historians today—identify a republic with classical city-states, such as Athens, Sparta, or Rome, which involved a high degree of citizen participation and which claimed a total devotion of the citizen to the city.[5] For these analysts, the modern governments of the West, which are found in large nations and which prize individual rights and private interests, cannot accurately be labeled *republics*. If one insists on using the term, it must be qualified and given a balancing modifier, so that we end up with a compound such as *liberal republic* or, for those inclined to show an edge, *bourgeois republic*.

Another simple name used in popular speech is *democracy*. But this term, too, while it is fairly widely employed by journalists and politicians, is resisted by most political analysts. As noted, Madison deliberately rejected it, identifying a democracy in a pure sense with the immediate rule of popular assemblies and, by extension, with an indirect form of government that provides no real check on the primacy of the immediate dictates of public opinion. (He had in mind here certain of the state governments of the 1780s, especially Rhode Island and Massachusetts.) Madison argued that democracies were incapable of deliberative decision-making; they "have ever been spectacles of turbulence and contention [and] have ever been found incompatible with personal security and the rights of property."[6]

The popular usage of *democracy* today, of course, is neither as strict nor as unflattering as Madison's definition. This change is not semantic, but reflects a greater acceptance of the legitimacy of a more active role for public opinion in governing modern liberal democracies. Still, Madison's conception of democracy has not been completely discarded. Most analysts find that the term *democracy* by itself overlooks the indirect character of the modern regime in the West, in particular well-established devices that are designed to restrain majority rule, such as bicameralism and judicial review. Hence the tendency either to attach the root democracy to some other word *(democratic republic)*, or some other word to democracy *(representative democracy)*.

Of the simple terms remaining, this leaves only the neologism *polyarchy*, coined by a modern political scientist.[7] It alone has escaped the fate of being made into a compound, as no one has yet dared to speak of a *polyarchical republic* or a *democratic polyarchy*. This result, however, does not appear to reflect this term's greater precision as much as its unfamiliarity to those outside the discipline of political science. If it ever gained greater currency, it would probably suffer the same fate as the others.

To the extent that language provides a window to reality, the constant recourse to compound designations offers an important clue about the underlying structure of *liberal democracy*. The use of two words suggests that this regime is not a pure or simple type but is instead based on a fusion of two governmental principles. In each of the compound terms employed, there is the germ of the same two sets of ideas. One of the words always points to the protection of rights, limited government, and deliberate decision-making processes—features that make up the core of modern constitutionalism.[8] (This set of ideas is rendered, at the risk of being laborious, by the word *liberal* in *liberal democracy*, by *representative* in *representative democracy*, by *constitutional* in *constitutional republic* and *constitutional democracy*, and by *republic* in *democratic republic*.) The other word in these compounds always points to rule by the people and to a democratic understanding of justice according to which government exists to promote the interests of the people as a whole (or the majority), not the interests of a select or designated minority. (This set of ideas is rendered by *democracy* in *liberal democracy* and in *constitutional democracy*, by *democratic* in *democratic republic*, by *representative* in *representative republic*, and by *republic* in *constitutional republic*.)

It is surely an annoying fact, especially for tidy minds, that no single, universally accepted name exists for the modern regime in the West. Yet the reigning confusion at least serves the purpose of reminding us of this regime's dual parentage.[9] In fact, liberal democracy's two constituent parts are sufficiently distinct that each one developed independently of the other. Prior to the establishment of the first constitutional democracies—which was largely an American innovation of the late-eighteenth century—there are instances of constitutional regimes that were not democratic, such as the British government after 1688, and of democratic regimes that were not constitutional, such as Periclean Athens, Geneva, and some of the early Puritan colonies in America. Until the Americans' successful experiment at combining these two principles into one form of government, most considered them to be not only distinct as a matter of historical practice but also incompatible.

Constitutionalism in Europe evolved from mixed regimes erected on a foundation of recognized social estates (royalty, nobility, and commons). Until the end of the eighteenth century, constitutionalism was widely understood to be dependent upon the existence of these estates. Constitutional government meant limited government in which arbitrary power could not be systematically exercised. To avoid arbitrary power, authority had to be divided among different political institutions—such as the Crown, the House of Lords, and the House of Commons in Great Britain—where each institution had sufficient power and confidence to hold its own against the others. This confidence could only exist where an institution had roots in the social structure of the community and was fortified by one of its great estates. This view had such currency in the eighteenth century that many Americans were convinced that if a constitutional government was to be established in the United States, it would be necessary first to create formal estates.[10]

A democratic government is one in which citizens all come from the same estate—hence, the word *estate* loses political significance. In its modern variant, a democracy is also one, according to Madison, in which the citizenry constitutes the "great body of the people." This kind of government emerged from a different tradition than constitutional government. It hearkened back to democratic republics such as Athens and Florence, although the modern variant added the crucial idea of equality of people founded in natural rights.[11]

For those concerned with protecting constitutionalism, the democratic or republican principle bore profound problems. As authority in a republic derived from one entity (the people), a republic lacked the diverse societal foundations necessary for establishing institutions able to balance one another. Moreover, the people were said to be impetuous and to care little for legal forms, especially when encouraged by demagogues who would inevitably grow up in their midst. Republics would destroy themselves by failing to check popular leaders, who from either ambition or ignorance would energize the populace to throw off regular deliberative procedures, opening the way to disorder or tyranny. The threat of the "popular leader" destroying a republic is central to almost all constitutional thinkers from Montesquieu through America's founders.

Just as proponents of constitutional government had doubts about republicanism, so, too, did many advocates of republicanism have reservations about constitutionalism. A republican government requires plenary authority in order to form the proper character of the citizenry. For republicans, the most important factor that accounts for the health of a republic is not its political institutions, but the mores of its people. Without certain mores, a republic could not exist or endure. In particular, a people had to possess the quality of "virtue," meaning that citizens had to prefer the city's interest to their own interest and be willing to sacrifice their particular will to the city's well-being. "Virtue," wrote Montesquieu in describing the character of republics, "is a most simple thing; it is a love of the republic." In a democracy, the love of the republic is the "love of equality": "the love of equality in a democracy limits ambition to the sole desire, to the sole happiness, of doing greater services to our country than the rest of our fellow-citizens."[12] The opposite of virtue for classical republicans is corruption, which refers to a preference for one's own particular interest over and above that of the city's. In Rousseau's terminology, the citizens of a republic had to be taught to prefer "the general will" to the "will of each."

The logic of this position is simple enough. Democracy means rule by the people (the majority). But if the people are corrupt, democracy is nothing more than a majority using the instrument of law to take unjustly what it wants. It is rule by faction. Such a system might be preferable to oligarchy (a minority taking what it wants) or tyranny (a single person taking what he or she wants), because it satisfies a larger number of people. But rule by majority faction can hardly be considered a desirable or legitimate system.

To foster and maintain virtue in a republic is no easy task. It requires special conditions and tight social controls that are in direct tension with the individual liberty sought under constitutional government. The city must be a "school" that forms and molds a certain kind of human being. This demands, first, that the regime be small—the size of a city- state, not a modern nation-state. Only where the city is of manageable proportion can the citizens come to love their fellow citizens and subordinate their own interest to that of the city. Second, the city's populace must be relatively homogeneous; the city cannot survive religious diversity or extremes of wealth and poverty, for these differences create conflicts, establish primary groups other than the city, and lead to a loss of virtue. Third, the city must be careful not to allow unlimited commerce, for commerce stimulates a desire for personal luxury. As Montesquieu wrote, "in proportion as luxury gains ground in a republic, the minds of the people are turned toward their particular interests."[13] Finally, the city cannot permit a free circulation of ideas, for certain ideas turn citizens away from the practice of their duties and promote corruption.

All of these conditions and social controls make for what today would be considered a closed society. Yet this kind of society was precisely the one that republican theorists maintained would promote liberty, because it created a people capable of self-rule. From a liberal or constitutional perspective, however, this kind of liberty for the city as a whole is purchased at the cost of liberty for the individual. The liberty of the republic is at odds with the modern conception of individual liberty.

Beyond seeking to assure the survival of the regime, republicans were also concerned with achieving human goodness. Liberal regimes, by allowing people to devote themselves primarily to private pursuits, produced a degraded human specimen—the despicable bourgeois depicted by Rousseau, whose only desire is for luxury and whose only passion is money.[14] A republic, by contrast, continued to be directly concerned, as an explicit object of political rule, with promoting a worthy or admirable quality to human life.

The understanding that constitutional and republican principles were distinct and in tension with each other can be seen not only from historical practice but also from the views of many political theorists. Among the great political thinkers prior to the nineteenth century, few can be counted advocates of liberal democracy. It is far easier to find theorists who were liberal without being notably democratic (Montesquieu, Hume, and Burke), or theorists who were democratic without being notably liberal (Rousseau).[15]

American Theorists of Liberal Democracy

American thinkers such as Thomas Jefferson, Alexander Hamilton, and James Madison were among the first to explore a theoretical foundation for combining constitutionalism and republicanism. Nevertheless, many anthologies of political philosophy exclude American founders from the category of major theorists, on the grounds that none of them elaborated a complete political theory. If this assessment is correct, it is at least partly because they devoted themselves not to general theory but to action in a particular case. Their actions, it might be said, have spoken as loudly and as reasonably as their words.

American thought on the nature of liberal democracy began in earnest with the Revolution and the writing of the first state constitutions from 1776 to 1780. Referring to the Virginia constitution of 1776, Jefferson observed that Virginia "was not only the first of the states, but, I believe I may say, the first of the nations of the earth which assembled its wise men peaceably together to form a fundamental constitution, to commit it to writing, and place it where everyone should be free to appeal to its text."[16] American inquiry into liberal democracy deepened during the debate over the formation of the national government in 1787-88, with the generally acknowledged high point being *The Federalist*. Two of the main claims of this work were, first, that it was possible to devise a sound form of government that was both republican and constitutional; and, second, that this regime could be established, not as a consequence of an accident in an out-of-the-way place, but by conscious design in a nation that could contend honorably with other world powers. Liberal democracy could thus serve as a model for the rest of the world.[17]

America's founders understood that to combine constitutionalism and republicanism in one regime required a reworking of the pure form of each of its two constituent elements. How these two elements could be grafted onto each other, what adjustments or modifications each element would have to undergo, and what new qualities might be needed to solidify the fusion— these were among the major theoretical questions of liberal democracy at its origins. They remain so today.

The main contribution of *The Federalist* to liberal democratic theory is to show how republicanism can be modified in a way that will enable it to become compatible with constitutionalism.[18] Experience had proven that pure democracies, in which decisions were made directly by the people, could not be constitutional regimes. A constitutional republic, therefore, had to be an indirect or representative form of government. Representation was also required, of course, to allow for a nation large enough to be able to defend itself against the powerful states of the modern world. After acknowledging this crucial, if obvious, point, *The Federalist*'s discussion of representation dwells mostly on the importance of representation in promoting the major benefits of constitutionalism: the protection of rights and the establishment of an effective government.

The Federalist's treatment of the basic principles of the structure of a constitutional regime is now widely regarded as classic. The foundation of authority in a representative democracy lies with the people. But this authority expresses itself through a written constitution, which then becomes the fundamental legal source of authority. There is a new distinction created between the constitution and the government, in which the "constitution [is] paramount to the government."[19] The written constitution establishes the government and apportions power among different offices or institutions, the officials of which are chosen directly or indirectly by the people. These institutions are so arranged that each has the means to protect its independence and integrity without requiring the support of a distinct estate in society. Public opinion carries great weight in the counsels of government, but the institutional arrangements provide the government with discretion and a degree of detachment from immediate popular pressures.

The elaboration of a representative government along these (or similar) lines is a large part of what we now call constitutionalism. Constitutionalism in this structural sense promotes deliberative decision-making and energetic government, which are important instrumental ends in their own right. It also fosters limited government that protects rights. *The Federalist* establishes the connection between government structure and limited government by showing first how a written constitution itself is a limit to arbitrary government, and second how rights are in danger in a popular government that lacks institutional safeguards and allows majorities to have their way too quickly.

Let us now turn to the other side of the equation: how constitutionalism needs to be adjusted in order to allow it to be combined with republicanism. Before confronting this question directly, however, it is necessary to observe how Americans were able to reduce the tension between these two principles by embracing a different understanding of constitutionalism from that found in Europe. Following the lead here of theorists such as John Locke, American thinkers staked out the revolutionary idea that certain basic rights attached in principle equally to all individuals—as stated in the Declaration of Independence.[20] By excluding titles of nobility, the American Constitution also signaled the elimination of a whole range of property and "rights" that existed in Europe. The Americans did not view the principle of equality as a concession that constitutionalism *had* to make to republicanism in order to secure a workable regime, but as an expression of the best form of constitutionalism.[21]

This American conception of constitutionalism, which was founded on the principle of natural equality, was not yet widely accepted on the Continent, where the idea of freedom, according to Tocqueville, was "conceived within the limits of classes and always linked to the idea of exception and privilege."[22] Many constitutionalists in Europe thus understood rights to include the historical privileges connected to the prerogatives of different estates, and they viewed constitutional government as a way of guaranteeing and protecting those rights. For many in Europe, therefore, the American example was the most dangerous and subversive possibility of all, not despite, but rather because, it demonstrated that a form of constitutional government could also accommodate the principle of equality.

On the basis of this understanding of constitutionalism, the American regime was emphatically constitutional in its design. In forming the compound between constitutionalism and democracy, *The Federalist* gives primacy to the former. The "protection of the diversity in the faculties of men, from which the rights of property originate," is the "first object of government."[23] These rights—rights founded on the principle of equality—are still threatened by democratic majorities. In affirming the primacy of rights as the end of the overall scheme of government—though not in our modern legalistic sense of judicial interpretations of a Bill of Rights—*The Federalist* also affirms the fundamental liberal idea of a delineation of public and private spheres and the separation of the state from civil society.

Let us now return to the question of adjusting constitutionalism to meet the requirements of democracy. Even with the reduced tension between these two principles under the American concept of constitutionalism, there is still a question of how republican government can be achieved in a constitutional regime. The republican element, as noted, had traditionally been interpreted to require not only equality but also virtue. It must thus be asked if there is a need for republican virtue in a liberal democracy, or, if not for republican virtue in its strict sense, then for another kind of virtue or a set of mores that we can call *liberal democratic citizenship*. And if there is some such need, who or what has the responsibility to promote democratic citizenship? What role are public authorities to play, and what implications does this role have for the liberal principle of the distinction between the public and private spheres?

It is on this point that we encounter a major limitation of *The Federalist*, for it does not thoroughly and systematically explore this set of questions. To be sure, it does not ignore the subject completely. For one thing, *The Federalist* clearly rejects strict republican virtue as the foundation for a liberal democratic system. In a constitutional regime designed to protect individual liberty, there can be no question of suppressing "the spirit of enterprise" or of promoting the "love of equality" of results. But whether *The Federalist* has anything more to say about citizenship, beyond rejecting classical republican virtue as the primary basis of community, has been a subject of considerable debate.

There have been two basic schools of thought among scholars on this question. According to one group, *The Federalist*'s only teaching on citizenship is contained in its negative message: the system needs no special kind of citizenship and can run on a proper channeling of people's lower passions. The "model" of government based on this view of human motivation is often referred to by these scholars as the

"Madisonian system."[24] This interpretation, first offered by historians, has more recently been seized on by "rational choice" advocates in the political science profession, who have been anxious to find support among the American founders for their idea that all significant political action can be comprehended under the same calculation of self-interest that underlies modern economics. According to a second group of scholars, this line of interpretation is false. It does not take *The Federalist* on its own terms, but attempts to stretch Publius—the Roman pen name taken by the authors of the work—to resemble certain interpretations of Thomas Hobbes or John Locke or Adam Smith. If there is such a thing as "the Madisonian system," Madison never proposed it. *The Federalist,* in this view, points to a positive idea of citizenship as necessary for liberal democracy, though this citizenship is of a different sort than classical republican virtue. Publius's references to the qualities of "esteem and confidence" in citizens required by liberal democratic government, as well as his numerous statements about the "ability and virtue" needed from the occupants of political office, are clear instances of this concern.[25]

There is more and more evidence today to support the soundness of the critique offered by this second group of scholars. Nevertheless, their conclusion does not go very far in defining the character of liberal democratic citizenship or in answering how constitutionalism can be modified to achieve republicanism. The scholars who are the strongest advocates of this view concede this point, for they do not purport to find in *The Federalist* anything remotely approaching a systematic exploration of the question of citizenship. To complete their argument about citizenship, these scholars must search among other writings or documents of the founders, picking and choosing among them to develop a coherent position.

There is a reason why *The Federalist* does not treat this question fully. *The Federalist*'s intention, we must not forget, was not to provide a comprehensive theoretical account of liberal democracy, but to establish the case for a *national* government in the United States. Given this objective, *The Federalist* was not obliged to treat every major question about liberal democracy, and it was especially likely to avoid certain matters that were to be dealt with chiefly by the states or local governments. The means of promoting citizenship fall mainly in this area, and they clearly involve a use of powers that opponents of the Constitution were least disposed to grant to the national government.[26]

A great error in interpreting *The Federalist* has been to treat it as if it were meant to provide a *comprehensive* view of the respective roles of public and private spheres in a liberal democracy. To be comprehensive, it would have had to discuss the role of state and local governments, which it does not. This error of interpretation is compounded when some attempt to equate *The Federalist*'s view about the role of the national government with the role of government in general. An interpretation of this kind inevitably distorts the views of the authors of *The Federalist* about the nature of liberal democracy and how it might be maintained, especially in regard to the question of how to secure liberal democratic citizenship.[27]

The role of citizenship in a popular regime was not, of course, an untouched subject in American political thought of the period, and some works made it a central theme. To cite from Jefferson's *Notes on the State of Virginia*, "it is the manners and spirit of a people which preserve a republic in vigor."[28] The people who wrote most often on this question, however, were those who had doubts about the Constitution or who were most interested in defending the prerogatives of the state governments.[29] This historical accident has led to a tendency to speak of a dichotomy in the American tradition between a concern for citizen character, which is seen as the exclusive province of the antifederalists, and a disregard for citizen character, which is said to mark the view of *The Federalist*. Yet this idea of a dichotomy, while it may have a certain elegance, is surely exaggerated, especially in its identification of *The Federalist* as an opponent of any notion of citizenship. If it is true that a comprehensive theory of liberal democracy may need to go beyond *The Federalist*, it does not follow that this "synthesis" would be fundamentally at odds with its position.

The First Philosopher of Liberal Democracy: Alexis de Tocqueville

The object of studying American writings as works of political science, as distinct from sources for different historical traditions, is to illuminate the nature of liberal democracy. From this perspective, no single American work of the founding period ever completed a systematic investigation of how to forge a compound between constitutionalism and republicanism.

The first author to attempt this task was Alexis de Tocqueville in *Democracy in America*. Not only was Tocqueville the first major political philosopher, inside or outside of America, to actually observe and study liberal democracy, but he is also one of the few of the select group of major theorists who can be called a "friend" of this regime. Although it is a fruitless exercise to debate who deserves admittance into a key club of great philosophers, it is nonetheless worth noting that many of the most prominent thinkers of the modern age (Hegel, Marx, Nietzsche, Heidegger) have been hostile critics of either liberalism or democracy, or of both.[30]

Judged in relationship to previous American thought, Tocqueville's work can be seen as a supplement to, if not a partial correction of, *The Federalist*.[31] *Democracy in America* treats both sides of the constitutional-republican equation without being limited, as *The Federalist* was, by the special requirements of performing a specific political task. To place *Democracy in America* in this higher category is not to say that it replaces the thought of America's founders or that it should be taken as more of an authority. Indeed, the whole idea of searching for authorities, which has a peculiar appeal in certain quarters, is a curious and ultimately fruitless mode of conducting political science. The object of a healthy political science is not to determine a priori authorities, but to pursue the best answers to the most important questions. It is in posing comprehensively the fundamental questions of liberal democracy—and thus introducing a logic of analysis— that Tocqueville is so helpful.

On the first question of how republicanism must be modified to be made compatible with constitutionalism—Tocqueville can claim little if any theoretical originality. He mostly restates the arguments of *The Federalist*, casting them at times in more general terms. Although the theme of the constitutional structure is important to Tocqueville in *Democracy in America*, it is far from being his central concern and makes up only one part of the entire work.

On the second question—how liberalism must be adjusted to be made compatible with republicanism—Tocqueville goes well beyond *The Federalist*. His principal concern was to elaborate the *moeurs* (mores), defined as "the habits . . . the beliefs . . . and the sum of moral and intellectual dispositions of men in society," which are needed among the citizens of a liberal democracy.[32] In presenting his account of liberal democracy in the United States, Tocqueville naturally devoted more space to American local institutions and civil law than to the institutions of the federal government, as the former provided a better vehicle for understanding the origin and development of American mores. Tocqueville's discussion of mores shows that the liberal principle of a separation of the public and private spheres, while it constitutes a fundamental juridical tenet of the regime, cannot do full justice to understanding all of the regime's requirements. A complete analysis must go beyond a study of purely formal or legal arrangements.[33]

Tocqueville's treatment of the mores that support liberal democracy has been widely misinterpreted. Especially in recent years, in the aftermath of the rediscovery of the theme of "classical republicanism," some American intellectuals seem to think that the moment one begins to speak of mores or citizen character, one must have in mind something akin to republican virtue. Modern advocates of republicanism thus often attempt to claim Tocqueville as one of their own. But they misread him.[34]

The mores that sustain liberal democracy, according to Tocqueville, are not uniquely republican; they include attributes that derive from *both* of its constituent parts. The "republican" side of liberal democracy points to the need for many character attributes that resemble aspects of republican virtue, while the liberal side depends on mores of its own, quite different than those that support republics. If republicanism requires a degree of civic-mindedness that is fairly widespread among the citizenry, liberalism requires citizens who possess common sense, a jealous spirit of independence, and, for some among them, a high regard for self and a sense of individual pride. Pride and spiritedness are qualities emphasized in aristocratic societies, which suggests that liberal democracy must be infused with elements alien to its own natural tendencies.[35]

Tocqueville goes further, however, and advances the analysis of liberal democracy to another plane. It is not enough—indeed it is often misleading—to view liberal democracy solely in terms of its two separate parts. Liberal democracy is more than a combination of liberal and republican elements; it is a compound or a new synthetic whole, and as such it has its own distinct needs and properties. The mores that support liberal democracy are thus not always either simply liberal or simply republican. Nor are the methods for inculcating its mores always derivative from either republican or liberal models. The analysis of liberal democracy, where it does not require a new vocabulary altogether, calls for a most careful use of liberal or republican terms in order to avoid confusing one part with the whole.

One of the distinctive supports of liberal democracy is something that is rarely noted or counted as a quality needed to sustain a regime: the active engagement in society of a certain kind of political knowledge. Tocqueville wrote that "a new political science is needed for a new world," and his work is an effort not only to create that political science but also to present it in such a way that it can be launched as a new enterprise in modern society.[36] This factor is so unusual—at least in contemporary analyses of liberal democracy—that it requires an introduction of its own.

The Role of Political Knowledge in Maintaining Liberal Democracy

How much conscious or active application of political knowledge is actually needed to maintain a liberal democracy? Stated differently, must a liberal democracy be continually superintended by political knowledge, or can it for the most part do without it? The answer to this question also determines in large part whether it is difficult or easy to maintain liberal democracy. It is perhaps surprising that there should be no consensus on so fundamental an issue. Rather, there are two diametrically opposed positions. One view holds that liberal democracy needs little if any conscious intellectual supervision; the other considers that superintendence is essential and that it is the major challenge in maintaining a liberal democratic regime.

According to the first view, a liberal democracy, once correctly established (which itself might be very difficult), is easily maintained. It can be constructed to produce a kind of self-regulating equilibrium. This view has several variants. In one, liberal democracy is a regime founded on human "nature," with "nature" understood as comprising the most common and powerful, and therefore the most reliable, drives: self-preservation and acquisitiveness. The institutions of liberal democracy can be built to function effectively by depending on nothing more than these drives. This is how Richard Hofstadter, for example, interprets the theory undergirding the American founding: "Since man was an unchangeable creature of self-interest . . . the Fathers relied upon checking vice with vice."[37]

A second variant of this position holds that certain qualities beyond these natural drives are needed to assure the proper functioning of liberal democracy, above all political moderation. But these qualities can be produced by a proper arrangement of the political institutions. Thus a separation of power, which forces ambition to counteract ambition, will teach leaders a sense of their limits. According to Jean-Claude Lamberti, this idea was central to the political thought of Montesquieu and the American founders: "A good constitution could generate the moderation of political passions and, in return, thanks to this moderation, the political system could function correctly."[38]

A final variant of this position refers more to the quality of life in liberal democratic society than to its political survival. It holds that a decent tone of life is a more or less automatic consequence of liberal democracy. Liberal democracy establishes a separation of state from society, and the things that assure a defensible quality of life—religion, morality, the arts—can be expected to flourish when left to develop freely in civil society. This is the view that Martin Diamond ascribes to America's founders: "they were apparently confident that, privately and without political tutelage in the ancient mode, the higher virtues would develop from religion, education, family upbringing, and simply out of the natural yearnings of human nature."[39]

These variants, and the possible combinations among them, represent very different pictures of the nature of liberal democracy. But in regard to the question of the role of political knowledge in maintaining this regime, all share a common view. All presuppose that if a liberal democracy is properly set in motion, it can continue on its own, without needing assistance from political knowledge. Liberal democracy is a regime capable of operating, so to speak, on automatic pilot.

The second basic position, which will be elaborated at greater length in the next chapter, holds that liberal democracy demands constant superintendence, even if its basic political institutions have been wisely designed. A liberal democracy, in this view, is far from being in perfect equilibrium. Its maintenance requires certain mores in the citizenry that do not flow automatically either from people's "natural" dispositions, at least as these ordinarily manifest themselves, or from the arrangement of the primary political institutions.

Somehow or other, therefore, ways must be found to produce and cultivate the necessary mores. This task, which I have been referring to as "superintendence," is complex and multi-faceted. It involves constructing the primary political arrangements with a view (in part) to their effect on mores; establishing secondary political and social institutions that promote helpful habits and practices; and devising intellectual and cultural strategies to foster supportive ideas, opinions, and beliefs. The task of superintendence cannot be fully institutionalized or written into a constitution or a set of laws. It is a variable enterprise that requires an ongoing adjustment and readaptation of secondary institutions and of intellectual strategies in such realms as religion, art, and education. As times change, the way to promote a favorable climate for liberal democracy must also change.

How the task of superintendence can operate in society is itself one of the chief objects of political knowledge. Political knowledge must become highly self-conscious, though in a practical way. Political science must include consideration of its own role in maintaining liberal democracy and of the means and mechanisms by which it can be inserted into society and made into an active force.

Friends of liberal democracy would clearly prefer the first, or automatic-pilot, view to be true, for the maintenance of liberal democracy would then be easier and surer. Proponents of a strict liberalism are apt to be especially attracted to this position. If the establishment of the state as a formal and highly limited governing instrument can provide for the survival of liberal democracy, and if no further conscious political thinking is needed to help direct society, then the political analysis need not extend beyond a treatment of the limits of state power and the proper arrangement of the primary political institutions. The sanctity of what Robert Nozick calls the "minimal state" and of the liberal principle of a separation between the public and private spheres would then be assured.[40]

For the same reasons, it is clear why the strict liberal might be reluctant to accept the position that liberal democracy requires a superintendence of mores. If superintendence is needed, then political analysis cannot accept the state-society distinction as the final word; it must systematically consider a larger system or whole that includes both state and society. For the liberal, this kind of analysis poses the uneasy question of whether a strict liberalism adequately supports liberal democracy. Moreover, the strict liberal is apt to fear that a form of political analysis that goes beyond the state-society distinction will open the way to influences hostile to liberal democracy. Once the wall between state and society has been breached, it is no longer possible as a practical matter to distinguish interventions designed to support liberal democracy from those designed to establish—or that would have the effect of establishing—a different form of government.

As any realist must acknowledge, however, wishing something to be true does not make it so. If anything, it is likely to lead to an acceptance of myths and a dogmatic insistence on the certainty of one's position. At the very least, the idea that liberal democracy is easily maintained rests on a high estimation of the capacity of basic political structures to resolve definitively the most vexing problems. At the heart of this view is the assumption of a mysterious invisible hand operative in politics, similar to the one that is said to govern the domain of economic exchange. Whether the political realm has been so blessed is certainly open to question.

If, on the contrary, it turns out that liberal democracy needs superintendence to survive—as I shall argue later that it does—then a different approach is called for. This approach need not, however, give cause for the kind of despair shown by strict liberals. It is grounds only for a frank admission of the difficulty, though not the impossibility, of maintaining a liberal democracy. Moreover, this problem should properly be viewed as one instance of the more general question of how to maintain different forms of government, as there is no reason to suppose a priori that maintaining any kind of regime is ordinarily a simple task. From this starting point, the question is not just whether liberal democracy is difficult to maintain, but how difficult it is to maintain as compared to other regimes.

Only a few general observations on this broader comparative issue can be offered here. On the one hand, in the considerable degree to which liberal democracy takes into account the powerful "natural" human drives of self-interest, it would seem to be easier to maintain than regimes that demand extraordinary efforts in character formation, such as a pure republic. This argument constitutes the "realist core" found in nearly all defenses of liberal democracy. Thus a liberal democracy, to follow Madison's argument in *The Federalist,* does not rely for its existence, as a certain kind of republic does, entirely on "moral or religious motives." Nor does a liberal democracy require—again unlike a pure republic—an equality of people "in their possessions, their opinions, and their passions." Liberal democracy is not averse to relying on "inventions of prudence" that seek to supply "by opposite and rival interests the defect of better motives."[41]

On the other hand, the task of maintaining liberal democracy is complicated by three special difficulties that result from the compound nature of this regime. First, the factors that support a compound regime are often complex and not easily discovered or understood. What certain simple governments, such as a small republic, require may be easy to discover, though perhaps quite difficult to put into effect. What a compound government such as liberal democracy requires may be difficult to discover, though perhaps relatively easy to implement. Liberal democracy is a form of government that, according to Hamilton, is "complex and skillfully contrived."[42] In comparison to other regimes, it relies more on political knowledge, not just to be established, but to be sustained. It has a greater need of political science.[43]

Second, liberal democracy often fails to generate enthusiasm for itself as an integral whole. Its intellectuals, who serve as the major interpreters in society of the meaning of liberal democracy, tend to view it from a "partisan" perspective that is either liberal or democratic. This partisanship is in part a result of liberal democracy's grounding in two different principles, each one of which independently can be an object of spontaneous attachment, whereas the compound can be appreciated only by a cooler and more detached analysis. The partisanship found among intellectuals also results from their concern to make liberal democracy more just, with justice understood as promoting either a liberal policy (more liberty) or a democratic policy (more participation or equality). This concern for just policies so preoccupies discussion that it becomes the prime focus of general political analysis in intellectual commentary and leaves little time or energy for investigating the question of the needs of liberal democracy as a whole. Although the conflict between liberals and democrats may often have the effect of making each party check certain excesses of the other, there is no guarantee in the end that this contest will produce an optimal balance.

Finally, liberal democracy generates not only partisans of its two constituent elements but also "friendly" opponents of the regime. Unlike the partisans, these opponents call not for the reform, but for the *replacement* of liberal democracy by another system—but in the name of one of liberal democracy's two primary principles. These opponents today are found almost exclusively among the ranks of democrats (or modern-day "republicans"), as almost no one on the contemporary scene openly rejects liberal democracy in the name of liberalism. The democratic critics argue that liberal democracy cannot be maintained in a way that accords with any reasonable standard of democracy, but must inevitably deteriorate into a kind of plutocracy that, according to Charles Lindblom, gives "disproportionate influence" to businessmen and permits a "molding of [mass] volitions" by corporations.[44] Or, in a slightly milder formulation, these critics argue that whatever advantages liberal democracy may once have possessed, a more democratic and progressive alternative is now on the horizon and, in Benjamin Barber's words, is "more inviting" than at "any time America has ever known."[45]

Liberal democracy is certainly not alone in having opponents of the regime living in its midst. But it may well be unique in the extent to which it accords them status and acclaim, elevating some to the very highest positions in the intellectual world. This embrace is a result not only of the liberal principle of tolerance but also of the fact that these opponents often speak most passionately for one of the regime's own basic principles. They are thus regarded as standing within liberal democracy, even when they acknowledge that they favor "fundamental" changes.

Political Science as a Social Enterprise in Liberal Democracy

As a compound regime, liberal democracy can be maintained only with great difficulty. It needs not only the usual sources of regime support (the "prejudices" of the community, a veneration of its laws, a demonstrated ability to promote people's interests) but also a new support: an enterprise in society devoted to understanding the nature of liberal democracy and to bringing that knowledge to bear in its behalf.

This kind of enterprise was once envisaged. It bore the name *political science*. For the authors of *The Federalist* and for Tocqueville, the *science of politics* or *political science* was, in its practical sense, knowledge directed at ascertaining the factors that maintain or destroy different forms of government. Reflection on this question validated, as a rational conclusion emanating from an inquiry into the nature of liberal democracy, the idea of establishing a self-conscious enterprise in liberal democratic societies to work for their maintenance and improvement. *The Federalist* speaks of the crucial experiment in America of determining whether governments can be established "from reflection and choice." Establishing a government on this basis requires a reliance on "the science of politics," which assists us in understanding the "means by which the excellencies of republican government can be retained and its imperfections lessened or avoided." Tocqueville continued on this same path by calling for "a new political science" to educate and guide liberal democracy.[46]

The academic discipline we know today as *political science* is, of course, no longer directly part of this enterprise. One branch of the discipline rejects it on the grounds that political science, as a science in some modern sense, cannot provide a sanction for any kind of engagement in the political world, let alone assist in making normative evaluations. Another branch, which has reintroduced "values" and "commitment" under a new postscientific understanding of social science, has as its chief proponents those who are unfriendly to liberal democracy.

Academic political science's abandonment of an enterprise supporting liberal democracy would be of no consequence if some other discipline performed this function. But none of the modern social sciences, or for that matter any of the humanities or professional schools, has directly assumed this task. To be sure, there are burgeoning public-policy schools in our universities that seek to resolve many of the concrete problems that society faces. But this is a quite different matter from supplying a grounding for the enterprise itself.

For the sake of liberal democracy, accordingly, it is important to conceive of a project for reconstructing such an enterprise. Some will ask what it should be called and where it should be placed in our universities. It may be too much to suggest labeling it *political science* and locating it in departments we know by that name. A suggestion of this kind is apt to prompt charges of a plot to politicize the profession or to commit academic treason by putting a tangible societal function (maintaining liberal democracy) on a par with a scholastic discipline (political science).

These charges might have validity if my suggestion were in fact to turn political science into an ideological instrument. But what I am offering for consideration is something quite different. It is to ask whether there is not a body of human knowledge that, in light of systematic reflection on the relation of knowledge to society, sanctions an enterprise of the sort recommended by the early theorists of liberal democracy.

2

How Liberal Is Liberal Democracy?

ALEXIS DE TOCQUEVILLE WAS BORN in another century, on another continent, under a different form of government. He is, nonetheless, "our" political theorist. He is ours, first, because he wrote about our age. An explorer of history more than geography, Tocqueville came to America to discover the modern era. As he told John Stuart Mill in 1836, "America was only the frame, my picture was Democracy."[1] Recognizing the scope and novelty of Tocqueville's project, Mill described *Democracy in America* as "the first philosophical book ever written on Democracy as it manifests itself in modern society."[2]

What struck Tocqueville most about the developed nations of the modern era was a growing equality. Equality for Tocqueville was a multifaceted concept. It referred to a sociological condition (the end to a privileged legal status for certain social orders and, by comparison to the past, a greater equality of economic resources); to a controlling political idea (equality among persons as the principal "symbol" of legitimate authority); and to a sentiment ("the love of equality" as "dominant passion" of the age).[3]

Other great theorists of the nineteenth century sought to map our age, but none set forth as clearly as Tocqueville what are still its fundamental political alternatives: (a) a hard despotism (resembling in some respects the totalitarian regimes of this century), (b) a soft despotism, in which the populace, sheeplike and despondent, quibbles over the shares of government-supplied largess, and (c) a bustling, energetic, albeit slightly rude, liberal democratic order.[4]

Tocqueville is ours, second, because he is the political theorist *par excellence* of liberal democracy. By a liberal democracy, Tocqueville meant a modern regime, encompassing an entire nation state, based on the principle of individual rights and governed by the great body of the populace.[5] Along with America's founding fathers, Tocqueville "discovered" liberal democracy in the realm of political thought, and he was the first thinker to provide a systematic treatment of this regime, studying in depth both its laws and its mores or culture.

Tocqueville is ours, finally—and here I speak as an American—because his major work, *Democracy in America*, is about the United States. Caution, however, is needed on this point. Tocqueville's interest in the United States was accidental, if not incidental. He came to America, as noted, to study the purest example of a social state of equality of conditions; while in America, he also discovered a model for the kind of regime that offered the best hope for the modern age (liberal democracy). America was a relatively successful example of this model, although it was certainly not the only or the best possible manifestation of it.

Despite Tocqueville's debt to America, the title of his book is almost misleading. Volume two, even on the surface, is far more a comparative study than it is a book about the United States. Volume one, while it explores concrete conditions in the United States, "uses" America, abstracting freely from its particular circumstances to understand the modern age and the possibilities for liberal democracy. Tocqueville was concerned not only with the "precautions taken by Americans to direct" democracy but also with the measures the Americans "had neglected." America's laws were "not the only ones that would suit democratic peoples," and Tocqueville "was far from thinking that we [Europeans] should follow the example of American democracy and imitate the means it has used to attain this end."[6] Tocqueville deliberately sets aside some of the most important aspects of the American case—for example, race, slavery, and the prospects for an enduring union. These were essential for understanding America, but they were not always germane to understanding the general character of liberal democracy.[7]

Tocqueville's immediate concern was with the debate about liberal democracy in Europe, and his emotional attachment was, quite properly, with his native France, not with America. Had there been a better place to study democracy than in the United States—say Australia or Antarctica—he would no doubt have tried to go there, giving the world *Democracy in Australia* or *Democracy in Antarctica* rather than *Democracy in America*. He would still, of course, have been "our" political theorist; but the fact that he chanced to turn his genius on the United States clearly makes his work all the more valuable to Americans.

Tocqueville is the political thinker of our age, of our regime, and even of our nation. One might therefore think that those living today who devote themselves to understanding liberal democracy in the United States—I am speaking of American political scientists—would have a serious interest in his political thought. But this is hardly the case. We have among us positivists who take their bearings from Weber or Comte; developmentalists who follow the "hard" Marx; and, increasingly, normativists of one stripe or another, who can be linked to Kant, to the "humanist" side of Marx, to the communitarian side of Rousseau, and to Heidegger. But we have only a small number of Tocquevillians. It is at least a curious fact that one of the truest friends of liberal democracy has so few adherents, whereas thinkers who were indifferent or hostile to liberal democracy do not lack for disciples.[8]

Some political scientists, to be sure, take great pride in making occasional references to Tocqueville, but it is usually for ornamental purposes. Tocqueville is the coffee-table philosopher of American political science; he is displayed in polite company to embellish a point or to impress others of one's good breeding. And as one might expect, he is admired not for anything as serious as an approach, but for his keen "insights." The more his insights are touted, the more his overall aim is ignored.

No one, of course, denies that Tocqueville was a perceptive observer of democracy. Wasn't it Tocqueville, after all, who said that in the United States there is "hardly a political question that does not sooner or later turn into a judicial one"—this, even before judges began to decide questions as controversial as when life begins?[9]

Was it not Tocqueville who said that two nations, the United States and Russia—the former characterized by "freedom," the latter by "servitude"— would each "one day hold in its hands the destinies of half of the world"— this, even before the term *superpower* had been invented?[10]

Wasn't it Tocqueville, in speaking of a waxing and waning of great and small parties, who all but discovered the notion of critical elections—this, long before it appeared as a "new" concept in the *American Political Science Review*?[11]

Wasn't it Tocqueville, this time speaking of the arts, who voiced alarm over "too many incoherent images . . . bizarre effects and weird beings of all sorts"—this, long before the advent of the music video?[12]

Wasn't it Tocqueville who worried about an increasing reliance on a few "abstract" and general words—this, before social scientists started using the term *system* and before modern college students attempted the bold experiment of compressing all human communication into the single word, *like*?[13]

And finally, wasn't it Tocqueville who stated that any effort to make men and women alike would result in "feeble men and unseemly women"—this even before the reaction set in against the modern, "sensitive" male depicted in the cinema of the seventies?[14]

One could go on. But if the accuracy of his predictions is to be the yardstick for measuring Tocqueville's thought, a fair assessment of his merits would have to take into account his mistakes as well as his good judgment. Of these, I will cite only one example, on which I have first-hand knowledge. Tocqueville wrote that "when only the rich wore watches, they were almost all excellent. Now few are made that are more than mediocre, but we all have one."[15] On first reading this statement in the sixties, it seemed remarkably prescient. A cheap Bulova at that time could not compare with an eighteenth-century Swiss masterpiece. But today a ten-dollar digital Casio is more accurate than its old Swiss counterpart, even if its snappy plastic encasement may not quite measure up on aesthetic grounds. Despite many penetrating comments about modern science, Tocqueville seems to have underestimated the possibilities of modern technology and erred in assuming that the inevitable inequality that exists in the aesthetic realm would hold in the technical realm as well.

Yet all this scorekeeping is in the final analysis of scant interest. If what we are seeking is factual knowledge of our own era, we would do better to open our eyes to what is around us than to pour over a book written more than one hundred and fifty years ago. After all, to learn by observing is not exactly an un-Tocquevillian activity. Besides, for understanding developments in our era, Tocqueville tells his readers that those after him would enjoy a distinct advantage; they would have lived through much of the modern age, whereas he wrote at its dawn, before many of its elements had assumed firm shape.[16]

To take Tocqueville seriously, it is more important to consider his approach than his predictions. Tocqueville can live for us today if we enter into the spirit of his project—if we begin the study of politics with his concerns in mind and look at liberal democracy from his perspective. What I propose for this chapter, accordingly, is to explore Tocqueville's understanding of the underlying character or structure of liberal democracy and of the role he envisaged for political science within this regime. These questions should speak to us today as much as they did to those who lived at the dawn of liberal democracy.

General Problems of Maintaining a Liberal Democracy

Tocqueville begins the study of politics not with a laboratory concern—how one can explain as much variance as possible among political phenomena—but with a, or I should say *the*, political question: the form of government under which one lives. In the modern age, given the choices Tocqueville claimed were possible, this question resolves itself into whether "we establish democratic liberty or [a species of] democratic tyranny."[17] The starting point for political science is thus supplied by a direct, common-sense perception of what is politically most important. Political science is designed, if not to tell us definitively what form of government to choose, then at any rate to help (so far as any general kind of knowledge may be able to help) to put our choice into effect.

Tocqueville does not hesitate to select liberal democracy as his preferred regime for modern times. Yet he also makes clear that it is the most difficult of the modern regimes to maintain. Despotisms "fit" more easily or naturally with the tendencies of modern times than liberal democracy. Maintaining liberal democracy, moreover, has a broader meaning to it than merely sustaining its political form. It also involves promoting a worthy way of life in society. This second aspect requires further elaboration.

Liberal democracy, more than most regimes, does not formally attempt to "stamp" or form its citizens or directly define an ideal life for individuals or society. It leaves the determination of the content of happiness to its citizens and thus to how they happen to develop in the autonomous realm of civil society.[18]

Tocqueville is perhaps best known for being among the first to penetrate this "formal" façade of liberal democracy and to demonstrate that liberal democratic societies are far more "defined" in fact than the formal principle of the regime suggests. He showed that the formal principle itself (the equality of people in their rights), along with modern commerce and Enlightenment ideas, establishes the supremacy of the common man in society and makes the tastes of the middle class the dominant standard of judgment. There is, accordingly, a common culture toward which liberal democracies tend, despite their formal neutrality about the way of life in society.

For all his efforts to pierce the veil of liberal democratic formality, however, Tocqueville did not dismiss the importance of the claim to allow a free development of society. Liberal democracy, while it sets in motion certain tendencies and constraints, does leave a fairly wide range of choice in regard to the way of life in society. Liberal democratic societies may not only develop in quite different ways, they also attain different levels of "civilization."

There are general reasons, familiar to readers of Tocqueville, why maintaining a liberal democracy is difficult, both in providing for its political survivability and keeping a defensible way of life. The strongest sentiment of the modern era is the "passion for equality," which lends more support to what Tocqueville called a "soft despotism" than to liberal democracy.[19] This passion generates pressure to define justice and liberty as equal or the same results. The consequence is an increasing demand to use the highest instrumentality of public authority—"centralized government" or, as we might say today, "the state"—to make conditions more equal. A constantly growing tutelary power develops at the center, which imposes more and more uniformity on society.[20]

Likewise, in regard to the challenge of maintaining a worthy way of life in democratic societies, powerful forces are at work in modern times to undermine a high level of civilization and pull society down to mediocrity, spiritual emptiness, and a diminished sense of human grandeur. Liberal democracy, of course, is not alone in this problem; the despotisms face it just as acutely. But the despotisms often find it in their interest to see civilization decline, as this can strengthen their grip on society.

To maintain liberal democracy, Tocqueville tells us, it is necessary to act against many of the most powerful tendencies of modern times, sometimes by directly opposing them, more often by prudently managing and deflecting them. This task requires more from us, more diligence, more intelligence—in a word, more political science—than is needed to maintain any other modern regime: "in the dawning centuries . . . individual independence and local liberties will always be products of art." Despotism, which in previous ages was difficult to maintain, "has been simplified; one may almost say it has been reduced to a single principle" (promoting equality).[21]

The efforts to maintain liberal democracy are almost always fated to be compromised. The ideas, institutions, and strategies that serve to check the harmful tendencies of modernity themselves risk coming under modernity's sway. Thus religion, which Tocqueville argued was so necessary for counteracting dangerous forces of modernity, is always in danger of being "captured" by democratic tendencies. Religion is helpful in keeping citizens' minds elevated above purely secular and material concerns. Yet there is more and more likelihood in democratic times that the worship of God will be associated with worldly concerns, be it personal monetary success or notions of social justice.[22] A similar difficulty exists in regard to higher education. The study of philosophy and the liberal arts, which Tocqueville took to be an important counterweight to certain unhealthy democratic tendencies, has been an avowed goal of many universities. Yet think how often these same universities, pressured not only by democratic impulses from outside but also by a democratic spirit from within, compromise that goal, whether it is to promote the latest idea of social justice or merely to satisfy the academic community's desire for drama and excitement.[23] Tocqueville's analysis of modern society explains and almost forecasts such failures.

The conflict between Tocqueville's recommendations for helping liberal democracy and his analysis of the fragility of his own proposed solutions almost makes his thought seem contradictory. It would be more correct, however, to say that his work is characterized by a tension—a tension that reflects the nature of political science as an enterprise in society. If the accuracy of prognostications were the exclusive and guiding objective of a science of politics, Tocqueville might have emphasized even more than he did the likelihood that liberal democracy would fail. The end of political science, however, is not set by criteria deriving from this idea of science, but from a human and a political objective: helping us secure and maintain a reasonable political regime.

This last objective surely relies on prognostication, as an inability to take account of our real situation will lead to futile, even tragic action. Yet a social science devoted exclusively to extrapolating trends, Tocqueville argued, suffers from two flaws. First, it is apt to claim too much for itself. If the end of the discipline is to state trends, then practitioners, in order to establish the importance of their discipline, are likely to exaggerate the force of trends and claim more for this kind of explanation than it can offer. Social scientists are "not content to show how these events have occurred, [but] pride themselves on proving that they could not have happened differently. "The overall effect of this mode of thinking on society is to promote "the doctrine of fatality"—that everything could happen only in one way.[24] As there is always some degree of freedom in the human situation, social scientists must take care that the idea of explanation that governs their conception of knowledge does not diminish people's belief in the freedom they possess.

Second, a political science devoted exclusively to extrapolating trends cannot perform one of the principal functions of the discipline. Political science should seek to assist "those who direct society" in choosing well and, in the case of liberal democratic leaders, help them to "educate democracy . . . regulate its movements and substitute a science of affairs for its inexperience."[25] To achieve this goal, political science must devote a good part of its attention not to what is most likely to occur, but to what would occur *if* certain actions were or were not taken. The elaboration of these "if-then" relationships, predicated not only on abstract norms but also on the functioning of a political regime, is the knowledge that can contribute most to this task, even if there is no certainty that this knowledge will always be taken into account.

The Limits to a Liberal Understanding of Liberal Democracy

In addition to the general tendencies of modernity that threaten liberal democracy, there is another, far less evident, reason why liberal democracy is difficult to maintain. The form or structure of liberal democracy—its way of ordering society—has the effect of concealing from those who live in it what is needed to perpetuate this regime, or even to consider regime maintenance as a problem.

A liberal form of government, following from its constituent formal principles, is characterized by a separation of the realm we know as politics from other realms of society, such as the religious, the cultural, and, to a much lesser extent, the economic. Politics, in the strict sense of the exercise of governmental power, is no longer supposed to control these other spheres. Where political authority attempts this control, it oversteps its rightful boundaries. Liberalism, in more familiar (if extreme) terms, erects walls between the political and the cultural and (to a lesser extent) between the political and the economic. It depoliticizes these realms, making them private rather than public. This separation is sometimes reflected in certain conceptions of our academic disciplines: political science deals with people in their relation to government, whereas sociology deals with people in their relationship to civil society.

Tocqueville defends, as a general principle, the liberal idea of the separation of these spheres. He shows that the idea of rights, with its concomitant principle of limited government, serves in the main to safeguard liberty in modern societies.[26] But Tocqueville does *not* claim, indeed his entire approach denies, that this principle can supply a full or adequate understanding of liberal democracy.

Tocqueville begins his study of liberal democracy from the premise that there is a "whole" that is prior, not in time but in essence, to the separation of state from society. This separation is not the foundation of a liberal democratic edifice, but rather—to continue the architectural metaphor—its first floor. The first floor is what we see upon entering—and most likely all that a polite host will wish to show us. But the entire structure rests on a deeper foundation, which must be the principal object of study in the analysis of liberal democracy.

As we descend with Tocqueville to inspect the foundation, we discover that, unlike the first floor, there are no walls between the political on the one hand and the cultural, the religious, or the economic on the other. Instead, there is constant interaction among these spheres that respects no formal boundaries. These interactions, far from being minor or incidental, hold the key to whether the foundation can support the edifice built upon it. On this level, there is no political science or sociology as these disciplines are sometimes demarcated in academic turf wars, but only a political sociology that encompasses them both.[27]

The legal or formal separation between the public and private realms is thus secondary or derivative. It is conditioned by a prior and more fundamental arrangement, which more truly constitutes the political aspect of liberal democracy than that which is formally assigned to the political realm under liberal principles. Yet Tocqueville does not take the step of dismissing the formal liberal principle as merely fictitious or as a cover for some more sinister design.

On this point, most modern commentators take a quite different view. They follow the analysis of Marx, who is celebrated by political scientists today for having exploded the liberal "myth" of the separate spheres and for having exposed the "formalism" of its liberties. For Marx, these various spheres are connected with one another, with all of them finally depending on the economic. The formal divisions are a fiction. Using a similar analysis, leading figures in American political science, such as Charles Lindblom, have discovered that the line between state and society in liberalism is not etched in stone. Excited by uncovering this nasty little secret about liberal democracy, they have since been running around telling everyone about it.[28]

Yet much earlier and from a different perspective than Marx, Tocqueville had discovered that the walls between the political and the nonpolitical are not primary. Indeed, he would almost certainly have objected to calling this insight a discovery, for analyzing the interrelationships among elements we today put into the boxes of society and state was basic to the kind of political science practiced by Aristotle and Montesquieu. Tocqueville can be credited, of course, for insisting on keeping this approach even when analyzing modern liberal regimes, but this hardly qualifies as a great intellectual breakthrough.

What then is the status of the formal liberal principle of separation in Tocqueville's analysis? Even though this principle is not primary, neither is it unimportant. Different principles, Tocqueville shows, work at different levels to produce different effects. The fact that something is not entirely true on one level does not mean that it is not true on another. Political analysis must seek to understand how doctrines operate on each level.

Knowledge on the level of the foundation, Tocqueville makes clear, cannot serve directly as an underpinning or grounding for this regime. The conclusions derived from an analysis of this level are too complex to be encapsulated in any formal or juridical principles. A liberal democratic regime needs a firm and comprehensible set of formal principles, capable of being stated clearly, so that citizens can consent to them to constitute the basis of a legal order. The formal liberal principle meets this standard and expresses the end of the regime on this level. It is not the whole story, but the whole story cannot be expressed in the formal principles.[29]

In light of his position on the character of liberal democracy, it is hardly surprising that Tocqueville has come under attack from partisans of both of liberal democracy's constituent principles. On the one hand, he has earned the dislike of many classical liberals (or, as we sometimes call them today, libertarians or conservatives) because he goes behind and beyond the distinction between the public and private and explores relationships in areas where no good liberal should tread. Thus, according to Milton Friedman, any idea that government has a role in educating citizens about right and wrong "is a totalitarian view opening the road to thought control [that] would have been utterly unacceptable to the founders."[30] Tocqueville allows for the possibility of modifying a pure separation in order to maintain a liberal democratic regime—even though he emphasizes that any strategy that involves a breach of this separation must calculate the threat that it introduces in the long run to the sanctity of the principle itself.

On the other hand, by showing that the liberal principle of separation is of such fundamental importance for liberty in the modern world, Tocqueville has earned the dislike of certain communitarians and socialists, who are only too eager to cast aside the formal lines of separation in order to get down to the real business of achieving economic equality or a more compassionate society. Tocqueville has proven especially difficult for proponents of these schools because he employs the form of their argument—the contention that a purely liberal perspective is not adequate—but for a different end: to promote limited government.

For Tocqueville the aim of protecting the freedom of civil society from the threat of state incursion is, paradoxically, too important to be left to the simple iteration of the formal liberal principle of separation. Principles are not self-executing; they do not enforce themselves in society. Real freedom requires an actual *power* in society to resist the state and a *will* among the citizens to limit government and protect rights. This power and will do not miraculously appear as a consequence of the mere act of assertion of an abstract principle; they must be promoted. How to achieve the human qualities and the social arrangements that work over time to support the formal principle of limited government is one of the major questions for political science in a liberal democracy.

Tocqueville had certain concerns about the formal liberal principle considered even on its own level. True, it asserts the primacy of rights and thus supports the autonomy of a private sphere in civil society. Yet the whole theory of individual rights is based on the recognition of the sovereignty of the community that organizes to form a government to protect these rights. The possible implications of this kind of sovereign power are frightening to contemplate. Under a feudal order, the central power was never in a position to protect everyone's rights, for it lacked the power to do so; that limitation, however, was also a protection against any kind of central despotism. But in a modern regime, the idea of sovereignty itself, even if bounded in theory by the idea of individual rights, poses an immense threat to limited government. There is no longer the same barrier to the power of the central authority, and no single individual can easily stand up to it. Nor may citizens always wish to do so. Herein lies the threat of a modern "soft" despotism. If the people come to believe in the idea that the government always faithfully represents their interests, "there is hardly any limit to the confidence they will repose in it."[31]

Tocqueville's response to the difficulties implicit in the formal liberal principle was to attempt to strengthen that principle's real political efficacy, even if this required on occasion moving beyond or outside of it. If liberalism by itself was not entirely adequate for building up the forces of resistance to collectivism, then other extraliberal elements had to be added. Social pluralism, secondary powers and associations, and complex institutional arrangements are all needed to promote the liberal end. The combination of liberal and extraliberal features, for the sake of maintaining liberal democracy, is one of the most distinctive aspects of Tocqueville's approach.[32]

The Superintendence of Liberal Democracy by Political Science

Tocqueville's study of the foundation of liberal democracy—the true whole prior to the whole as stated by its formal principles—helps account for the complexity of his work. He shows us that what happens in one sphere (e.g., the religious, the artistic, or the philosophic) affects what happens in the others (the economic and the political). The formal or juridical boundaries, from this perspective, are not primary. Liberal democracy depends upon a certain political culture, which is a product not just of law, but of philosophic and religious views, of habits and sentiments. The creation of a supportive political culture is not, however, automatic; the interaction between the private and public spheres does not necessarily regulate itself in a way that supports liberal democracy.

The private sphere must, accordingly, be superintended by a self-conscious effort. The immediate response is probably to think of the state as the best agency to perform this task. But if this task is handled chiefly by the state, in particular by the central authority, it would add to centralized power and contribute further to conceiving of "government as the sole, simple, providential, and creative force" in society.[33] Even where the central state can be used effectively, its benefits must be carefully weighed and discounted against the long-term effect of people's overall reliance on government. The means of promoting liberal democracy cannot habitually be contrary to its ends and still succeed in promoting those ends.

Superintendence, accordingly, requires other strategies besides the direct use of state power and other actors besides the state. Where the state does act, it will often be preferable for it to proceed obliquely and indirectly—not by overt regulation, but by quietly influencing the conditions that encourage or discourage certain activities over the long term. This is "public policy" exercised in its most subtle and often its most efficacious way.[34]

Tocqueville's analysis of this delicate task of superintendence in a liberal democracy resolves itself into a simple question: How can those in society's autonomous or private spheres act to maintain the regime in which they enjoy the privilege of acting in autonomous spheres? How can people use their freedom in a way that enables them to maintain their freedom? This is one of the fundamental problems of liberal democracy. It can only be dealt with—solved would be too strong a word—by and with the aid of political science.

Political science, as an enterprise in society, has a distinct role. It takes the place of a portion of the tutelary power that is assigned to the state in nonliberal regimes. Political science performs this task not, obviously, by physical coercion—not even the *American Political Science Review* possesses this kind of naked power—but by inserting itself into society on the strength of an appeal to reason. Reason indicates where political science fits in society and how it is needed. Whatever its theoretical aims, political science also has this clear practical function. It aims to influence "those who direct society," which in a liberal regime refers not just to political legislators or elected officials but also—among others—to religious leaders, poets, scientists, film producers, social philosophers, historians, and social scientists.[35] Because authority is so widely dispersed in a liberal democracy, its legislators are also widely dispersed.

It is to the leaders in these fields that Tocqueville poses the question that guides the enterprise of political science in a liberal democracy: What is the poetry, the art, the jurisprudence, the philosophy, the music, the theater, the history, and the social science that supports and sustains a liberal democracy and that allows those who live in liberal societies to enjoy their liberty in those fields? Clearly, this formulation is paradoxical. A liberal regime frees certain realms from direct political control or regulation. In a formal sense, it depoliticizes them. But it is this very circumstance that makes it necessary that these same realms be freely repoliticized—not formally or by law, for this would threaten the juridical principle of the regime, but informally by means of a process of self-regulation guided by political science.[36]

Are there, then, no truly autonomous realms in society? Is it not possible to speak of art for art's sake, religion for religion's sake, philosophy for philosophy's sake, or social science for social science's sake (i.e., for understanding the operation of society)? There is no simple answer to this question. These activities can clearly proceed for the most part on their own. Modern artists may devote themselves to self-exploration, the religious to serving the Deity, philosophers to multiplying linguistic distinctions, and social scientists to elaborating correlations. The formal autonomy that liberal democracy grants to these realms is designed to promote a great deal of actual autonomy.

Yet in the final analysis, no realm of thought or activity is entirely autonomous. What goes on in each of these realms ultimately affects the foundation on which the political order rests, even if this is denied or ignored. And none of these realms can enjoy its autonomy without existing in a physical place that permits and protects it. Every human activity must have a "home"—which, for all practical purposes, means a political regime. Accordingly, unless one's sole concern is for the "Heavenly City" without regard for life on this earth, it is necessary to consider how that home can be secured. Political effects eventually result from almost every important human activity, whether that fact is openly admitted or not.

If the overtones of this view of the primacy of the political sound menacing to those concerned with the liberalism of liberal democracy, this reaction only confirms the special difficulty liberal democracy faces in sustaining itself. In a regime of formally autonomous spheres, those in each private sphere will be inclined to insist that their activities are entirely private and lacking in any public dimension; or, if they concede a public dimension, they will say their activities affect the culture—understood as the sum total of serious activity in the autonomous spheres—but not really the political order. People proclaim their autonomy without pausing to acknowledge the political externalities of their activities, especially the political externalities of activities in the moral and intellectual realm. But the most important externalities are moral and intellectual.

Another, and virtually opposite, tendency Tocqueville observed is becoming more prevalent in many areas of society today. Some intellectual leaders in the private spheres, far from insisting on the nonpolitical character of their activity, are the loudest in denouncing an apolitical posture and the first to call for a full political commitment. Religion, or art, or education must in the first instance be committed and political. However, the source for these various calls for the politicization of culture is not systematic political science, but other intellectual doctrines in society that supply politically oriented ideas and offer political programs.

According to Tocqueville's analysis, there is a certain space in the intellectual map of society that is open to ideas that influence how "those who direct society" think about politics. Tocqueville sought to fill this space with political science, understood as a rational inquiry that investigates the relationship of doctrines, actions, and structures to maintaining different forms of government. To the extent that political science is unable to occupy this space, it either lies vacant or is filled by other modes of thinking, based, for example, on ethical or scientific or historical reasoning. Today, it is more and more these modes of thought, rather than political science, that set the agenda of our thinking about politics. These other forms of reasoning are less helpful than political science to maintaining liberal democracy—indeed, they have often been indifferent or hostile to it.

Conclusion

Maintaining liberal democracy requires the diffusion of political science in society. Political science as an enterprise working in behalf of liberal democracy seeks to induce the leaders of each major area of society to consider the relationship of their activity to maintaining the regime; political science is a perpetual gadfly for liberal democracy. As part of a liberal education, it aims to inculcate a way of reasoning that makes students conscious of the connections of private activities to the maintenance of a regime. As a research or academic enterprise, it seeks to supply some of the general answers to this question, or at any rate to set an agenda for their discussion in different contexts.

Liberal democracy depends on creating a society in which people, operating in the relative autonomy of their formally private spheres, do not generate consequences that turn against the regime that supports their formal autonomy. Maintaining both the formal lines and the political culture that supports them is a difficult task. Everyone is prepared, when it suits them, to call attention to the threats to liberal democracy that come from any breach of the formal lines of separation, but many refuse to give serious consideration to the requirements of character that support the regime. It is often said today that liberalism is threatened by the growth of a new religious moralism that seeks to scale the wall between politics and culture. Yet in focusing on the threat to liberalism that comes from suggested uses of state power to regulate private spheres, we may forget to ask whether those who operate in many of these spheres have not almost invited this response by their stubborn unwillingness to promote the political culture needed to support the regime in which they live.

It would be tragic if our only choice were one between a harsh corrective action that threatens the principle it wants to rescue and an indifference that continually invites this threat. Tocqueville's political science offers a way of escaping this awful choice. He is our political thinker, and we need him today as much as ever before.

3

Traditional Political Science

MODERN POLITICAL SCIENTISTS often divide the history of the discipline into two great epochs: the era of what they call "old" or "traditional" political science, which began with Plato or Aristotle in Athens in the fourth century B.C. and which continued until well into this century; and the era of "modern political analysis" or of the "behavioral persuasion," which began with Charles Merriam and Harold Laswell in the 1930s and which achieved dominance in the profession by the 1960s.[1] Honored, therefore, are those of the last generation who lived through such a momentous intellectual revolution.

If this version of the history of the discipline can be accepted, then traditional political science, which lasted for some twenty-three centuries, has a long and distinguished list of practitioners. Inevitably, in any attempt to present a single coherent view, a selection of some kind, no doubt somewhat arbitrary, must be made. The traditional approach, I will say, is best represented in the works of Aristotle, Montesquieu, and Tocqueville. These authors focus the study of politics on a direct, common-sense encounter with what they hold to be politically most important: the form of government or regime under which one lives. Political science takes its bearings from this encounter. It concentrates on regimes—on their quality, their character, and on the "sources of [their] destruction and preservation."[2] The regime or form of government is the most inclusive concept of traditional political science; it refers to the form or the shape of a society, as fixed by who or what rules, and by the principle of justice and the sentiments that dominate society. The efforts of different groups or parties to constitute a regime—to win power and to have their own view prevail—make up the central source of conflict in political life.[3]

Modern political analysis, by contrast, begins with what its adherents define as the irreducible unit of politics: the "power act."[4] This starting point enables political science to avoid the errors and misconceptions that flow from relying on a category like the regime, which, it is claimed, represents a "reification" based on a metaphysical assumption.[5] By beginning with the power act as the unit of study, modern political analysis can broaden the study of politics and focus attention on the political aspects of all human activities, be it the family, the country club, or the founding of a political state. Modern political analysis thus aims both to clarify and to enlarge the scope of the discipline.

A number of political scientists, however, have recently called into question the advantages claimed for modern political analysis over the traditional approach.[6] But before any comparison between them can be made, a statement of the method of traditional political science is needed, which I shall attempt to provide in this chapter. In an effort not to prejudge the merits of the two approaches, I avoid wherever possible referring to the first approach as *old* or *traditional*, as this might carry the implication that it is obsolete. I prefer to call it simply *political science*, reserving the adjective *traditional* for those instances when it must be distinguished from the modern variant.

The political science of Aristotle, Montesquieu, and Tocqueville is made up of three interrelated parts: (1) an analysis of conditions or place (historical sociology); (2) an analysis of regime types and what maintains or undermines them (general political science); and (3) an analysis of what maintains or undermines regime alternatives in a specific context (American politics, French politics, Iranian politics, etc.). In addition, Aristotle has a fourth part, an analysis of the best regime, that is not explicitly found in the political thought of Montesquieu or Tocqueville. In this chapter, I shall survey the three parts of political science that are shared by these authors, relying where possible on Tocqueville's work in order to maintain the focus on liberal democracy.

The First Part of Political Science: A Knowledge of Place

The first part of political science consists of a study, for want of a better term, of place. A knowledge of place seeks to understand the constraints and developmental forces at work in the world both in time (a historical era) and space (a people or a nation). It aims to situate actors in the relevant context—in Tocqueville's words, "the fatal circle"—within which they must choose.[7] This general field of study comes closest to constituting the subdiscipline we know today as historical sociology or political development.

The Historical Era

When considering a historical era, political analysis focuses not literally on a time period as such, but on a broad commonality that operates within a historical context. Aristotle distinguishes clearly between ancient times and modern times. Montesquieu divides the history of the West into the ancient period, the feudal period, and the modern Enlightenment period. Tocqueville gives each historical commonality the name "world" or, following the historian François Guizot, "civilization."[8] When Tocqueville speaks of modern times, he is not referring to the contemporary civilizations of the American Indians or the Africans, but to "the Christian world," meaning the areas of the modern world influenced by Christianity and the Enlightenment.[9] In studying the modern world, Tocqueville attempts to describe the forces that have shaped its character—such as Christianity, the Enlightenment, and commerce—and the common developments that are taking place within it.

Tocqueville's approach to the study of civilizations relies on a general analytic scheme of the basic causes of social life developed by Montesquieu. Montesquieu divides the causes into two general categories: "physical causes" (geography, climate, placement in relation to others), and "moral causes" (which derive from human beings interacting with one another and their environment). The moral causes consist of such elements as religion, manners, the way of thinking, the economic-technological state, civil law, and the "political law" (the laws or traditions that determine the arrangement of political offices and distribution of political power). These different moral causes relate to each other in complex cause-effect relationships.[10]

In this scheme, the weight of the different causes is constant, in the sense that a virgin people put in the same place and subject to the same circumstances would, except for accident, be constrained in their development in the same way. But once a particular civilization is launched, there is an interplay among the various causes in each context. Consequently, key elements of the moral cause—above all religion, manners, and the way of thinking—evolve in distinct ways in each civilization. This distinctness consists of both a different weight for each cause (for example, physical causes count for more among the Native Americans than the Europeans) and a different character for each cause (the Christian religion has different effects than Islam).[11]

The weight and character of the causes in any place may be explained in part by a historical inquiry that traces everything back to some "original" time. This is one reason why systematic historical studies suddenly become so important for Montesquieu. For the current analysis of any particular civilization, however, the relationship among the causes is always distinct. The causes cannot therefore be applied to a particular case as part of a rigorous theory in which their respective values are known in advance, but only as general categories of analysis, whose specific content and relationship must be discovered empirically in each context.[12]

Tocqueville was less interested than Montesquieu in a general study of civilizations and focused more of his attention on the modern era. The most striking fact about modern Christian-Enlightenment civilization, he argued, was found in the development of a broad socioeconomic condition (a "social state"), which he originally called "democracy," meaning here a growing equality of conditions that contrasted sharply with the hierarchical arrangement of the preceding "aristocratic" period.[13] Analysis of a social state can be of considerable value. A social state sets in motion certain tendencies that operate across all societies, which allows one to speak at a certain level of analysis of the character of life at one time, irrespective of the specific regime, and compare it with the character of life under another social state, irrespective of the specific regime.

In the end, however, Tocqueville makes clear that this kind of analysis ignores the most important question, which is the character of the political regime. While the social state limits the choice of political regimes, it does not determine it. It was for this reason that he later regretted having used the term *democracy* to refer to a social state, for *democracy* is ordinarily associated in the first instance with a form of rule, not a socioeconomic condition. "Democratic government," he wrote, "can mean only one thing: a government where the people more or less participate in their government."[14] The modern social state of equality of conditions is compatible with at least three different regime types. Because the political issue is more fundamental than the sociological one, developmental knowledge should ultimately be in the service of political knowledge.

The Nation and Genius of a People

After situating human development in history, an analysis of place seeks to locate it in a narrower context of geography, as the character of a nation or people. A people is formed initially in a nation, but some part of a people may leave for colonies. The part that leaves takes with it certain of the original characteristics. Tocqueville can thus speak of differences in the New World among Anglo-Americans, French-Americans, and Spanish-Americans, each people having its own particular developmental forces at work within it, much as a civilization does. All nations of the Christian-Enlightenment world are influenced by the general social state of equality, but each nation has its own special situation and history, which gives it a particular character.

The analysis of the nation is thus a second lens to fit on top of the analysis of a civilization. In comparing peoples or nations of the same civilization, the basic causes operate with less variation, so that it is possible to be more refined about the specific factors that help account for differences. For example, groups of French, Anglos, and Spaniards came to the New World, but produced quite different results. These differences, according to Tocqueville, owed something to different geographical circumstances, but the main factor was a particular moral cause: the Anglo-Americans, because of a set of mental habits that derived from being a self-governing people, were rapidly able to put themselves in a dominant position.[15]

As in the case of his analysis of a civilization, Tocqueville's study of each particular nation makes use of a scheme of basic causes. Here, Tocqueville took the division between physical and moral causes and then subdivided the moral causes into two basic categories, yielding a three-cause model: the physical environment (geography, resources, proximity to other powerful nations, etc.); mores (beliefs, sentiments, and way of thinking); and laws (civil laws and the political law, meaning the arrangement of political offices and power).[16] These causes again have no fixed weight, but assume their precise character in light of the history of their interaction in each setting.

The most important and enduring constraint at work in a nation or people is its mores. The sum of a people's mores, where it assumes an identifiable form, is referred to variously as the "genius" of a nation, its "national character," its "general spirit," or—to employ a contemporary term—its "political culture."[17] This concept is central in the search for a knowledge of place.

Nations are not eternal. The nations about which Tocqueville speaks (e.g., France, Spain, England) did not always exist. They were products of a historical process. Obviously, what was created and evolved could be destroyed or altered. Nevertheless, these nations do exist now, and they have formed peoples with certain characters or dispositions, the staying power of which is very strong. Even if the legal boundaries of these nations were to change, these character traits would remain in evidence for some time and act as a powerful constraint on whoever defines or imposes the political law. (There may, of course be subcultures within a legal state that may be distinct and not share the dominant culture.)

Because the genius of a nation is so important, it can be used in some cases in a way that *almost* suggests the idea of determining or explaining the form of government. Thus Tocqueville observes that the original inhabitants of New England "left to their descendants the habits, the ideas, and the mores that are most fitting to lead to the flourishing of a liberal democracy." In a similar vein, *The Federalist* comments that "no other form of government [but a liberal democratic form] would be reconcilable with the genius of the people of America."[18]

Yet in the final analysis, the genius of a nation does not determine the political regime. The concept, even as used in these statements, is employed not so much to explain the act of instituting a form of government as to set forth the dominant reality a legislator faces in a given situation. Traditional political scientists used the concept of genius to help understand the likely consequences that would follow *if* a certain action were taken, not to predict which actions actually would be taken. The concept was never designed to suggest that legislators are compelled to choose in a certain way. What it can tell us is that an attempt to institute a form of government greatly at odds with the prevailing genius might have little chance of succeeding; or that if such a government is to have a chance to succeed, it might only be able to do so with the application of an unusual degree of coercion.

The genius of the nation is thus a central constraint in almost any situation. But it does not fully bind human action. No matter what the prevailing genius, one can imagine those coming momentarily to power imposing a political law very different from one that seems to grow out of or fit with it. One can also envision this effort leading to chaos or disaster or, under certain circumstances and with enough guile or coercion, to a government that might actually prevail. The possibility of a swift, decisive, and successful change in the genius of a people, however, is something Montesquieu preferred to associate with the rare circumstance in which a political ruler has near-total authority, as in the case of conquest: "A conquest may destroy pernicious prejudices, and lay . . . the nation under a better genius."[19] Because the political law is itself a major cause of the genius of a people, the result of instituting a new political law, even one at odds with the prevailing genius, is a change in some degree of the genius of that people. The genius is always changing—albeit usually slowly.[20]

The analysis of place, accordingly, can take us only so far. It can tell us about the basic disposition of a nation at any given time, and it may even provide a strong clue about how most people are likely to think. But it cannot tell us in advance how either political leaders or the people will act in specific situations. This limitation in the explanatory power of a knowledge of place is not unduly troubling to practitioners of political science. The aim of political science is not to develop deterministic explanations for the benefit of other scholars, but to elaborate a mode of thinking that can be of assistance to potential legislators, helping them to understand what actions would be wise or foolish or for the good or the harm of a nation. The concept of genius thus has great value, notwithstanding its inability to account for what takes place in history.

In many situations, there is a rough match or equilibrium between a prevailing genius and a certain form of government. Acknowledging that match may be the only viable choice, or at any rate the only choice that would not entail undue coercion. As Montesquieu wrote, "it is better to say that the government that is most conformable to nature is that in which its particular disposition fits best with the disposition of the people for whom it is established."[21] Proceeding with due regard for the genius is a major part of political prudence, and it in turn has an important bearing on political ethics.[22]

A systematic study of the situations facing political actors does not, of course, exhaust all normative issues. In any situation there is some margin of choice. The risks one might wish to run must include consideration not only of the probability of success but also of the worth of the alternatives. Nevertheless, a political ethic that disregards prevailing constraints cannot even begin to calculate the effects of any action. It is therefore defective, unless one is working according to an ethical system that ignores the concerns of this world and considers only a sacred realm beyond.

A deeper reason why an analysis of place cannot produce a full explanation of how individuals will act is human freedom, used for the moment in the strict sense of human beings not being fully determined in their action by any combination of factors in their environment. Environmental conditions may incline people to act in certain ways, but individuals will sometimes break with the expected pattern. "Their nature," Montesquieu writes, "requires them to be free [or self-initiating] agents."[23] Freedom is thus a source of change in the case of all of the moral causes; it is one of the main causes of these causes.

Self-initiating action can influence society by altering the character not just of the political law, but of any of the moral causes. An action or idea having an important effect on the religion, the way of thinking, or the state of technology will end by having implications for the genius of a people and eventually its political order. To cite two major examples, Christianity and the Enlightenment profoundly affected the genius of various nations, indeed virtually created new civilizations. Lesser changes in religion and philosophy have also had important effects.

The most usual and most dramatic ways, however, in which legislators' self-initiating action affects society is through the effort to define or impose a form of political rule in society. The political law is the moral cause that most immediately and directly determines the sum of moral causes, and it is the cause to which people are most attracted when attempting to change society. It has this character because political power is immediately authoritative. Political power directly commands the other realms—that is, it rules—in a way that no other moral cause does.

What I have been calling here man's freedom or self-initiating action, refers, to repeat, to the mere descriptive fact of being undetermined, and consequently to the fact that actions may set off effects that can change the whole environment. Action of this kind should not, however, be equated with freedom in a higher sense of knowing what one is doing and thus of having a reasonable chance to accomplish an intended end. In fact, action that is free in the first sense is often not free in the second one. Most action that changes society occurs without people having any real intention of doing so; or it occurs where people have such an intention, but act without knowledge or skill and end up producing consequences they never contemplated; or it occurs where people, having such knowledge, act to benefit themselves, without regard for society as a whole. In all of these cases the actions, while free, are blind in respect to achieving any political end, or at any rate indifferent to achieving any end for the good of society.

To have a reasonable chance of achieving an intended end, people must take account of the reality of their situation. Supplying a knowledge of the processes at work in society, so that legislators might achieve their objectives and achieve them for the good of society, is the practical object of traditional political science. Traditional political science is usually addressed to, or designed to influence, legislators in the usual sense (statesmen and politicians), especially when they deal with the political law as founders or constitutional reformers. The centrality of political power in defining society—not to mention that those who hold political power control people's security and material well-being—justifies this focus on political action as it is ordinarily understood. Yet actions affecting any of the moral causes can influence the genius of a people and thereby alter the political law. This opens up the possibility of indirect legislation deriving from nominally nonpolitical realms. One can therefore consider the realms of civil law, religion, political theory, and philosophy as being potentially political realms ("regimes," as it were, that affect political regimes in the conventional sense); and one can consider jurists, religious leaders, political scientists, and philosophers as being potentially the most powerful princes. "For developed peoples," Tocqueville wrote, political theory "creates—or at least forms—the basic general ideas, which in turn form the conditions in which statesmen act and which originate the laws these statesmen believe they have devised."[24]

Because individuals exercise self-initiating action at the point of attempting to establish political laws, a developmental knowledge cannot fully explain the form of government. This limitation was not a problem for political science, as the pursuit of causal knowledge was not its ultimate end. A knowledge of place was not an independent discipline having its own criteria of importance, but one part of political science.

Many of the controversies today concerning the nature of explanation in the social sciences only emerged when practitioners of historical sociology began to associate political science with an effort to account for nearly all social phenomena by determined causes and that treated anything that cannot be explained as a "residual" that lies beyond rational discussion in a realm governed by arbitrary normative choices. For traditional political science, however, science does not end with historical sociology. Historical sociology leads up to other kinds of analysis that seek explanations of a different sort. Long before one arrives at purely normative questions, there is still a great deal of room for systematic inquiry.[25]

Identifying Forms of Government

The discussion above raises the question of whether the regime should be identified with the genius of a people or with the political law. The initial response is probably to favor the political law, not in a legal sense, but in the empirical sense of discovering who actually holds power in society. Thus, where a king governs, the system is a monarchy; where the people govern, it is a certain kind of democracy; and where a "power elite" or an "establishment" governs, even behind the veil of a democratic constitution, the system is an oligarchy. On further reflection, however, this approach seems to simplify things too much, for it ignores the role played by the genius of a people in shaping the way of life in a society.

Political science approaches the complex problem of identifying the regime by considering both the political law and the genius. Simplifying greatly, there are two possible categories in the relationship between these two factors. In one category, the genius either supports or is not systematically opposed to the political law; this situation is one, roughly speaking, of congruence or equilibrium. In a second category, there is a conflict between important parts of the political culture and the political law; this is a situation of incongruence or disequilibrium.

For the first category, the regime can be identified with the political law. Included here are cases as different as those in which the genius has slowly evolved to prefigure and support a regime (as with liberal democracy in the northern states of the United States in the 1780s) and those in which the rulers may have brutally pacified and transformed a political culture, creating a new one that is more or less in step with the government (as in the case of Cuba since the 1960s).[26] Congruence in this sense should not be equated with regime stability, as it is only one factor that contributes to that end. Thus, a political culture that actively supports the political law may nevertheless contain elements that will destabilize it. Too great a love of equality, for example, can destroy a democracy.[27] Alternatively, a political law that is congruent with the political culture may still be fatally flawed on its own terms, leading to turmoil and instability; this was the case, Tocqueville noted, with many of the state governments in the 1780s.[28]

The second category poses greater problems for identifying the regime. Situations of incongruence are found under colonial arrangements and hegemonic spheres of influence, where an outside power may impose and support a government that is alien to the dominant political culture. (Such has been the case with many of the communist regimes in Eastern Europe set up by the Soviet Union after World War II.) Or it may occur where a domestic force holds immediate political power and is strong enough to maintain itself despite significant opposition from the political culture, as in Shah Pahlavi's reign in Iran (1953-1979) in the face of a growing undercurrent of Islamic fundamentalism. In disequilibrium situations where those in power seek not merely to hang on, but to perpetuate their political law, a race takes place between the power holders' deliberate (and often brutal) efforts to bring the political culture into line, and the tendency of the political culture to defeat the political law, either by sustaining an opposition or by gradually modifying the law's operation until it has been virtually captured by the spirit of the political culture. Often there is movement in both directions; the political culture shifts to support the political law, and the political law changes to accord more with the political culture.

Disequilibrium should not be equated with regime instability, though it is usually a major contributing factor to it. In some cases, those in power possess such formidable means of control that they are known to be capable of meeting any threat. The result can be a stable regime, at least for a certain period. Even though all cases of disequilibrium present the problem of governing without consent, they obviously must be judged quite differently; they include cases as different as those of an enlightened despotism that seeks the good of society and a brutal tyranny that aims only at exploiting the populace.

The importance of the political culture in determining the ultimate fate in many situations has led some to the idea of classifying political cultures as regimes (e.g., a democratic political culture or an authoritarian culture). These efforts can only go so far, however, because a genius falls short of being a full-fledged or well-articulated idea of rule; rather, it is a set of habits and mores that operates as a constraint, often showing itself more by what it opposes than by what, precisely, it requires. The shape a regime will assume can never really be known until there is some articulated notion of who should rule, either by a government or by a group or party that aspires to govern.

How, then, does one identify the regime in a situation of disequilibrium? The task is a difficult one, but the difficulty reflects not so much the inadequacy of conventional terminology as the ambiguity of the situation itself. Because disequilibrium is the most noteworthy fact about the case, the best description of the regime is a statement of the components of the conflict. To illustrate, we find two notable discussions of disequilibrium situations in Tocqueville's analysis of the United States. The first treats the late colonial period, in which the political law was formally monarchic but was already being eroded or modified by a more democratic genius. The second treats the United States as a whole in the 1820s, where Tocqueville identifies a disequilibrium between the (generally) liberal democratic principles of the national government and a political culture in the South built on habits and mores deriving from the institution of slavery.

How one identifies a regime in disequilibrium may thus depend on the circumstances and on the practical purpose for which the identification is intended. In dealing with a government in areas where those in formal power make authoritative decisions, the political law may be the decisive analytic consideration. In dealing with elements of society that the government does not fully control, or in looking ahead at prospects for change, the genius may be the more important consideration. The possibilities mirror the complexities of political life itself.

The Second Part of Political Science: General Political Science

The second part of political science consists of identifying regime types and of studying the factors or causes that support or undermine them. This part may be referred to as general political science, as it constitutes the core of the analytic study of political phenomena.

A regime type—for example, liberal democracy or monarchy—is not an actual, particular regime, but a concept or abstraction. In Tocqueville's terminology, it is a "general idea," meaning a concept that identifies a set of things that shares something essential.[29] A regime type refers in the abstract to a way of ordering a society expressed in terms of who rules, according to what end or principle, and dominated by what sentiment or passion.

Political scientists begin to learn about regime types by analyzing particular cases. It was by studying the United States, for example, that Tocqueville derived or abstracted the regime type of liberal democracy. (As it turned out, the United States was the only extant example of this kind of regime.) Particular instances serve to help one grasp a general type. But it is not the statistical average of existing cases that best defines a type. The average may not fully reveal its nature, as there may be too few cases in existence, or the cases in existence may be too tainted by particular and accidental characteristics. A general type, correctly drawn, represents the model that is least adulterated by the particular and thus the one that is best able to provide general guidance without introducing error.[30]

General political science begins by setting forth a list or a classification system of regime types. Aristotle and Montesquieu each developed a typology that did not rely formally on historical periods, whereas Tocqueville's three-regime schema was tied more specifically to the modern historical era.[31] For all of these thinkers, a regime type is a specific kind of whole in which certain things go together and certain things do not. Ascertaining the things that go together, above all the factors that support or undermine each regime, is the principal concern of general political science. Clearly, many factors that support or harm a regime are not unique to it. All regimes, for example, would have reason to value knowledge of military and administrative sciences. But the supports that differentiate regimes—the things, for example, that contribute to upholding a feudal aristocracy as distinct from a small republic, or a republic as distinct from a liberal democracy—are not only more revealing about the character of regimes but also the most difficult social phenomena to understand. Political science is the most elusive of all the social sciences.

When political scientists look at a particular case in order to learn about a regime type, their objective is different from that of the ethnologist or the anthropologist. The aim is not to describe all the laws or mores of a given society or to dwell on the customs that appear the most curious. The political scientist is selective, attempting to isolate the elements that work to maintain or undermine the particular regime being studied, and then to ascertain the extent to which these elements might support the general regime type, outside of that particular context.[32]

The knowledge of general political science is also different from that sought under the first part of political science (a knowledge of place). The political scientist is interested here in establishing abstract, analytic relationships about what maintains or undermines different regime types. These relationships or laws are of the following type: if more (or less) of A, then more (or less) of B, all other things being equal. For example, Tocqueville contends that the more a people in a liberal democratic state can learn and develop the art of associating with one another, the more liberal democracy will be secure. Montesquieu gave this general method its most systematic expression in his discussion of the key human passion that he postulates to undergird each regime type: honor (or preference for one's self) for a monarchy; virtue (or love of the country) for a republic; and fear for a despotism. He then proceeds to explore the means—the civil laws, customs, and form of education—that would work to promote each of these human passions.

The objective of the first part of political science (an analysis of place) is different. When referring to a particular place, the aim is to understand the cause or genesis of an actual state of affairs in that specific context: B happened because of A. For example, in Tocqueville's famous chapter "The Principal Causes That Tend to Maintain a Democratic Republic in the United States," he seeks to explain why a liberal democratic order came to exist in the United States. He attributes this result to the mores of the original inhabitants, to the economic system, to certain key civil laws, and finally to a wise set of legislators, who, mindful of the democratic genius of the people, instituted a liberal democratic constitution. When referring more generally to models of development, a knowledge of place aims to devise categories and relationships that can be used to explain what has happened in a number of cases (or what is most likely to happen) whenever certain conditions apply. Explanations here take the following form: where we find a certain thing (A), B has generally followed (and is most likely to follow). For example, Montesquieu, who had never been to New York City, wrote that "wherever there is commerce, there we meet with gentle manners," and Tocqueville argued that where one finds a general equality of conditions (a democratic social state), there will be a strong tendency for people to be suspicious of secondary institutions.[33]

Sociological explanations (or predictions) of this last sort do, of course, state general relationships or laws. As such they are akin in form to the relationships sought by general political science. But the set of relationships studied under developmental sociology is different, as the objective is to inquire into what has happened or what will happen and to discover explanations or laws that cover the largest number of historical cases with the greatest degree of accuracy. By contrast, the laws sought by general political science do not aim to discover what has occurred or what is actually likely to occur in history, but instead to state hypothetical relationships about what maintains different regimes: if A is done, then B would be more likely to follow. Whether A itself is likely to be done is a different question—and not the essential one. The knowledge of general political science is not sought principally for predicting what actually goes on in history, but for use by those who possess it—for their understanding and, more importantly, for its application to society. For this last purpose, the relationships of greatest interest sometimes involve matters that do not occur very often, but that would be of great importance to society if they occurred.

The knowledge of general political science does, of course, have a predictive aspect to it. Where a measure is taken that is accounted for under one of the relationships studied, then we can say, all things being equal, that a given consequence will probably follow. The larger the number of such relationships and the more often they have reference to events, the better general political science will be able to predict. Hence, there is a substantial overlap between a knowledge of place and general political science. But, to repeat, the knowledge of general political science is not sought in the first instance to explain or predict historical events.

What, then, is the relationship of general political science to the real world? If it does not seek to predict in history, in what sense does it connect to reality? General political science, it would seem, takes on a social reality insofar as it is applied and put into effect. Its utility depends on the extent to which those who direct society have been influenced by it and choose to make use of it. Admittedly, most political activity takes place without reference to general political science. But this fact has no bearing on its validity.[34]

The reason why political science is so little used is a matter about which one can only speculate. Certainly, it cannot be fully explained by the difficulty or expense of applying political science. There are many instances in which it could be quite easily employed, and the average political scientist can be had for a much lower rate than a lawyer, a doctor, or a mechanic. A better reason seems to be that most of those who act in politics have never been exposed to political science or, if they have been, are not able to appreciate its potential benefits. Finally, it may also be that a guiding concern of political science —the good of society as a whole—is not usually a high priority for those in positions of power.

The differences between the objectives of historical sociology and general political science are important. Students of historical sociology tend to measure the worth of explanation by actual historical results; they address themselves to what *has* happened or what *will* happen. Students of general political science are more concerned with what *would* happen (or what becomes more probable) on the assumption of doing a certain thing. These assumptions obviously cannot be outside the realm of human possibility, for then the discipline would no longer be science but fantasy (or science fiction). The assumptions on which knowledge is sought must involve conceivable actions (even if these actions are improbable) that could take place under conceivable circumstances (even if these circumstances are unlikely).

The worth of lengthy inquiries into improbable actions taken under unlikely circumstances has been long debated and contested. However, certain political scientists have clearly seen value in an analysis that elaborates a regime type without considering the usual constraints that are in operation. It is in making this kind of inquiry, for example, that Aristotle sketches his best possible form of government. Yet that form of government, however improbable, does not rest on any assumption about human beings or human relations that Aristotle did not believe could exist under the best of conceivable circumstances. It is not based on an ideal or a wish that humans beings might be better or more just than they can be. For this reason, even Aristotle's best regime remains in many respects surprisingly realistic.

Regime types are not of a fixed number. Certainly, their practicality as choices depends on conditions that vary in history. Certain arrangements may, because of technical capacities, seem improbable in one era—indeed might be difficult even to conceive—yet emerge as possibilities in another. Liberal democracy, as a society in which the majority of all people is middle-class, could not be considered probable in ancient Greece, for the greater part of the population was always poor. New kinds of regimes, developed perhaps with the help of political science itself, may also be invented, as *The Federalist* argues was the case for modern representative government.[35]

The emergence of new possibilities does not necessarily imply a change in the fundamental standards by which regimes are judged. But it may lead to changes in the evaluation of particular regimes, for the qualities embodied in various regimes may be arranged and combined in new or unforeseen ways. For these reasons, political science must from time to time be recast—or, as Tocqueville put it, "a new political science is needed for a new world." Furthermore, many of the practical relationships that political science explores, if they are to be helpful or interesting, will have to be adapted and altered to fit into concrete terms of the times in which ones lives. The political science of large nation-states has a different set of practical concerns than the political science of city-states. Political science is thus always in some measure being updated. It has no final version.

From an immediate practical standpoint—from that of aiding a would-be legislator—the regimes of greatest interest to the political scientist are those that represent actual possibilities in one's time. For speculative or theoretical reasons, however, some are disposed to contemplate the full scope of human possibilities and to make comparisons among them. Tocqueville, for example, sometimes judges modern democratic regimes against the regimes of an aristocratic social state, even though he makes clear that these judgments cannot directly guide any practical choice.[36]

The study of regime types that are not current possibilities is, nevertheless, more than an academic exercise. It is important to keep alive the full range of possibilities, if only for another day when conditions may have dramatically changed. Moreover, the study of any complex regime, such as a liberal democracy, has much to gain from a consideration of other possibilities, even if they are not fully viable under present conditions. The effort to maintain any regime involves discovering and cultivating, not the specificities toward which it inclines—for these are often what leads to its destruction or degradation—but the specificities that promote it. Liberal democracy, as one of the more complex and heterogeneous regimes, can benefit from drawing on a number of different regime principles. It has something important to learn from the calm and orderly calculations of interest of modern commercial liberalism, the virtue or communitarianism of small republics, and the sense of individual pride of European aristocracy.

The Third Part of Political Science: The Political Science of a Particular Place

The third part of political science aims at attaining knowledge of how to maintain or undermine alternative possible regimes in a particular place. Knowledge of this kind is the focus of study for the various area or nation specialties, such as American politics, French politics, British politics, Iranian politics, and the like. The analysis here normally begins with the actual regime in place and then asks how that regime could be maintained (or undermined) and how other possible regimes could be established and maintained.

The focus of the third part of political science differs from the first two parts. Unlike the first part (a knowledge of place), but like the second (general political science), the study of the political science of a given nation focuses on regimes and regime alternatives. The knowledge it seeks is not historical explanation or prediction, but knowledge of a hypothetical sort: what would happen if something were done; for example, what steps taken in China or France or Iran would shore up (or undermine) the existing regime. Yet this part of political science differs from the second part in that it focuses not on general regime types, but on regimes as they might exist in a particular place, as constrained by its particular history and character. Knowledge deriving from the first part of political science is thus highly useful for those concerned with the regime analysis of a particular nation.

Practitioners of this third part of political science immerse themselves in the study of their chosen nation or area, becoming expert in its political system, culture, and history. They bring to their studies whatever general methods or tools they happen to have acquired along the way. For traditional political science, however, the status of this third part of the discipline and how it relates to the other two parts of political science must be made conscious objects of reflection.

The political scientist, we have seen, can abstract from a particular case (e.g., the United States) to learn about a general regime type (e.g., liberal democracy). But is this whole process any more than an intellectual exercise? Does the elaboration of general regime types have any practical use in concrete cases? The worth of general political science clearly depends on its applicability to specific cases. The third part of the discipline is thus the part that tests the worth of the science as whole. All action takes place in the realm of particulars. No one lives in a general regime type as elaborated in a book of a political scientist, but in particular regimes established in a particular place.

In each place the regime question presents itself to political actors in terms of a choice among distinct possibilities in a specific context: what are the alternative regimes possible *here*, what are the supports available or conceivable for each alternative in *this* place, and the like.

There is, nevertheless, a link that exists between particular cases and general types. When deliberating about concrete alternatives, legislators sometimes conceive of their choices, at least in part, by reference to general types, and they use the knowledge of general types to throw light on particular situations. The American founders thus identified and expressed many of the key problems they faced in general terms; they asked whether it was possible to "find a republican remedy for the diseases most incident to republican government"—not merely an American remedy for the diseases most incident to American governments.[37] They made conscious use of "a science of politics" by which "the excellencies of republican government may be retained and its imperfections lessened or avoided."[38]

Of course, the American founding was no abstract exercise in liberal democratic model-building. Much of founders' task consisted in fitting a political law to a particular circumstance, which in many respects lay beyond the guidance or direction of general political science. One of the great discoveries of the Founding—what we today know as *federalism*—was initially not a formulation of general theory, but a response to the unique aspects of the situation at hand. Almost immediately, however, this accidental discovery became an object of conscious reflection—a general idea—that can be counted as one of the most significant improvements that the founders added to the "science of politics."[39]

The use of political science obviously presupposes its existence. There was a time, before political science had been discovered, when human beings conceived of political things almost entirely in terms bounded by their own particular community or culture—its gods, its ways, and its customs.[40] When political science, or something akin to it, was discovered in Ancient Greece—when people began to express the problem of political rule in terms of common forms that could be conceived of outside of one's own community— then it became possible for ideas about general regime types to have an effect on particular cases. This is the world in which we in the West now live.

Digression on the Theoretical Debate on General Ideas and Particulars

The status of the third part of political knowledge hinges on the relationship of general ideas to particular cases. This relationship raises a fundamental philosophical issue that has provoked one of the most important theoretical debates of the past two centuries. That debate has shaped, and continues to shape, the development of the social sciences.

The relationship of general ideas to particular cases was a major theme for Aristotle, Montesquieu, and Tocqueville. In Tocqueville's case, it was *the* fundamental metaphysical question. He speaks of the need for human beings, in their effort to make sense of the world, to use general ideas "to enclose a great number of analogous objects under a single form." Yet he immediately adds that a reliance on general ideas is fraught with problems, even where care is taken to avoid using empty or sloppy categories. The reason is that "there are no beings exactly alike in nature: no identical facts and no rules which can be indiscriminately applied to in the same way to several objects at once." The use of general categories therefore inevitably distorts our understanding of specific cases. Each case is unique, but the use of general ideas risks making us regard them as being somehow the same.[41]

This metaphysical problem has a further aspect to it. When human beings become conscious that they are making use of general ideas, they can exercise a degree of control over how much stock they put in them in interpreting the world. General ideas—concepts such as *state, progress*, and *class*—can be either frequently or sparingly employed as human tools for grasping reality. Not that the average person troubles himself or herself daily with this kind of problem, but philosophers and theorists do. And their judgments of how much trust to put in general ideas have an important influence on how—and how much—general ideas are actually used in society. Furthermore, because the way people conceive of the world has a profound influence on how they behave, it follows that philosophic views about general ideas ultimately affect reality. Philosophy, in some degree, makes reality—at least that portion of it that we as human beings can fashion according to the use of our intelligence. Tocqueville's particular worry was that modern intellectuals had come to rely far too much on general ideas and that the application of this mode of thought threatened to impose a sterile homogeneity on society.

The problem raised by the relationship between general ideas and particular cases is not, of course, confined to politics. Trainers train athletes, educators educate students, doctors treat patients. The worth of all of these activities ultimately proves itself in its application to individual cases—to the training of a certain athlete, the education of a certain student, or the treatment of a certain patient. As every trainer, educator, or doctor knows, no two cases are exactly alike. The approach employed therefore cannot derive entirely from general rules, but must grow partly out of experience with the nature or genius of each individual case. At the same time, these fields of inquiry rely on bodies of general theory that are held to be relevant to specific cases, albeit in different degrees.[42]

The applicability of general ideas to particular cases depends in large part on the degree to which the particular cases actually share something in common with one another. Political scientists today treat the act of voting—at least within a single nation—as a general idea, on the grounds that there is sufficient commonality in this act among different voters to allow for the development of interesting generalizations. Whether political regimes share enough in common for there to be a general science of regimes has for some time been a matter of dispute. Given both the relatively small number of cases involved in regime analysis and the differentiating impact of the genius of each nation, it is no wonder that some should ask: "Is a science of comparative politics possible?"[43]

Among those who often question whether such a science can exist, according to Tocqueville, are political leaders, exactly the people who he thought "should be practicing this science." Practical political leaders tend to regard the "field of politics as too variable and too much in flux for there to be the fundamentals of a science. The facts of each epoch, the conditions of each people . . . can only usefully be considered on their own terms."[44] On a more theoretical level, certain German theorists, such as Herder and Hegel, developed the idea that the essence of consciousness itself is expressed through the ethical realm *(Sittlichkeit)* of each people. This line of thought suggests that the genius or culture is the highest unit of social analysis.[45]

The theoretical position that calls into question the possibility or utility of general political science rests on one or more of the following three contentions: (1) that each case is so particular or special that no knowledge of regime types is possible; (2) that, even if general knowledge might shed some light on particular cases, it cannot be of assistance in the fundamental political choices, which are choices not of regime type but of fulfilling a particular mission or destiny (e.g., whether to spread a particular religion, give expression to a particular idea, or engage in imperial conquest); (3) that, even if general knowledge could be of some value, admitting this is dangerous and unwise, for the likely result will be to favor the development of an enterprise of abstract theorizing that remakes the world without regard to the particularity of each place.

Even though these three objections to general political science are different, it is easy enough to conceive how they could be brought together on the level of a partisan intellectual debate. Such a development occurred in Europe in the reaction to the French Revolution, with the formation of a party or school known variously as organicism, romanticism, traditionalism or sometimes conservatism. For this school, the excesses of the French Revolution resulted directly from the unrestricted application of general theory or rationalism to political life. At fault were certain tendencies of the Enlightenment, which overvalued the worth of general ideas. The consequence was a mode of thinking and acting that sought to impose more and more homogeneity and uniformity on the world.

Today, at a great distance from this conflict, the modern historian is apt to say that, not rationalism itself, but *one* form of rationalism was a cause of the French Revolution. But at the time, first the proponents and then the opponents of the Revolution identified the particular expression of reason that promoted the Revolution with Reason itself. In this struggle, the debate about the relationship of general ideas to particulars became polarized. Rationalism was associated with an adoration of general ideas, traditionalism with a rejection of them and a celebration of the particular. For a time these positions seemed to preclude a rational or nonpartisan investigation of the relationship of a general science to particular cases.

Traditional political science, by its activity of elaborating general types, necessarily rejects the basic tenets of an extreme conservatism. But this position does not preclude accepting a great many of its insights. Indeed, Montesquieu was one of the major sources for the development of traditionalist ideas, criticizing the universalism of "those bold flights that seem to characterize the works of the present age" and giving great weight to the unique elements of each place; and Tocqueville directly incorporated much from traditionalist thought into his presentation.[46] Political science in its classic expressions therefore never shared the premises of many sciences of politics that emerged in the eighteenth and nineteenth centuries.

The great controversy between rationalists and traditionalists has had a decisive impact on subsequent Western thought. Nineteenth-century traditionalism led to the historical school and then to historicism, which together have transformed Western consciousness nearly as much as rationalism had done in the seventeenth century. The historical insight continues to influence social scientific thinking, especially in the contemporary school known as hermeneutics, which emphasizes the particularity of cultures and even of human perceptions.[47] No version of political science today can avoid taking account of these developments or go back to previous formulations. Nevertheless, there is still much to be learned from the way in which traditional political scientists treated this question.

The Third Part of Political Science (resumed)

In light of this discussion of the relationship between general ideas and particular cases, we can now return to a fuller treatment of the political science of particular places or nations. The status of this part of political science involves considering two questions: (1) whether general ideas (regime types) can be applied to particular cases, and (2) whether, assuming that they can be, these ideas provide guidance on highly significant (or the most fundamental) issues.

On the first question, traditional political science holds that general ideas can be applied to particular contexts, but only to a certain degree and in a certain way. As the discussion of a knowledge of place indicated, civilizations or peoples can be discussed or analyzed in terms of general causes (e.g., geography, mores, and laws); but exactly how these causes operate in each particular context is something that must ultimately be understood by a study of that particular case. The transfer of general knowledge to particular contexts is therefore a delicate task, one that resembles an art as much as an exact method. Propositions of general political science can only be introduced in a certain way into specific contexts. Because each context has its own profile, general theory can provide only partial guidance. And even with that guidance, some aspects of each case will escape the relationships studied by general political science. General political science does not cover—it was never intended to cover—all of reality. General political science is a body of analytic theory, to be consulted and employed by legislators in the full awareness that general rules do not fully apply to each particular case.[48]

The name we can give to the concept of applying general theory to particular cases is *translation*. Translation in this context consists in searching for the analogous materials in particular contexts that work to produce a parallel effect to that suggested by general political science. The method proceeds roughly as follows. On the level of general political science, we consider the form each cause should assume in order to support a general regime type—for example, the kind of institutions, civil laws and mores (political culture) that would support liberal democracy. We then move to a particular case. Here, with the aid of a knowledge of place, we sketch the actual way each cause operates in that context, asking what are the effects of the existing institutions, civil laws, and mores on the regime in place. We then consider the extent to which the causes in the case at hand parallel what general political science suggests for supporting a regime. Thus in regard to mores or political culture, we would ask how the actual political culture in a nation comports with the political culture that general political science tells us supports the chosen form of government. To the extent it does not, we ask how to proceed, as part of a strategy either for shoring up or undermining the existing regime, to establish the culture for the chosen regime. In dealing with these questions, we look at the materials that exist or might be developed in that place to produce the intended results.

This approach relies very heavily on the elaboration of regime types and the study of their properties in the abstract. It is different from a nominalist approach that uses particular cases or statistical averages of a set of cases. The nominalist approach can help point up the relative importance of different causes in producing certain effects, but it cannot, like translating from a general type to particular contexts, suggest a course of action that will have the desired effect in any particular case. The only kind of advice it can give is to transfer a certain set of laws, institutions, or beliefs from one place to another. But this advice can be meaningless or even harmful.

The causes of each nation—though we can give them general names— operate in distinct ways in each place. As a result, the form of each cause that produces a desired result will differ from case to case. For example, no two geographical situations are the same. Insofar as geography may be a significant determinant of society, it follows that different mores and laws will be required to obtain a similar outcome in two different places.[49] Similarly, because the mores of each nation are different, the same laws or institutions will function somewhat differently according to the context.

A transference of mores—which Tocqueville considered the weightiest of the causes in modern civilization—would in theory come closest to being able to produce the same effects in different settings. But this only poses a problem; it does not offer a solution. Laws and institutions (at least in their external forms) are objects that can be moved from one place to another. The same is not true of mores. What can be physically transferred (laws) thus seldom produces the same effect, whereas what might produce the same effect (mores) cannot be physically transferred. Instituting mores to support a given regime is not a mechanical process, but one that involves all the difficulties of translation. Certain mores might over time, through a series of steps, be replicated in the same form in different places; others can only be reproduced analogously, by finding something in one context that produces a parallel effect in another, though perhaps by assuming a very different outward form.

Traditional political science was sensitive to these difficulties. To ignore the need to translate concepts into specific contexts could result in failure, as Tocqueville pointed out in the case of Mexico's ill-fated effort to adopt the American model of federalism in its Constitution of 1824: "When they [the Mexicans] borrowed the letter of the [U.S.] law, they could not at the same time borrow the spirit that gave it life."[50] In the same vein, Tocqueville contended that American laws, even those he esteemed most, should not be taken as exact models for European liberal democracies: "I am very far from thinking we should follow the example of American democracy and imitate the means it has used to attain this end, for I am well aware of the nature of a country and of antecedent events on political constitutions."[51] Montesquieu gave this theme its most general expression: "[The laws] should be adapted in such a manner to the people for whom they are framed that it should be a great chance if those of one nation suit another."[52]

Political science systematically explores the limitations of the applicability of general ideas to concrete cases. Yet while it acknowledges these limitations, it still sees an important role for general knowledge. Political science parts company here with more radically particularist or hermeneutical schools. It does not deny that there is a spirit or—to use contemporary vocabulary—a grammar to each culture, but it holds that general categories of analysis provide a way to begin to look at different cultures and to assist legislators in making important political choices. From Tocqueville's perspective, moreover, there would seem to be a peculiar irony in the growing emphasis today on hermeneutical approaches. These approaches stress the idea of difference just when differences are becoming less pronounced, at least in the West. This new situation allows for an easier translation of general ideas into specific contexts and makes political science potentially a far more helpful enterprise in the modern era.[53]

Turning to the second question, we find that while the political science of a specific nation may be guided in some measure by general political science, we have not yet determined whether general political science can provide guidance on the most fundamental kinds of choices. In other words, can the study of American or French or British politics look ultimately to an analysis of regime types, or must it look to some other ground? Can general political science discover what is most significant in particular cases, or must that knowledge come from some other source? The problem here can be illustrated by thinking briefly of two classic cases. Ancient Athens is generally classified as a democracy. Yet Athenian leaders often claimed that what was most fundamental about the city was a distinct Athenian trait, not something that derived from its being a democracy or from any quality it shared with other democracies. As Pericles said, "We love the beautiful . . . we are bold and daring."[54] Rome provides another example. Rome in its early period can be classified as a certain kind of republic. But in calling it a republic, does one grasp what may be most distinctive about that people—a particular character that drove it to the conquest of the known world? Such unique or "special" characteristics, some argue, constitute the essential nature of specific regimes, not the qualities that derive from a general regime type.

Traditionalist thinkers developed this line of reasoning into a broader critique of general political science. General theory, if it is not false, is surely of secondary importance. To the extent we insist on using general types as our main instrument for grasping reality, not only do we misunderstand particular regimes, but we also run the risk in the end of imposing a sterile homogeneity on the world around us—of fostering what Ernst Troeltsch termed "a world of superficiality and Pharisaism."[55] The deepest reality of any nation, in this view, must be expressed in terms of its particular characteristics or destiny, and the regime choices a nation faces can only take on meaning as people rely on the ideas and the vocabulary rooted in a particular context. If, accordingly, there is an important kind of knowledge for legislators, it cannot derive from general political science, but must come from an immersion in a single tradition and an understanding and appreciation of its unique character or spirit. The study of particular nations or areas—we should no longer call it the political science—must be grounded in the history of distinct cultures.

A discipline of politics so conceived might look for guidance much more to the first part of political science (a knowledge of place). But it would part company with any attempt to explain the genesis of particular cultures in terms of general categories, stressing instead the unique and specific creative acts that form each people. For the pure traditionalist thinker, particularism is not only a fact of life but also something to be cherished and cultivated—indeed, it comes close to constituting the ultimate social value. Individuality exists, but it should also be willed.

No one has given a better statement—I shall not necessarily say defense—of this position than Troeltsch. He identifies it with "the German mind" and calls it "Romanticism." Romanticism is a mode of thought "directed to the particular, the positive: to plastic and superpersonal creative forces, which build from time to time a spiritual Whole, and on the basis of that Whole proceed from time to time to create the particular political and social institutions which embody and incarnate its significance." The ground of romanticism is in a certain understanding of history, according to which the historical process is seen as "an ever-moving stream, which throws up unique individualities as it moves, and is always shaping individual structures on the basis of a law which is always new."[56]

Traditional political science acknowledges elements of this view—up to a point. It stresses the importance of the constraints of particular places; and, especially in the case of Montesquieu, it goes a long way, in the name of a certain understanding of liberty as the development of individuality, in valuing diversity.[57] In one of his most well-known statements, Montesquieu writes: "It is the business of the legislature to follow the spirit of the nation when it is not contrary to the principles of government; for we do nothing so well as when we act with freedom and follow the bent of our natural genius."[58] The *natural* here is given a second meaning, not as a universal, common standard that applies to all individual beings (and against which they may perhaps be measured or judged), but as an inner impulse from which grows something specific to each being. There is much in each situation, Montesquieu argues, that lies beyond the reach of general political science and its laws. In these areas, there should be a strong deference to the "spirit" that prevails in that place.

Montesquieu's statement should, nevertheless, be read not only for what it says about the limitations of general political science—which has been the usual way of reading it—but also for what it says about the potential use of general political science. General political science focuses on discovering laws and relationships that maintain regimes. These laws can be applied to specific situations through the method of translation, and they should be applied. The spirit or genius of each place should set the standard only to the extent that it "is not contrary to the principles of government." The implication here is that the spirit—the second meaning of nature—does not fully displace the utility of a common analytic scheme.

Whether the most fundamental choices in particular situations can always be expressed in terms of general regime types, or whether they may involve something unique or particular, must remain an open question. But the need to resolve this question theoretically may be less important than it appears. Political science is knowledge that establishes its worth, not by how much of reality it explains, but by how well it could serve us if we chose to apply it. General political science is not offended by the fact that a great deal of reality may lie outside of its purview, or by the fact that its laws may not have direct applicability to every situation. If it can be of significant assistance, it has served its purpose.

Certain nations have managed to surmount the difficulty of a potential conflict between a particular destiny and a general standard by asserting that their particular destiny involves the realization of a general standard. Of course, only a handful of nations are even potentially troubled by this kind of question. These are the nations that lay claim to having a grand destiny, which is what marks them out, certainly by their own account, as distinctive. Among the liberal democracies today, three nations appear to be in this group: Great Britain, the United States, and France. Great Britain boasts of having given the world constitutional government, the United States of having given it liberal democracy, and France (on occasion) of having given it some other kind of democracy. Of all modern political tracts, *The Federalist* stands out in its effort to combine political science and a special historical mission for a given people. It argues for the reasonableness of liberal democracy, but it also lays claim for the "glory of the American people," who have pursued "a new and more noble course" not only for themselves but also "for the whole of the human race."[59] Political science must be completed by being put into action in specific cases.

Political science is general knowledge about politics that can regularly prove highly useful on important matters. But it does not claim to provide complete guidance on every political matter in every case. This may seem a significant concession of its limitations, but it says no more than that it can only take us so far. The error is to ask more from it.

Traditional Political Science: Fact or Fiction?

Auguste Comte, the founder of positivism in social science, once argued that the best indication of whether a body of knowledge has advanced from the murky realm of philosophic speculation to the solid ground of science can be seen from how a discipline is usually taught in the universities. A body of knowledge is more likely to have attained the status of a real science when it is organized according to an approach or method and not according to the ideas of different thinkers. Who said what is a secondary matter, of interest chiefly for historical curiosity. By contrast, when a body of knowledge is presented in terms of the alternative views of past thinkers, this is a signal that its basic method is a matter of dispute and that the discipline has not moved beyond the phase of mere philosophical speculation.[60]

By presenting here the common elements of an approach to traditional political science, I can doubtless be accused of inventing a science where none existed. The charge might go as follows. Although it is possible to speak of a common method for *modern* political science, wherein researchers toil under rigorous common standards, it is no more than a piece of fiction to conceive of premodern analysis in such terms. Premodern analysts had their own method and system.

To establish the idea of a common approach for Aristotle, Montesquieu, and Tocqueville would, I concede, require a far more thorough investigation than I have attempted in this chapter. But if I had undertaken this task, I would no doubt have lost myself in the sort of exegesis of texts that so often makes these writers inaccessible to anyone who might actually wish to put them to practical use. In my defense, I can only say that I am not the first to remark on the similarity of these three authors' analytic approach. The famous French *doctrinaire* Royer-Collard, on first reading *Democracy in America*, immediately observed that "to have a point of comparison, it must be taken along with Aristotle's *Politics* and [Montesquieu's] *The Spirit of the Laws.*" We can establish independently that Tocqueville attempted to model his own political science on Montesquieu's. Montesquieu saw himself as the great heir of a supple comparative method reminiscent of Aristotle's, rather than a purely deductive approach based on either stoic or modern natural law.[61]

To compensate for my failure to offer a full account of these authors, I should at least indicate the points that seem most to call into question the idea of a common approach. First, a notable difference seems to exist between Aristotle on the one hand and Montesquieu and Tocqueville on the other in regard to the character and status of the first part of political science, a knowledge of place. Although readers of *The Politics* have long remarked on the importance of both context and sociological variables in Aristotle's analysis, they have also pointed out that Aristotle gives less attention than modern thinkers to the developmental or historical aspects of sociological analysis. It is easy, however, to exaggerate this difference. Aristotle calls attention to the great contrast between old and modern times and makes clear that regime choices that were possible in a previous era have become, for reasons of development, virtually impossible in his own; and he stresses the importance of the great intellectual changes (the invention of rational approaches to politics) that had intervened since ancient times.[62]

More importantly, the variation among these thinkers on the question of development may owe less to any fundamental disagreement than to a change of conditions that altered the category of development itself. Aristotle elaborated the category of development as far as it could be at the time. But the rise in the West of Christianity and later of commerce, modern science, and technology provided the basis for a systematic inquiry into development that was no more than a formal possibility in Aristotle's times. Western civilization was now launched on a more determined course than had ever been the case. Montesquieu and Tocqueville were merely giving this category the fuller and more systematic attention it now deserved.

Second, there seems to be an important difference between Aristotle and Montesquieu on the one hand and Tocqueville on the other in regard to their use of general political science. Tocqueville appears more directly partisan in his analysis. Aristotle and Montesquieu rank regimes, but they go on to discuss how each regime type can be maintained. They hold that in the variety of circumstances in societies, a number of regimes might be considered legitimate or at any rate necessary. They therefore offer advice, and even write a bit rhetorically, about how each regime, while continuing to be maintained, can achieve its most just possible form. By contrast, Tocqueville reserves his counsel for legislators of liberal democracy, for which he is a clear partisan; and he never systematically explains how a soft or a hard despotism could be maintained (though his advice is often apparent just beneath the surface).[63] Here again, however, the variation among these thinkers may owe more to changed circumstances than to any fundamental disagreement of method. Tocqueville's analysis of the modern era rests on the claim that there has been a decisive change in conditions since the time of Montesquieu. The advent of the democratic revolution meant that the viable alternatives in the modern world were fewer and more simplified, that only one of these alternatives was worthy of choice, and that choosing liberal democracy was possible in every modern context. "There will be no room," Tocqueville wrote, "except for democratic freedom or the tyranny of the Caesars."[64] This extreme analysis might have legitimated his more partisan approach and given some support, deriving from the general method of political science, to a more rhetorical style.

Finally, there would seem to be differences, this time perhaps among all three thinkers, regarding their standards of evaluation—on the status, for example, of individuality and on the ultimate meaning of justice. Discussing these differences and exploring how far they might actually derive from changed conditions rather than fundamental disagreements are subjects for another inquiry. Yet even here, the existence of different standards does not by itself preclude a common approach to the analysis of political phenomena.

4

Modern Political Science

IN THE VIEW OF THOSE who concern themselves with the state of the discipline, political science has recently entered into a period of critical self-examination. Today, according to Gabriel Almond, there is an "uneasy separateness" in which "the various schools and sects of political science now sit at separate tables, each with its own conception of proper political science."[1] The so-called behavioral persuasion, which reigned supreme in the seventies, has since come under challenge, on one side by an approach that claims to be more precise and scientific (rational choice) and on the other by an approach that is openly committed to raising political consciousness and promoting values (new normativism).

There are two basic questions that underlie the current self-examination. One involves an epistemological controversy, common to other disciplines in social science, about whether knowledge in the social sciences consists of elaborating cause-effect relationships (the empiricist view) or of grasping and explicating the grammar or meaning of human action in diverse cultures (the so-called hermeneutic position). The other is more specific to political science and has been summed up by the simple query: "Knowledge for what?"[2] It concerns the longstanding difficulty in political science of defining the discipline's central questions of inquiry and stating the ends or purposes for which knowledge is sought. My focus in this chapter is on the second question, which is prior to and more important than the first. It is necessary to have an idea of what one wishes to know before considering how one can know it, although these two issues are admittedly connected. I shall consider the basic ways in which the question of "Knowledge for what?" has been answered in the discipline over the past two decades. Because a rigorous intellectual history at today's early date is impossible, I have chosen instead to reflect on how this problem was presented to me during my own education in political science. My experience, if not altogether typical, has nevertheless exposed me to most of the important developments in the discipline.

The Science of Politics in the Sixties

According to the conception of social science that I encountered in my first undergraduate political science course in the sixties, scientific knowledge in the social realm—and the emphasis then was clearly on the idea of science—consisted in the elaboration of actual causal connections among social phenomena. Social science (the formulation was Max Weber's) seeks "to order empirical reality in a manner which lays claim to validity as empirical truth," with the ordering intended to explain "the relationships . . . of individual events in their contemporary manifestations and . . . the causes of their being *so* and not *otherwise*."[3]

Beyond causal knowledge of this kind, social science could not go. It could not instruct us directly about normative questions, however much it might help to clarify implications by showing causes and consequences. In addition—and this I found surprising—social science could not offer any guidance about which social phenomena to study, because it provided no internal criteria of significance. What political science investigated, accordingly, had to be determined by a standard external to science itself. Among those espousing the scientific approach at the time, two schools of thought proposed a program of what should be studied. One was based, for want of a better description, on quasi-scientific grounds and probably could be traced back to Comte; the other was based on practical or humanistic grounds and could be traced to Weber.

For the quasi-scientific school, the criteria of importance derive from a conception of knowledge modeled on the hard sciences. In this understanding, the quest for scientific knowledge in any field begins by demarcating the phenomena under its purview. One then proceeds to look for laws that explain the greatest *amount* of phenomena in the field or that achieve the greatest *certainty* in what is explained.[4] Thus if political phenomena are defined as a subset of social phenomena consisting in "acts performed in power perspectives" or relationships "that involve, to a significant extent, control, influence, power, or authority," then importance is a function of what promises to add the most to the systematization or certainty of our understanding of this data.[5] Political scientists of this persuasion in the sixties were given to sketching broad analytic theories designed to help systematize knowledge, the most widely employed of which were structural functionalism and systems theory.

For the second or humanistic school, the scholar should seek to acquire scientific knowledge of those things that experience with the political world reveals to be humanly important or interesting, either to the scholar or to his or her culture. In this view, importance is a function not of the quantity of political phenomena explained, but of what we take to be significant. What is studied will differ from culture to culture, from generation to generation, and from scholar to scholar. This view points to a more malleable content for political science than that outlined by the quasi-scientific view, but this does not make it any less scientific: one can be systematic in what one chooses to study without choosing what to study on the basis of what can be made most systematic.[6]

Although these two schools differed on the criteria for establishing significance, the scientific scholars I met dismissed any idea of a conflict between them. Scientists at the time were engaged in a common struggle, bordering for many on a crusade, to rid the discipline of metaphysical and value-laden concepts and to establish a genuine *science* of politics, often referred to as behavioralism or the behavioral persuasion.[7] The two modes of determining importance were also considered complementary in the decisive respect of promoting scientific progress. Concepts derived from efforts to systematize knowledge could be brought to bear in understanding humanly important problems, and scientific findings of the important human questions could be incorporated into the general theories. At some point the top-down and bottom-up approaches would meet to form a grand general theory.

The focus in the sixties for those scientists who subscribed to the humanistic school varied somewhat from scholar to scholar. But one question stood out as preeminent: how to maintain liberal democracy. As Sidney Verba explained in a retrospective on the political science of the sixties, "we were concerned with the question of why some democracies survive while others collapsed."[8]

Verba offered two reasons to account for this focus. First, these scholars lived through an age in which liberal democracy was severely tested. The faith that motivated Americans during World War I—the belief in the solidity of democratic systems and a confidence that liberal democracy would spread to other nations—was shaken by the dramatic rise of nondemocratic ideologies after the war. These ideologies challenged liberal democracies not only from the outside, as adversarial regimes, but also from the inside, as large domestic parties or mass movements. As a result, many were in doubt about the ultimate fate of the democratic cause. In Verba's words, "the survival of democracies in the developed world was problematic. . . . Social science at the time [the sixties] was still trying to solve the puzzle of the pre–World War II replacement of democratic regimes with totalitarian ones. . . . We were concerned with those attitudes that were supportive of a democratic regime."[9]

A second reason that accounted for the centrality of the question "What sustains democracy?" can be linked, paradoxically, to the lingering influence in the profession of traditional political science. Establishing this connection requires a brief digression. By traditional political science, I have in mind not the caricature of normative and legalistic reasoning drawn by many scientists, but an approach to the *analysis* of political affairs. Under this approach, the subject matter of the study of politics is not something for the researcher's private determination, but emerges from a common-sense encounter with the political world. People's particular political concerns vary with time, place, and objective, but these concerns reflect certain abiding questions, the study of which informs an understanding of the fundamental political problems.

The focus of political science under the traditional conception is on the study of regimes or forms of government. Far from being a narrow or legalistic concept, the regime or form of government refers not just to what we ordinarily mean by governmental institutions, formal or informal, but more generally to the way of life of society. What is political in the broadest sense is not always exhausted by what governments are empowered to do, for what governments may or may not do is itself determined by the regime and constitutes one of its most important characteristics.[10] Moreover, what shapes the character of a society, including its principles or arrangements for the exercise of public offices, often originates from what is ordinarily conceived to be something other than political acts (or even power acts)—from realms we know as economic, cultural, religious, familial, and intellectual. The study of the influence of political principles on these realms, and of these realms on the form of government, is at the core of traditional political analysis.

To be more precise, the more empirical or analytic aspect of traditional political science focuses on the factors that support or undermine various types of regimes. Its normative aspect—this modern terminology is itself slightly alien—is concerned with ranking regimes, determining the character of the best regime or the best regime generally practicable, and determining the best form (normatively) of each regime. We find these two elements—the empirical and the normative—in Aristotle's program outlining the content of political science: "Let us study what sorts of influence preserve and destroy states, what sorts preserve and destroy each particular kind of constitution, and what the causes are that make some states well administered and others not. Once we have studied this, we shall perhaps be more likely to see with a comprehensive view, which constitution is best, and how each must be ordered, and what laws and customs it must use to be at its best."[11]

The important question for the political scientists of the sixties who were guided by the humanistic standard—how to sustain liberal democracy— thus turned out to be one instance of the fundamental empirical question of traditional political science. This congruence offers corroborative evidence for the primacy of a common-sense understanding of political life as the study of regimes. It also reflected a continued reliance on traditional categories of analysis. As Gabriel Almond wrote in 1980, the "theory of democratic stability to which *The Civic Culture* contributed is in the most ancient of intellectual traditions [related to] the mixed government model celebrated in Aristotle, Polybius and Cicero, and later influential in the development of separation of powers theory."[12] Although modern political scientists tried to banish the tradition from the formal study of politics, they continued to rely on it as something with which the well-educated would presumably be familiar.

The dominant view of political science in the sixties, then, was of a science devoted to discovering causal laws among political phenomena. What should be studied—that is, what was important—was held to be either that which covered the greatest quantity of political phenomena (or covered it with the greatest prospect of certainty) or else that which the political scientist determined to be important from a human perspective. The latter approach focused on the question of how to maintain liberal democracies and thus led to a search for a theory that would explain how liberal democracy worked.

Ethics and Explanation

To understand how political science has evolved since the sixties, it is necessary to look not only at the formal questions the scientists posed but also at the kinds of answers they gave. In their search to discover what maintained liberal democracy, the scientists insisted, in sound empirical fashion, on studying the supports of liberal democracy that could be observed in existing regimes. To justify the expense and novelty of their approach, they attacked the prevailing prescientific models of liberal democracy that derived from classical or orthodox democratic theory. They chided classical theorists for beginning with "larger political units," for "reifying institutions," and for inquiring into "how men ought to act," instead of focusing on the only real empirical data available to us, which is the observable behavior of individuals.[13] This focus on the behavior of individuals, together with a certain theory of human motivation, was what gave the scientific movement its name of the behavioral persuasion.

Beginning from the data of individual behavior, the scientists elaborated realistic, no-nonsense descriptions of liberal democracy. The model they developed later came to be widely known as democratic revisionism or pluralism.[14] Under this model, the attitudes and behavior patterns said to support liberal democracy were at variance with the idealistic norms (supposedly) upheld by orthodox democratic theorists. Liberal democracy rested on rather low or dismal foundations, which many scientists, bent on purging the discipline of false idealism, did not hesitate to expose. Major studies found that voting behavior had little rational content and that political stability resulted from a large degree of political apathy. Even more strikingly, one of the most celebrated books in political science of the decade, *The Civic Culture,* revealed that liberal democracy depended for its existence on the (false) belief by elites that voters can discipline leaders and the (equally false) belief by voters that elites can be checked by the public. For the whole mechanism of liberal democracy to work, according to this book, political leaders "must believe in the democratic myth that ordinary citizens ought to participate in politics and they are in fact influential." At best this myth has "some truth to it"; but fortunately, "whether true or not, the myth is believed."[15]

For all the realism or toughness of these models, however, much of the scientific literature of the period took a curiously optimistic position in regard to the future for liberal democracy. Many studies posited liberal democracy as the natural end state of political development, the regime toward which the forces of history were taking us.[16] This odd marriage of a highly realistic view of what sustained liberal democracy with a Pollyannish view of its prospects fit the way of thinking of many scientists. Precisely because pluralism rested on what was said to be humanity's basic psychological nature, and not on fragile ideals, liberal democracy was thought to be the most natural regime, even though this low foundation for liberal democracy was not universally accepted or applauded.

Given this low foundation, an intense debate quickly developed over the purpose of political knowledge and its mode of presentation. The debate focused on the theoretical or ethical question of the relationship between the scientific approach and liberal democracy—or more generally between social science and the support of any kind of regime. Interest in this question was heightened by the possibility that science might uncover findings that, though admittedly circulated in an unreadable prose, could prove harmful to liberal democracy, whether by stimulating popular disaffection, by "liberating" citizens from certain beneficial beliefs, or by encouraging leaders to act on premises that might damage the system. Although this result would be a matter of indifference or satisfaction to those opposed to liberal democracy, most scientists at this time, as adherents of liberal democracy, had to acknowledge at least the possibility of a conflict between their commitment to science and their fundamental political beliefs.

Some scientists dealt with this problem by sketching a role theory for the activity of social science in society. This theory held that, in one's capacity as a political scientist, one's highest commitment was to science. The scientific chips had to be left to fall where they may, without any modification or adornment for ethical or political reasons. It was in one's role as a citizen, not a scientist, that one could express preferences. If it turned out that there was a conflict between the two roles, if science undermined liberal democracy, then so be it; the conflict was irresolvable.

Most scientists I met at the time, however, refused to be pushed to this theoretical extreme. They argued that the alleged conflict between science and liberal democracy was merely a hypothetical possibility that was played up, mostly by disgruntled partisans of classical liberal democratic theory, to embarrass scientists and discredit their enterprise. Given the threats that existed to liberal democracy, scientists insisted that the search for what sustained it had to be conducted rigorously and without sentimentality—the very qualities demanded by the scientific method. Democracy could not be grounded on anything less than the truth, the whole truth, and nothing but the truth, as presented scientifically. In the end, there could be no conflict between science and democracy, for both were based on the same principles.

This issue might have been put to rest, at least as far as the scientists were concerned, except for the fact that one of the most respected scholars of political behavior, V. O. Key, nearly joined ranks with the critics. In his last book, *The Responsible Electorate*, Key advanced his "perverse and unorthodox argument . . . that voters are not fools."[17] Although some scientists chose to read Key's argument as merely an attempt by one scientist to correct his colleagues by offering new scientific evidence, there was clearly much more at stake. Key intended to raise the question of whether, at least in instances where scientific evidence was not decisive, political scientists could afford to proceed entirely as scientists, ignoring the possible long-term consequences of their findings on society. Interpretations holding that political behavior was moved by irrational forces might become harmful self-fulfilling hypotheses by encouraging political actors (candidates, campaign consultants) to emphasize use of irrational techniques.

The implications of Key's view went far beyond the immediate question of how to interpret voting behavior. The deeper issue concerned the nature of political science as a form of knowledge and as an enterprise in society. As an important part of human knowledge, political science is an active part of reality that necessarily has social consequences. A social science that does not consider its effects on society, or include a reflection of its potential function, not only fails to account fully for its own empirical subject matter but also abdicates some measure of political responsibility.

If, however, political science is to be self-conscious about its place in society, where does this lead? Is the only alternative to the scientific view a narrow, partisan approach that serves, somewhat like an ideology, to advocate a certain form of government and promote certain values? Is there no position that can somehow account for and do justice to both the normative and empirical aspects of the enterprise? These questions remained well beyond the scope of inquiry of the behavioral movement.

Political Science Today

What might an undergraduate student today, curious about the same question of what constitutes political knowledge, discover from his or her education? Not everything in the political science curriculum, of course, derives from abstract developments of theory. The content of courses still relies heavily on tradition and on judgments of importance based on concrete problems. And yet today's undergraduate—and certainly today's graduate student—would also find that a great deal of what is taught, and certainly how it is taught, bear the influence of theoretical views of the nature of social scientific knowledge.

The dominant theoretical view in political science today, as in the sixties, derives from the modern scientific idea. This position no doubt reflects the scientific character of graduate education of the sixties and seventies. Accordingly, most political scientists probably subscribe to the idea that social science establishes the method of inquiry but not the standard of relevance, which is a matter for the researcher's own choice. This view has encouraged growth in the number of questions pursued, while at the same time casting doubt on any attempt to define a substantive core to political science—other, that is, than the sum total of interests of those who do research in the field. A glance at the roster of panels at recent meetings of the American Political Science Association quickly confirms that the profession today displays a range of interests that could be described as catholic, if not undiscriminating.

Yet those of a scientific persuasion do not choose their subjects of study randomly or in isolation. Even though the predominance of the scientific approach today may make scholars less conscious of the problem of what establishes criteria of significance, the direction of scientific research is set ultimately by the same two general standards that operated in the sixties: a quasi-scientific and a humanistic standard. Only now, both of these have a different focus than they did two decades ago. The quasi-scientific standard is based more on rational choice than on behavioralism, while the humanistic standard focuses not on the question of what maintains liberal democracy but on a new question of how liberal democracy measures up against certain standards of justice.

Rational Choice

The quasi-scientific standard continues to be heard in exhortations to build theories that promise to be powerful, either in the sense of organizing sizable amounts of political phenomena or of providing genuine predictions once certain assumptions are satisfied. In the study of American politics, there has been a decided shift in the last decade in favor of the latter idea of constructing models that, given their assumptions, can lead to clear and indisputable deductions from stated premises. If anyone ever gets around to it, these deductions can then be checked against actual behavior. This general approach goes by the name of rational choice.

Rational choice today is gaining ground on behavioralism, perhaps even replacing it, as the preferred scientific approach. This fact can be ascertained not just from a casual observance of the major journals, in which symbolic equations are increasingly crowding out statistical presentations, but also from the allocation of teaching positions in political science departments at major universities, which has recently been favoring the disciples of rational choice. There have even been rumors in some places of purges of behavioralists. But if the significance of the rise of rational choice for professional advancement has become apparent, its theoretical import is less clear. Rational choice, as the scientific alternative of behavioralism, challenges behavioralism in the two major ways in which that movement has been understood in American political science.

In one of its meanings, behavioralism is used synonymously with empirical political science, albeit an empirical political science that focuses on repeated, visible and quantifiable acts of individual behavior (or on motivations that can be measured and quantified). The behavioral approach, according to Robert Dahl, seeks to explain "the empirical aspects of political life by means of the methods, theories, and criteria of proof that are acceptable according to the canons, conventions, and assumptions of modern empirical science"; in David Truman's words, it "aims at stating all the phenomena of government in terms of observed and observable behavior of men."[18] Under this approach, the effort is to observe human behavior and then, on the basis of these observations, derive statistical generalizations (laws) of behavior. These laws refer directly back to actual human behavior; they are in effect the tallies of observed regularities.

Rational choice conceives of the scientific project quite differently. It begins with a simple assumption about human behavior—that people are utility maximizers, ideally where utility can be expressed in terms of a common unit of measurement. This starting point allows one to deduce logical conclusions about what behavior is (or would be) without having to deal directly at every point with observed behavior. Rational choice thus involves a good deal of abstract theorizing—modeling and game playing—that has no immediate empirical dimension. The power of the approach derives from its being able to draw precise conclusions from its own axioms. Its underlying premise is that the initial assumption (and thus the deductions) are sufficiently accurate, at least under certain circumstances, to throw a good deal of light on actual human behavior. This premise, of course, can only be verified on the basis of tests of the fit between the models and observed human behavior. These tests must be based on a method other than rational choice itself.[19]

In a second meaning, behavioralism is used synonymously with modern political psychology, understood either as straight concern for safety and income (the view of group theorists such as Arthur Bentley and David Truman) or as a search to fulfill certain unconscious needs and desires (the view introduced into American political science by Harold Laswell). The latter emphasis on the nonrational or irrational sources of behavior has had by far the greater impact on the behavioral movement. Behavior, according to Laswell, originates either from deep subconscious drives (in the form, for example, of "a passion to dominate") or from psychic needs, reflective of subconscious fears or desires, that are stimulated from the outside, whether by socialization or by techniques of mass persuasion. The individual is conceived as being acted upon, subject to control or manipulation from advertising or propaganda. Even though modern democracy may have released the mass of humanity from ignorance and superstition, it still requires, in Laswell's words, "the development of a whole new technique of control, largely through propaganda."[20]

Modern political psychology, especially in this last sense, constitutes the foundation of the "realistic" understanding of human behavior that undergirded the pluralist model of liberal democracy. This model also linked together the two basic meanings of behavioralism. Political scientists sought to adduce behavioral laws (statistical tallies of observed regularities) that were explained by a behavioral (nonrational) view of human motivation.

Rational choice is based on a different understanding of human motivation. It postulates an individual who acts *on* the world and brings to it a faculty for calculating his or her own utility. The individual is not regarded as driven by irrational impulses or as being easily controlled or manipulated from outside. The individual is rational, albeit in a purely instrumental sense. The change in the discipline from behavioralism to rational choice can therefore be viewed in some measure as a change from Freud to Bentham, or from psychology to economics.[21]

The sharp differences in behavior that would seem to flow from these two models have been lessened somewhat by rational-choice theorists' investigation of information costs. A consideration of these costs brings rational-choice theory closer to behavioralism in some of its practical conclusions, because individuals will often not find it worthwhile to spend time and effort becoming well-informed. In voting, for example, a healthy dose of rational ignorance can often be expected; the voter—if he or she finds it rational to vote at all—may discover that it is more cost-effective to rely on superficial information or on simplifying devices, such as party labels, than to invest time and effort carefully studying candidates' position papers. But this practical convergence does not alter the fundamental difference in perspective between the two approaches.

Rational choice was developed for scientific reasons, on the grounds that it is a more powerful approach than behavioralism and can lead to a more rigorous body of theory. Its original attraction, nevertheless, owed a great deal to the belief that it mitigated the conflict between political science and liberal democracy. Rational choice called into question the emphasis on irrationalism that was found in the behavioral models. It thus appeared to rescue liberal democracy from its grounding in demonstrably false myths. What made rational choice especially attractive was that it achieved this ethical advantage not by relying on the idealistic motives posited in orthodox democratic theory, but by adopting a highly realistic view of the individual as a calculator of self-interest. When it comes to realism, therefore, rational choice has nothing to be embarrassed about next to behavioralism. The new realism of rational calculation has displaced the older realism of behavioral manipulation. Still, it is not clear if liberal democracy in the end is much safer when grounded in narrow calculation than in irrationalism. The choice here would seem to be between citizens and politicians as either mercenaries or fools, where the fool at least can sometimes be tricked into believing in a common good.

Observing the bitterness of the disputes between adherents of behavioralism and of rational choice, one might get the impression that these two schools of modern science are arguing over the two great human alternatives. But from the perspective of traditional political science, this battle appears to be little more than a family quarrel. Both modern political psychology and rational choice are heirs of an individualistic-hedonistic psychology, differing only in their views of how the individual seeks gratification. Neither takes seriously the idea that the prime motive of political action derives from a distinctly political or social source—from a concern for what is just or what is theoretically (or theologically) right for the regime or community.

It is worth pausing to consider this difference between the psychological assumptions of modern and traditional political science. Modern political scientists have dismissed the contention of traditional political science that there are distinctly political (or political-theological) sources of behavior on the grounds that this view leads to idealistic assumptions about human motivation, where idealism refers to instincts identified as being nice, helpful, or safe. But this characterization of traditional political science is false. While traditional political science can account for behavior that is more public-spirited than anything contained in the modern view, it does *not* paint an idealized picture of human conduct. Quite the contrary, it aims to account for behavior that is harsher or less amenable to reason than anything explained by rational choice or behavioralism—for example, the intense anger and desire for retribution connected with the sentiment of injustice, or the passionate disputes that derive from alternative understandings of religious and metaphysical questions.

A psychology that begins from a political or social motivation possesses a distinct logic of its own, different from that of the individualistic, hedonistic assumptions of both rational choice and behavioralism. This point has recently been rediscovered and given the new name of "cultural theory." According to Aaron Wildavsky, cultural theory "is based on the axiom that what matters most to people is their relationships to other people and other people's relationships with them." It follows, according to Wildavsky, "that the major choice made by people (or, if they are subject to coercion, made for them) is the form of culture—shared values legitimating social practices—they adopt."[22] Substitute "political" for "cultural," "regime" for "form of culture," and "understanding of justice" for "shared values legitimating social practices," and one is back in the world of (traditional) political science. The terms of traditional political science may sound old-fashioned, but it is difficult to say that they suffer very much from inaccuracy or imprecision when compared to the modern terminology that has taken their place.

The idea that the political has its own roots, distinct from purely economic considerations, is the starting point of traditional political psychology. It is at the core, for example, of Aristotle's discussion of political disputes and sedition; and its most eloquent modern statement, curiously enough, comes from the famous Marxist thinker Antonio Gramsci: "One may speak separately of economics and politics and speak of 'political passion' as an immediate impulse to action which is born on the 'permanent and organic' terrain of economic life but which transcends it, bringing into play emotions and aspirations in whose incandescent atmosphere even calculations involving the individual human life itself obey different laws from those of individual profit."[23]

Rational choice appears today in two forms: a hard and a soft variant. The distinction turns on whether the utility that drives human behavior is posited in advance (the hard variant) or whether it is derived empirically (the soft variant). For adherents of the hard variant, who claim to be the more scientific, individuals are said to be interested in maximizing specific motives that can be expressed in terms of a common unit, such as money or votes or position. These motives are already known, or at any rate are posited for the sake of allowing rigor in developing the science. The model for rational choice in this respect is the discipline of economics, and in some of their bolder statements rational-choice theorists would merge politics into economics to form one larger discipline of social behavior.

Economics is remarkably simple, even economical, in its premise about what motivates economic behavior. It proceeds on the assumption that utility can be measured in terms of a single common unit. In the formulation of the famous classical economist Alfred Marshall, "an opening is made for methods and the tests of science as soon as the force of a person's motives . . . can be approximately measured by the sum of money which he will just give up in order to secure a desired satisfaction, or against the sum which is just required to induce him to undergo a certain fatigue."[24] Economists admit, of course, that this assumption of the individual as a utility (profit) maximizer is a simplification of actual behavior that can prove false or misleading in the case of certain individuals and cultures. They nonetheless defend their method of abstracting and simplifying on two distinct grounds: first, that it represents a fairly close approximation of a great deal of actual behavior; and second, that it focuses attention on the efficient allocation of resources, which is the end or good of the discipline. If rational choice is to have any hope of approaching or equalizing the science of economics, it will depend on the degree to which these same two defenses can be applied to the study of political phenomena. The record to this point suggests that there are definite limits to how far this new science of politics can go.

To take up the first defense, it is the contention of economists that the assumption of profit maximization will usually explain the essential part of actual behavior in the economic realm. This observation is borne out, they insist, by considerable empirical evidence and by the helpfulness of the predictions based on this assumption. In the words of a leading economics text, "the theory that assumes profit maximization to be the sole motive will produce predictions that are substantially correct."[25] There is considerable disagreement, however, about whether the greater part of political behavior can be accounted for by an assumption of maximization of interest, and even more disagreement about whether the most important parts of political behavior—actions that shape political life and political institutions—can be so understood. Recently, proponents of the behavioral approach have taken the lead in attacking rational-choice theorists by resurrecting this older argument. Thus Robert Inglehart, after making an obligatory bow to the "major contributions" of rational choice "to our understanding of how politics works," points out that "the incompleteness of models that ignore cultural factors is becoming increasingly evident." Inglehart cites the importance of factors such as religion (e.g., Muslim fundamentalism) and ideology in accounting for basic developments in the world.[26]

When confronted with these charges, adherents of rational choice readily concede that their assumption often does not hold true, and that—to move the question to a system level—there may be forms of government or cultures for which it is less applicable than others. Rational choice accordingly has not been used very much in attempting to explain differences among regimes, but has largely been confined to analyzing politics in modern liberal democracies, in which a pursuit of material self-interest is said to constitute a large element in political life. To bolster their case, rational-choice adherents have been among the most insistent in interpreting *The Federalist* as a work inspired by an economic theory of behavior. Thus Morris Fiorina, in the second edition of his book *Congress: Keystone of the Washington Establishment*, notes the similarity of the founders' thought to his own: "The self-interest assumptions that underlie the analysis in *Keystone* are much the same as the assumptions that underlie the architecture of the American political system."[27] This interpretation, incidentally, is the same as that of the radical critics of the Founding, as both have an interest, though for different reasons, in presenting the founders' thoughts in its narrowest economic light.

Even in the case of liberal democratic regimes, however, many have questioned how much political behavior is actually illuminated by the assumption of a maximization of interest. The utility of the rational-choice approach has been challenged, not only for how well it accounts for policy changes but also for how well it describes behavior in the case of its favorite institution: the U.S. Congress. Certain rational-choice advocates have responded by modestly claiming that their approach is but one tool among many available to political science; but not to carry their modesty to excess, they usually add that rational choice, as the most rigorous and scientific tool, deserves to be exhausted before other approaches are introduced. Even this modest claim, however, must be weighed in light of the opportunity costs for the discipline of according primacy to rational choice. In becoming bewitched by greater power or rigor in what is explained, the political scientist may focus too much attention on those aspects of human behavior amenable to this type of analysis. And even where political scientists avoid the error of treating the unexplained part of political behavior as derivative of the explained part, they may not adequately develop the techniques needed to understand other parts of political behavior. According to Richard Fenno, "not enough political scientists are presently engaged in observation. . . . The question is a disciplinary one. Observation-based research is a rarity in the *American Political Science Review*."[28]

There is another sense in which rational choice cannot quite emulate economics in its use of interest maximization. The great power of economics, as Marshall indicated, is not only that it posits human motivation to be based on self-interest but also that it has a single and fungible unit to which all interest can be reduced: money. This common unit of measurement enables the economist to devise predictive models that move across the whole range of economic activity. But in politics there is no single common unit to which all self-interested activity can be reduced. The unit rational-choice theorists employ shifts according to the arena being studied. Sometimes it is money (when discussing voters); other times, votes (when discussing members of Congress); other times, power (when discussing bureaucrats). These units are not only different, they are incommensurable. At best, therefore, hard theories of rational choice allow for predictive models of political behavior in different arenas, but they cannot tell us how these arenas relate to one another. One cannot know when a person will exchange money for votes or votes (reelection) for more power. A unified theory is thus beyond the reach of rational choice today in a way that makes it very different from economics.

The other ground on which economists defend their premise of simplification of human behavior relates to the normative implications of economic models. Most economists accept, almost as a matter of course, two basic assumptions: that (by and large) the impulse of each individual to maximize his or her utility (profit) is not inimical to, but actually promotes, economic efficiency; and that a more efficient economic result is more desirable than a less efficient one, subject to certain possible qualifications based on considerations of distributional equity.[29] These assumptions, simple and obvious as they seem, have an important bearing on the value of economic models, because they insure that the models deal with the *summum bonum*, or "highest good," of economics: the efficient allocation of resources. Using these models, economists can devise alternative scenarios, see how existing arrangements compare with hypothetical alternatives, and search for the option that achieves the best allocation of resources. Herein lies part of the attraction of economic analysis. Economic models are helpful not only in explaining what is, but also in providing useful hypothetical advice about what one might wish to do. To be sure, these models would have no utility if they had no explanatory value, but, because of their normative implications, they have an interest that goes well beyond their ability to explain existing behavior.

Rational choice has great difficulty in rivaling economics on this score. The starting assumptions of rational choice and the models that derive from them do not tell us what is important or good. We cannot assume, as in economics, that individuals pursuing their private utility produce the public good; and we do not know from the models themselves, as we do in economics, what the good is. Thus, the assumption of rational-choice theorists that Congressional representatives act to achieve reelection and maximize their electoral margins tells us nothing about how representatives should act or for how Congress should be arranged. If anything, these models are helpful in obliquely suggesting certain things to be avoided. In any case, the standards of what to promote or avoid are not supplied by the assumptions of rational choice, but remain entirely external to the model. Rational-choice models thus lack the kind of normative implications characteristic of economic models. To the degree that rational choice fails to deliver on its promise of being descriptive, it loses much of its interest.

Some rational-choice theorists, it is true, adopt a strict economic perspective and argue that the end of politics, like the end of economics, is the most efficient allocation of resources.[30] Almost all who take this position go on to posit a view of the state that assigns government a minimal role and that aims to keep the widest range of activities in private markets. Insofar as rational choice has become associated with this laissez-faire position, it has acquired the reputation of being, in Almond's description, the "hard right."[31] Yet this position is not a necessary postulate of rational choice. Merely because the end of economics is efficiency, it does not follow that the end of politics must be the same thing. Indeed, quite a few rational-choice theorists separate themselves from any idea that politics must follow an economic perspective and seem almost embarrassed or apologetic about the crudeness of their colleagues. They use rational-choice models to analyze the operation of institutions, but they adopt any number of different ends for society, including in some cases egalitarian ends that call for a very active role for the state.[32]

Let us now turn to the soft variant of rational choice. Under this variant, while people are said to calculate their utilities, the ends they pursue (their schedule of preferences) cannot be derived from rational-choice theory itself. Schedules of preference must be discovered empirically, from what people actually value in any particular society at any particular time; goals can range from a selfish pursuit of material gain to an unselfish concern for the public good. Rational choice is then used as a tool of analysis, calculating utilities on the basis of what is found to be valued.

The soft variant of rational choice, by its own acknowledgment, is derivative of empirical studies of the basic values in any particular context. Even after these basic values are discovered, however, it is often difficult to produce precise models, because the schedule of preferences cannot be reduced to a common quantifiable unit. Moreover, because the schedule of preferences is not intrinsic but is formed by society, it is subject to change. Many important political struggles are conflicts not over the distribution of a good under the existing schedule of preferences, but over what the schedule of preferences itself should be. Rational choice in its soft variant constitutes a lower-level tool of analysis, which is helpful only as long as the existing schedule of preferences remains in effect. It is therefore subordinate in importance to a more fundamental kind of inquiry which aims to discover the factors that form and change preferences. Rational choice itself provides no help in this kind of inquiry.[33]

Because the soft variant of rational choice concedes so much to other approaches, many of its adherents seem to think that it must therefore cover the whole of political life. What soft rational choice loses in rigor, it must make up for in breadth. Yet, while the relaxed assumptions of soft rational choice may expand its horizons, it still does not properly grasp the full range of political behavior. The starting point of its psychology remains individual rational calculation, even when the individual is said to be calculating a public-regarding value. Rational-choice psychology still misses the distinctive aspects of behavior rooted in a political or social logic concerned with the character of the regime as a whole.

For all of the differences between rational choice and economics, rational choice nevertheless possesses many of the advantages of economics. It is powerful, to the degree that its assumptions hold, and its models provide insight into what would happen under circumstances that do not now exist. Like economics, it allows one to consider behavior under alternative sets of arrangements and can therefore be used to generate hypotheses about political behavior in different contexts. Rational choice thus seeks the kind of explanation that is of interest to those who must deliberate. In form, if not always in content, it seeks the type of explanation sought by traditional political science.

The Humanistic Standard of Science: The Postbehavioral Critique

According to the modern view of science, no science can lay claim to establishing its own criteria of relevance. Rational choice proposes what amounts to a quasi-scientific standard by concentrating on a neutral standard of what produces the greatest scientific certainty. Many, however, continue to insist on orienting scientific research according to humanistic criteria—that is, by deciding what is important politically and then using the best scientific techniques to treat these questions.

Using this humanistic standard, what emerges today as the central question for inquiry? A review of the literature establishes that the question that was the focus of the discipline in the sixties and seventies—what sustains liberal democracy?— has lost its place. According to Verba, "the concerns expressed in *The Civic Culture* [the focus on democratic survivability] were products of their times . . . just as political beliefs change, so do the concerns of political scientists."[34] Verba maintains that in the study of established liberal democratic regimes, the focus today is on the policy process and the policy performance of governments, not on their maintenance.

Policy performances must ordinarily be analyzed, if not ultimately judged, in light of certain standards. We find, accordingly, that political inquiry today often proceeds by asking about the extent to which policies in liberal democratic systems measure up to certain substantive values. Any value might conceivably be employed as a subject for scientific investigation, but researchers naturally emphasize the values that they deem highest or most worthwhile. In practice, as noted in chapter one, these values tend to be either liberal or democratic, with the greater emphasis today probably being on democratic values. By democratic values, political scientists generally have in mind equal and sustained participation in political and economic decision-making and an equal distribution of social resources, chiefly wealth. These values are referred to variously in the literature as "full procedural democracy," "substantive justice," and "human development."[35]

Typical of this last approach are the works of Charles Lindblom and Robert Dahl. Lindblom in *Politics and Markets* assails the absence of genuine democracy in modern liberal democratic states and apologizes for his earlier defense of liberal democracy (or pluralism). Liberal democracy is guilty of its association with capitalism and its "inequality of income and wealth." To promote greater equality and end the "hegemony" of the business corporations, Lindblom advocates a "new pluralism" (Pluralism II) that aims to put "both pluralism and democracy under socialism."[36] In a well-known essay entitled, appropriately enough, "On Removing Certain Impediments to Democracy in the United States," Dahl urges us to focus on the extent to which citizens actually enjoy "equal opportunities for expressing preferences" and possess equal shares of income and wealth (a key element of "substantive justice").[37] Dahl's essay, which shall be discussed at length in chapter six, is representative of a whole line of thought that aims to make performance according to these egalitarian standards the central focus of the study of modern liberal democratic societies. To be sure, nothing in this general approach of measuring policy performance against a set of values implies a commitment to any particular set of values. Just as one need not support liberal democracy to ask what maintains it, so one need not be an opponent of it to ask how it measures up to standards such as procedural democracy or substantive justice that may be foreign to it. Any standard, from the Right or Left, could be employed.

There are, however, important implications for the character of political science in making this *kind* of question, rather than the regime maintenance question, the central focus of political analysis. Substituting this new question for the old one has had the effect of changing the orientation of the discipline in a way that makes it less favorable to liberal democracy than it was in the sixties. Now the very wisdom of maintaining liberal democracy is implicitly at issue.

This unfriendly attitude toward liberal democracy can be explained by looking at two factors: the historical situation, and developments *within* political science. On the first count, most political scientists today, in contrast to the sixties, no longer begin with the premise that the major liberal democracies are in jeopardy of succumbing to retrograde forces, either from within or without. The threat to liberal democracy has diminished, providing the luxury, in Dahl's words, of making the "gap between criteria and performance" the central focus of their inquiry. Yet it would be incorrect to say that the recent literature of political science has described the condition of liberal democratic regimes as one of happy stability. The theme of crises in performance, especially for the United States, has enjoyed wide currency. Whenever liberal democracy was experiencing difficulties, many political scientists were only too eager to point this out, as in Walter Dean Burnham's claim that "the general crisis of the American political system remains a cardinal reality of our time."[38] These "crises" are viewed, moreover, in a different light than in the sixties, when the concern was with averting problems to save liberal democracy. Today's problems are depicted, sometimes almost gleefully, as a logical result of fundamental inadequacies and injustices of liberal democracy. Thus, for John Manley, the advanced pluralist system in the United States is characterized by "persistent inflation and unemployment, the forced retrenchment of the so-called welfare state, and the deepening of gross inequalities."[39] For Lindblom, such crises may offer, paradoxically, an opportunity for liberal democracies to redeem themselves: "Our best, yet dismal, hope for structural change is through a transitory catastrophe."[40]

These accounts clearly bespeak a diminished regard for liberal democracy, which is said to be thwarting the realization of the highest values. This view has different sources, from the acknowledged grounding of values in Marxism (whether structural or humanist), to certain deontological approaches, to recent hermeneutical treatments of liberal democracy. The attack on liberal democracy, however, has also resulted from developments *within* the discipline of political science, in particular from the response to the picture of liberal democracy as it was sketched by the first generation of scientific scholars.

When the scientific approach achieved dominance in the discipline in the sixties, it came under attack for creating a vacuum in regard to normative concerns. A vocal group, later known as postbehavioralists, charged the discipline with neglecting what Christian Bay called the "*ought*-side" of human thought and with limiting political science to the study of observable behavior. Behavioralism, Bay argued, made social science "conservative," in the sense of favoring the status quo against any liberating alternative. By failing to consider values, the political scientist inevitably ended by promoting the prevailing values of "his profession . . . and of his government, at least on the more basic policy objectives and assumptions."[41]

While not saying exactly how political scientists could discover the "oughts," Bay left no doubt that his prized concerns—justice, democracy (equality), and human development—were not being well-promoted by liberal democratic systems. Even though most political scientists could not be induced to abandon their commitment to science, political theorists could nevertheless liberate many of their more practical-minded colleagues from their prevailing prejudices and make it "respectable or even mandatory" for them to serve higher values rather than liberal democracy.[42] Theorists could perform this function not so much by directly challenging the scientific approach as by changing the agenda of scientific research. Scientists could be persuaded to use their techniques to study where and how modern liberal democracy fell short of realizing fundamental values.

Although the postbehavioralists' charge that scientists were unconcerned with values—picking them up, as it were, off the street—was a gross caricature, it exposed a weakness in the formal scientific position.[43] In asking what maintained liberal democracy, the scientist as scientist professed no view about whether liberal democracy was worth maintaining. This "don't care" posture proved difficult to sustain in the seventies in the face of postbehaviorist accusations that it represented a moral abdication to the reigning regime. Still, one may wonder why it was that so many chose not to defend liberal democracy, but to become its critics—or, if not to attack liberal democracy outright (for that would mean trodding in the forbidden fields of normative concerns), then to acquiesce in a new agenda of scientific research set by those who rejected it. Why was it so often assumed that the high ground on the values question was occupied by those hostile to liberal democracy, so much so that to be concerned with values was equated with being against liberal democracy, whereas to be for liberal democracy meant one was an insensitive, unimaginative empiricist? It was no doubt liberal democracy's misfortune to be the first system subjected to scientific analysis, leading some opponents of the scientific approach to attack liberal democracy as well; but there had to be a deeper reason for the opposition to liberal democracy.

Part of that reason can be found in the response in the discipline to the pluralist model. Although some critics of liberal democracy argued that the pluralist model missed the injustices that were implicit in society's elusive "second face of power," most never disputed the validity of the pluralist model.[44] Liberal democracy was pluralism, so much so that the two terms could be used interchangeably. The problem was not with the inaccuracy of the description, but with what it implied about the worth of liberal democracy. If liberal democracy was a mere struggle among self-interested groups, if voters were deluded, if the system rested on patently false myths of which intelligent statesmen had no inkling, on what basis could this form of government be defended? The pluralist account of liberal democracy, in short, supplied all that was needed for a normative critique. Opponents of liberal democracy had merely to take the stark realities of the pluralist model and expose them to the light of day. Scientists who devised the model were accused of being partisans of that system, and their indifference to higher values was held up to scorn. Here at last stood Frankenstein's monster naked before its creator's eyes.

Few of the scientists could have been prepared for such attacks. They had devised their model at a time when most political scientists were defending liberal democracy. Their realism under these conditions had represented a harmless iconoclasm, shocking enough to help win them reputations but without posing any immediate threat to liberal democracy. Everything appeared in a different light, however, when the scientists became pillars of the establishment and when their model was accepted as the real thing. Their understanding of liberal democracy, it turned out, was not quite as neutral or harmless as they had supposed. A defense of liberal democracy, which hitherto had not been seriously at issue, was suddenly demanded. Now, however, many were disinclined to provide one.

During the sixties and seventies, the scientific scholars who had devised the realist models of liberal democracy were attacked from two sides—sometimes for being bad empiricists, more often for being defective normativists. The latter charge was also much easier to slip: all one had to do was abandon liberal democracy and claim that the purpose of the models had been to describe and explain liberal democracy, not defend it. One could go much further (and many did) to alleviate the pressure from critics by agreeing readily that the description of liberal democracy suggested its indefensibility. New research and analysis could be (and was) undertaken to discover the gaps, now said to be growing, between criteria and performance, leading to a shift in the dominant descriptive account from the old Pluralist I model (realistic, but not hostile to liberal democracy) to the sleek and updated Pluralist II model (engineered to appeal to those with a taste for socialist humanism and Gramsci).

The New Normativism

The critique of scientific political science launched by the postbehavioralists proved highly influential, so much so that many of those criticized ended by joining their critics. This critique had both a hard center and a soft periphery. For those in the hard center, a science of politics is itself objectionable; values must consciously direct our efforts. For those in the soft periphery, the scientific idea remains sacrosanct, but the research questions must change in order to test whether the chosen values are being promoted. This normative orientation strengthens the scientific project by, in Dahl's words, "suggesting criteria that will help empirical investigators to judge the relative importance of the questions they might undertake to study."[45] So natural has this last change appeared that many advocates of the scientific approach, ever suspicious of any kind of normative inquiry, may be unaware of the source of their own research agenda.

The common origin of the two strands of this movement justifies referring to them by a single name: the new normativism.[46] Although originally associated with the postbehavioral critique from the Left, the new normativism is an approach that today has its practitioners on the Right as well.[47] Its defining feature is not any particular ideology, but an approach that makes the focus of political science the measurement of policies, often considered singly, against certain standards. Regimes are then judged, either implicitly or explicitly, by their performance on these standards.

It is this method that today undergirds one part of political science.

Another part is supported by a more strictly scientific idea, in the form of rational choice. These are the two main poles of political science today, and neither one has in view an explicit project to maintain liberal democracy.

5

Reconstructing Political Science

TO JUDGE BY THE THEORETICAL DEVELOPMENTS of the last two decades, political science today would have to be diagnosed as suffering from acute schizophrenia. Its dominant personality has been shaped by a drive to create a science of politics that aims to maximize the amount of political phenomena explained. For many in the discipline, however, this approach is unsatisfactory because it lacks an immediate anchor in any human concern. The reaction against the hard scientific view helps account for the second personality of modern political science: its commitment to promoting certain values. Political scientists who once relegated normative questions to the realm of the rap session now wear their commitments as a badge of honor and a rebuke to backward colleagues who have not yet realized the fashionability of "having values."

The Dr. Jekyll of pure science has helped produce the Mr. Hyde of the new normativism. The result is a discipline that risks swinging between a barren concern for the trivial and a dangerous quest for the utopian. These excesses are moderated in practice by the welcome refusal of many practical-minded scholars to follow the implications of the discipline's abstract theories. But it is uncertain how long common sense can hold out against these theories in the absence of a foundation that can relate the empirical to the normative.

Traditional political science, I have suggested, comes closest to supplying such a foundation. But it has been attacked and misunderstood, often by those who should be its friends or allies. And even when small parts of it are rediscovered, they are given different names, as in the approaches known as the "new institutionalism" (which is hardly new and not especially institutional), "cultural theory" (which is much the same as regime theory), and "state theory" (which repeats elementary points that were known well before 1980).[1] There are, no doubt, historical reasons that can account for the sometimes extraordinary efforts made to avoid any implication of borrowing from traditional political science. But in this chapter, it is better to leave these old disputes and turn to how traditional political science compares with some of the other approaches surveyed.

Traditional Political Science and the New Normativism

For proponents of the scientific viewpoint, traditional political science is often lumped together with the new normativism. To these scientists, both approaches occupy the same space in the discipline as metaphysical inquiries that deal in some fashion with values. There is therefore no essential distinction among them. Perhaps they arrive at different conclusions or preach in different ways, but metaphysicians have always divided into quarreling schools.

It is only, however, in the thin universe of positivism that all normative approaches are equated. Outside this universe everything changes, and how one goes about addressing normative concerns becomes as important, perhaps more important, than whether a normative component of any kind is present. Once this point is granted, any resemblance between traditional political science and the new normativism is purely formal. The two are distinguished, and distinguished sharply, by the way each applies values to political life. Traditional political science addresses normative issues in a way that makes it closer in many respects to scientific political science than to the new normativism; it tightly limits the direct application of values, opening up a wide range for empirical determination of what many today rush to put in the realm of purely normative considerations.

Traditional political science begins its inquiry with the question of what supports or undermines regimes, whereas the new normativism begins with the question of how discrete policies measure up against chosen values, such as equality or economic efficiency. Traditional political science addresses the question of values in political life not directly, but in the first instance in terms of a choice among forms of government. It weds the value question to a consideration of regimes and what maintains them. The new normativist, by contrast, poses the question of values directly, with the regime issue often ignored or treated cosmetically. To take Bay's revealing formulation, the aim of the inquiry is to ask how "every law and constitutional clause" measures up to certain norms. The pure standard is applied to every question or major policy area, and the quality of a regime is judged more or less by a summation of these responses.[2] In some contemporary works of political theory, which adopt what is sometimes called a deontological premise, this approach is particularly prevalent. Look through works such as John Rawls's *A Theory of Justice* or Robert Nozick's *Anarchy, State, and Utopia*, and one finds almost no discussion of real-life societies. These books are all about justice, but hardly ever about real political regimes. The theories of justice follow in a long line of thinking about certain problems, with excellent philosophic pedigree, but they in no way fit the approach, redolent of Aristotle, Montesquieu, and Tocqueville, that I have identified as traditional political science.

The difference between these two approaches profoundly affects the character of political analysis. Under traditional political science, the choice of the form of government is the most important political question, so all other matters must be considered initially in this light. The first question of political analysis is how each policy affects the form of government, not how each policy measures up to certain norms. The choice of regime in any particular case involves asking which regimes in that context are within the realm of reasonable possibility, what is their rank order, and what might be prudent to attempt under the circumstances. Abstracting here from the question of prudence—which is usually the guiding consideration—it stands to reason that among the regimes possible in any case, the choice should go either to the regime that is highest in rank or to one that, though not the highest, is less prone than those that outrank it to degenerate into a lower type.

To rank regimes clearly involves consulting standards beyond the forms of government. It is here that one must consider pure values, such as fairness, virtue, or human development. The ranking of regimes proceeds by measuring the degree to which different forms of government embody the best mix or package of such standards. In making any ranking, however, it is necessary to include what is actually needed to establish and maintain each regime. Regimes, in other words, must be taken as wholes or complete systems, which means considering not only their aspirations but also the things needed to sustain them.[3] The fundamental political choice is thus not one among standards, but among forms of government, for it is the form of government (with the standards contained in it), not the standards themselves, that actually orders the life of a society.

The political scientist must therefore investigate what makes each regime a whole or a system. The things that serve to maintain a regime have a certain justification, the more so as they are essential to its survival. What is needed to sustain any regime, not under exceptional circumstances but on a regular basis, will be considered just—relative, of course, to that regime's point of view.[4] Even in the better regimes, certain of these sustaining features cannot be considered right or conducive to human development when judged independently in light of some general standard. This fact must be underlined, as it marks a limit to the possibilities of political life. For that very reason, it shows both why it is insufficient to make the direct application of pure standards to individual policies the decisive criterion for investigating normative questions and why it is necessary to develop a political approach to ethical or normative questions.

The fundamental political choice always relates to the form of government. Any issue having a significant effect on maintaining or undermining a regime must first be considered politically—which is to say by reference to its influence on preserving or destroying the regime. There may, of course, be alternative means for maintaining a regime, with some being equally effective; to the extent this is the case, the means may be weighed and judged directly against abstract value standards. But this approach has then been sanctioned by a prior political judgment.

For traditional political science, the distinction between regime issues and policy issues is fundamental. The regime refers to how a society is constituted or what it is, whereas a policy refers to what a government decides to do (or, more broadly, allows to be done). When, for example, the U.S. government faces a decision of how much money to provide for loans for college students, this is a policy matter. Whatever decision is reached—and the differences might of course be very important—the United States would still be the same form of government.

This example seems to suggest a neat compartmentalization between policy and regime questions, in which regime questions are matters of "high" politics, such as a revolution or a coup, and policy questions are matters of "low" politics, such as emission standards for automobiles. But reality is not so simple. Regimes can often be changed without revolutions, or the revolution can be the final stage of a process that has been prepared long in advance. And strategies, sometimes delicate, can be devised to alter the actual character of the regime, usually in its civil aspect, before directly redefining the public principle of rule—or in rare cases without ever directly confronting it. These subtleties often make the distinction in practice between regimes (how a society is politically constituted) and policies (what the government decides to do) difficult to perceive. What is presented publicly as a mere policy change might be a measure that is designed to change—or that will have the unintended effect of changing—the form of government. To the degree that a policy has the effect of precipitating a change in regimes, it is in reality a regime question, no matter whether it is offered or even consciously perceived in that light.

One of the main tasks of traditional political science is to identify developments that fall into the category of a substantial regime question and distinguish them from policy matters. Because the paramount value question relates to the form of government, every issue having a material effect on the maintenance or transformation of the regime should be considered first in this light; the analysis here in principle is an empirical, not a normative, kind of inquiry. To judge things first in terms of their impact on the maintenance of the regime is to adopt a distinctly political logic. This logic escapes today's autonomous ethical or normative approaches, which proceed directly from principles of justice or right to definitive judgments of policy.

Nothing said about traditional political science thus far means that value questions are confined to the initial choice of regimes and never raised thereafter. This would inappropriately limit the scope of normative concerns. Not every political action or problem bears in any significant degree on regime maintenance. For matters that are substantially neutral in regard to regime maintenance (i.e., policy questions), political analysis will have recourse to other grounds for making judgments, consulting general principles of right or justice or efficiency. The realm of policy issues is both enormous and enormously important.

What applies to policy questions, in the sense of the distribution of resources, applies as well to the goal of human development. Traditional political science investigates the relations of regimes to human development, ranking regimes in large part by what promotes human development. Once a selection of regimes is made, however, political logic holds that the focus should turn largely to what is needed to maintain (or destroy) the form of government, and no longer only to what promotes human development. Traditional political science recognizes that even in a regime committed to enhancing human development, what sustains the regime will not in every instance be the same as what promotes human development.

The fact that traditional political science does not trumpet norms in the same direct way as certain modern normativists might lead some to conclude that it lacks any ethical dimension. This conclusion would be unfair. Traditional political science, even when investigating what maintains regimes, seeks to keep as close to the surface as possible the broader point that regimes are to be chosen by their worth as measured against certain standards; and after the choice of regimes is made, it urges that standards should be directly consulted where no substantial regime effects are involved and where latitude exists in what maintains the regime. Each regime should be made as just as it can be; but it can only be made so just and still remain itself.

The logic of traditional political science and that of the new normativism would be the same if it turned out that what promoted a standard such as substantive justice on matters of policy always involved asking the same question as what maintains a regime. But this supposition does not hold for any abstract principle of justice. What maintains any real regime cannot be fully known by asking what maximizes an ideal principle of justice, and what is needed to maintain any real regime will not correspond in each case to what promotes an ideal principle of justice. This conflict exists in some form in every regime, including the best regime. The maintenance of political regimes always exacts a price in the world of moral concerns.

This view gives traditional political science its realistic character. It invites comparison here with the behavioral approach, which also prided itself on realism and which adopted its pluralist model in opposition to the allegedly idealistic precepts of classical democratic theory. Nothing in the kind of realistic conclusions reached by scientific analysts, however, could have shocked anyone the least acquainted with traditional political science, as distinct from a few grade-school civics teachers. If there were faults in the pluralist theory—as many scientists now concede there were—they resulted in part from the scientists' eagerness to push their tough and realistic conclusions beyond what the facts would bear. This empirical error, if it was one, in no way calls into question the premise of realism itself. Critiques of the science of politics by new normativists have had the regrettable effect of bullying many in the discipline into abandoning realism as penance for the scientists' original sins. Guilt has never been a foundation for a sound intellectual enterprise.

Criticisms of Traditional Political Science

Traditional political science has served as a convenient foil for modern political science, being blamed for any number of errors, real or imagined. Its two chief crimes are said to be its conservatism and, for want of a better term, its "a priorism." The charge of conservatism is based on the claim that by focusing attention on the analytic question of what maintains and undermines regimes, traditional political science leads to an unreflective adherence to existing systems. Yet it is difficult to see why this question works in favor of maintaining any particular regime. The choice in favor of any regime is based on an evaluation that must be made prior to and along with this analytic question. If anything, traditional political science forces one beyond a soft reformism that deals only with specific issues to confront the more basic question of the defensibility of the existing regime itself. The fundamental theoretical posture of traditional political science is always "ballots or bullets" or the choice of the form of government.

Perhaps the charge of conservatism is meant to apply less to the choice of the regime than to the approach traditional political science employs after a regime is chosen. By stipulating that policies should first be judged politically in light of what maintains the system, traditional political science provides an excuse for delay by imposing a double test on any policy. It calls for a check on the regime effects of policies before their justice or efficiency is considered. This process, it is said, impedes the progressive movement toward a just society, which ought to proceed by the single test of judging each policy proposal in light of a preferred standard of right. There is no denying that a double test, if applied with a covert partisan aim, could serve unjustified conservative ends. But applied honestly, this approach asks no more than that the consequences of actions be judged on the grounds of what is most important to conserve or destroy, which is the regime. Any other approach is piecemeal and relies on unexamined assumptions of what holds a society together.

Finally, the charge of conservatism rests on a confused premise that equates the question of what maintains a regime with what maintains the status quo or promotes short-term stability. Traditional political science treats these as two distinct issues, having only a limited bearing on each other. What protects the status quo may or may not help maintain the regime. For example, dismantling segregation in the South in the United States clearly upset the status quo and caused instability; but it did not thereby run counter to any general propositions of political science about what maintains liberal democracy. Because traditional political science is analytic, not descriptive, it always holds up the status quo to the external mirror of the model of the regime. In this sense, it is anything but conservative. Stability as a goal is largely a consideration of prudence. It may have something to recommend it where one has opted for the existing regime, for the simple reason that instability opens the door to accidental possibilities for a regime change. But this judgment in favor of stability is only a rough rule of thumb, which is subordinate to a broader analysis of how well the status quo works to maintain the regime.

The other general charge against traditional political science is its "a priorism." Traditional political science presents us, the argument goes, with a closed matrix of regimes that it has artificially constructed and then asks that we define actual regimes without seeing how they perform. The criticism of a closed system may be taken up first. Traditional political science proceeds on the basis that in each society there is a deeper structure—or struggle over a deeper structure—that aims to, or has the effect of, forming or defining society, including its basic policy tendencies. The core of the regime is defined by who rules, by the passion that dominates in the society, and by the basic principle of justice or overarching belief that moves those who hold the preponderant influence in society. Traditional political science further posits that the actual regimes can be grouped or analyzed in terms of a limited number of general regime types, even though each actual regime is in some sense unique. Neither of these assumptions, however, amounts to saying that the matrix of regimes is closed. New things may be discovered about regime types, and certain characteristics manifest themselves differently in the course of history. Moreover, new regime types on occasion emerge—for example, liberal democracy in the eighteenth century, or Marxist-Leninist regimes in the twentieth century. Regimes are thus not of a fixed number, and we are constantly learning new things about them. Political science is a body of knowledge that can never be completed.

The other aspect of the charge of a priorism is that traditional political science does not take policies seriously enough. It defines the regime without looking first at its specific policies, whereas it is the sum of the policies or performance that best defines any regime. A regime, in this view, is what it does, and what it does is best determined by a summation of its policies, not by some prior idea of its nature. Answering this criticism requires understanding the sense in which traditional political science seeks to relate regimes to performance or output.

Performance is analyzed as a set of general tendencies of regimes. These tendencies are usually discussed along three dimensions: (a) the principle of justice—for example, that a democracy tends to an egalitarian standard of distribution, an oligarchy to an inegalitarian standard, (b) the policymaking capacity—for example, that democracies are often mutable or unstable in their policies, whereas aristocracies are patient and fixed in their objectives, and (c) the foreign policy orientation—for example, that a fascist regime will tend toward expansion, whereas a traditional monarchy will favor caution. These are tendencies, however, and do not determine each and every output. On certain key matters, the regime may very strongly favor a given outcome, but—depending upon the regime—it may leave open or provide only minimal direction for large areas of policy. To say, for example, that a regime is a democracy cannot tell us specifically what policies it will adopt in every field. No general theory of regimes is capable of prediction in this sense.

When we look at particular regimes, therefore, we find that the policies undertaken by a certain government are not always constrained by its general form and may vary considerably from the norm. Policies, moreover, are made by individuals, who are never fully determined by a regime structure and who, under certain circumstances, may act in ways highly uncharacteristic of it. The classic case is supplied by Thucydides' presentation of Sparta under the leadership of the daring Brasidas, who was far more Athenian than Spartan in both his style and his policies. It is always possible that such a leader may fundamentally change the character of the regime in the direction suggested by his leadership, although this did not occur in Sparta after Brasidas's rule. Gorbachev's reign in the Soviet Union provides an interesting case for the study of this same question in modern times. Neither drably Soviet in his style nor orthodox Leninist in his policies, Gorbachev is very much the Brasidas of his time—with what results one cannot yet say. Situations in which the leaders act in direct opposition to the norms of the regime are, almost by definition, unusual, but they are certainly not unknown.

Traditional political science accordingly does not equate the regime with its policies. The regime refers to a structure that goes deeper than specific policies; that structure gives rise to general policy principles, but not to each and every policy. The regime itself does not change with every major policy shift, including policies that are at variance with its own tendencies. The form of government is the cause that, more than any other cause that humans can deliberately choose, gives immediate shape to the society. But there are other causes at work in specific societies that can change or alter the "expected" outcome.

It follows, therefore, that there must be two levels of analysis—one dealing with the form of government, the other with policy. These two levels are linked, in the double sense that the form of government generates policy tendencies and that policies at variance with the regime can precipitate a change in the form of government. In any regime, however, each level operates with a certain autonomy. The failure to understand the distinction between these two levels and to give each its proper weight leads to two different kinds of errors. One is to overinterpret the significance of the regime and to hold that every major policy must reflect its principles or logic. In this view it is almost impossible to conceive of change other than by overt revolution, which makes it very difficult to take advantage of opportunities that might eventually lead to regime change. The other error is to underestimate the significance or influence of the regime and to identify the immediate policies as the only real element of political analysis. Under this approach, the risk is that one will exaggerate change and rush—perhaps tragically—to identify temporary or ostensible signs of movement with a fundamental change of regimes.

Traditional Political Science and a Science of Politics

Traditional political science, though normative, limits the direct application of value considerations to a far smaller sphere than the new normativism. It relies heavily on empirical inquiry and thus shares a great deal with the behavioral movement that once spurned it. Nevertheless, though a frequent ally of the behavioral approach in the analysis of political phenomena, traditional political science diverges substantially from it on many theoretical issues.

The starting point for traditional political science is not, as it is under the scientific approach, a matter for each researcher's personal choice. In the scientific view, we begin in a world in which we know nothing other than that there are certain data (in the case of the political world, power acts) that constitute reality. These data have no structure or meaning that can reliably be grasped by direct human perception. We construct our concepts by discovering connections and interrelations through scientific tests, or we impose certain tentative boundaries on the data in order to learn about something we designate to be important to us. For traditional political science, by contrast, the human perception of the concept of the regime and its primacy is the starting point. The way we perceive and structure the world is part of the data of reality, indeed its most important part. The perception of the importance of the regime, confirmed by the repeated experience of knowledgeable people after a certain point in human development, is not something to be mistrusted, but accepted and built on. It is a fact established or known phenomenologically.

Knowledge of regimes and what works to maintain or undermine them is the principal aim of the analytic part of traditional political science. Political science at this level looks for general relationships or laws of causality along the following lines: A (the presence of a certain factor, be it physical, economic, cultural, or political) tends to promote (or undermine) B (a given type of regime), or A promotes B under a certain set of conditions (e.g., underdevelopment or development). What maintains regimes can be studied in large measure in isolation from normative considerations. The question of regime maintenance can, of course, be set aside when studying other matters, such as the efficiency of different policies or arrangements. But these other questions can only be properly studied *after* one has checked on the regime issue and determined how (or whether) it affects the matter at hand. To consider other matters independently of the regime is to take them out of their most important context. A study of the most efficient administrative arrangement, or the ideally competitive party system, or even the perfectly competitive economy, is at best an abstraction, at worst an absurdity. Administrative arrangements, party systems, and economic systems do not exist by themselves, but within political regimes. The regime is prior in importance to any of these systems.

The search for the causal relationships between factors and regimes involves, but is not limited to, the study of observable behavior and cases. The most helpful laws of causality involve going beyond the sum of all actual cases to describe the analytic properties of regime types. One normally proceeds by looking at the available cases (e.g., liberal democracy as it appears in the United States, Great Britain, and France) with the end or object of drawing inferences about general types (liberal democracy). The particular cases are the concrete instances through which one attempts to see the general type, which has the status of what we have called a general idea—that is, a concept derived from an effort to identify what various particular cases have in common and what distinguishes them as a group. Where no actual cases exist of a certain phenomenon, it is still theoretically possible to construct a type by delineating in thought what its characteristics would be if and when it existed.

A regime type, although a concept or abstraction, should be distinguished from certain understandings of ideal types, which are sometimes conceived as arbitrary constructs posited by the social scientist for the sake of study. A regime type is meant to identify something that is real by giving a name to characteristics that distinguish what is essential about a group of cases, even though no case is exactly the same as any other in the group or a perfect expression of the general type.[5] A regime type should also be distinguished from a model in the economic sense. The economic model is a construct that does not aim to represent or grasp reality; it deliberately breaks reality down into simpler parts with a view to enabling one to deduce clear and predictable results that can prove helpful. A regime type is not in the same way a deliberate simplification; it aims to identify the thing in all its complexity, though not to the particular complexities of any specific case. The regime type of liberal democracy thus refers to the general characteristics of liberal democracy insofar as one can identify them, though not to the exact qualities and characteristics of one particular nation.

Analysis of cases by statistical means (i.e., counting each case equally and using this data base to establish or disconfirm hypotheses), while often the soundest point from which to begin, does not always enable one to capture fully the character of a general idea or to ascertain genuine causal relationships between forms of government and the various factors. The cases (forms of government) are systems of the most complex sort in which the number of variables usually exceeds the number of cases, making the introduction of statistical controls often implausible or impossible. Moreover, as each case is found in a particular historical context, it is tainted by the particular and the accidental, so certain cases may be of less value than others in developing general theory. To minimize these problems, the political scientist naturally welcomes more cases in order to increase the likelihood that statistical information will prove helpful. Yet because the numbers of examples is often so limited, it is difficult to establish many genuine causal relationships between factors and regimes without going beyond statistical analysis. The political scientist will therefore introduce common-sense criteria that allow certain cases to be excluded and others to be considered as more revealing of the nature of a form of government. The aim is to strip away from existing cases factors that are artifacts of the particular case in an effort to comprehend the type at the most general level.

Nor is it likely that the existing cases contain all of the possibilities. The fact that certain factors have in the past helped maintain a certain type of regime does not mean that other factors, untried or unobservable at the present time, might not support that regime as well or better while at the same time further promoting a standard such as human development. For traditional political science, the object is not descriptive but analytic; it is to penetrate to the logic of the types and deduce causal relationships between factors and types in a way that would enable one to say how they relate, even where no existing cases can prove or disprove the deduction. These relationships, where they cannot be tested by observation or by facts currently known, must stand as tentative hypotheses, subject to being shown plausible or doubtful by future experience or by the discovery of new facts about existing or past cases.

A descriptive political science that looks only at existing cases and does not abstract to regime types might well be too conservative. Classical democratic theorists, such as Madison, Tocqueville and John Stuart Mill, clearly considered it part of their task to seek out the best possibilities for liberal democracy. They often delineated laws or mores, not yet fully realized in any existing regime, that would contribute to the maintenance of the system and that, within that system, would contribute most to an objective such as human development.

In leaving immediate empirical reality, there is always the danger of slipping into a kind of naïve idealism by positing relations that could not exist. Unrealistic claims of this sort, advanced by weaker theorists, provided the grist for the behavioral scientists' caricatures of classical democratic theory. Yet the fact that a technique can be misused hardly makes it invalid. The aim of traditional political science is to explore *genuine* possible relations, even if they are not actual. The spirit in which this kind of analysis takes place is obviously crucial. A realistic approach differs notably from many new normative inquiries today, which generate connections that satisfy a favored standard of justice and then, almost as an afterthought, introduce cosmetic arguments about regime maintenance. In this category must also be placed so many of the airy sketches of modern small republics and third-force models between liberal democracy and communism.

Traditional political science also differs from the scientific approach in the intended use of its knowledge. Advocates of the scientific approach have conceived the ultimate aim of knowledge in two radically different ways: massive social engineering and benign academic detachment. The first view, espoused by a few of the pioneers of the scientific approach, had as its goal the reconstitution of society. According to Howard Laswell, "the task is nothing less than the drastic and continuing reconstruction of our own civilization, and most of the cultures of which we have any knowledge."[6] Political science would not only provide the knowledge for this enterprise but also supply the personnel in the form of trained political psychologists who would become the real leaders of society. The generation of scientists of the sixties renounced this grandiose enterprise, settling instead on the more modest academic goal of explaining variance, with the expectation that this knowledge might ultimately have some social utility. Pure political scientists today tend to write mostly for other political scientists. Those more interested in practical matters have been segregated into public-policy schools. For the first time, the profession is large enough and wealthy enough to supply internally the rewards to motivate its members, regardless of any considerations of practical utility. It is at least a curiosity that the modern scientific view of political science, which began as an enterprise with such extravagant claims of practical application, should have retreated so deeply into the ivory tower.

Traditional political science is unlike either of these two scientific views. It differs from the Laswellian approach, not in eschewing all practical intent, but in working in a far more modest way through instructing and assisting actual or potential statesmen and legislators. In addition, traditional political science views the matter of politics in a different way, not as something that can fully be subdued and mastered, but as something having a certain shape or integrity of its own, which can be directed and guided but not fully controlled. Traditional political science also differs from the more academic view of the modern idea of science. It has the practical aim of serving society and being an engaged enterprise within it. (If traditional political science has a purely academic aspect to it, it consists of the internal discussion among theorists of how much this enterprise might reasonably hope to accomplish and of how best to make knowledge active in society.) Ironically, traditional political science, which was accused by the first wave of scientists of being too detached from reality, has been attacked by the second wave of scientists for being too interested in immediate policy and institutional questions. Traditional political scientists have shown a much greater interest in training students for practical careers (rather than for reproducing political scientists) and for seeking alliances with the more practically oriented public-policy schools.

Explanations Favored

Given the importance it assigns to this practical aim of aiding legislators, traditional political science favors certain kinds of explanations that under a purely scientific approach have no special status. Of course, traditional political science is concerned with attaining the most scientific knowledge possible respecting the relationships of factors (e.g., physical, economic, technological, cultural, legal, and institutional) to regimes. Knowledge of these relationships is necessary for intelligent choice, because choice begins by considering what is possible and thus what limits or constrains action. Yet because traditional political science aims to assist legislators, it seeks to connect physical and economic correlations to explanations that legislators feel they can use and that relate to their experience with the world. The explanations legislators seek, though they may have a physical or economic component to them, are those that are expressed finally in terms of human (i.e., cultural, political, or psychological) motivations. These explanations have a privileged status.

The reason why traditional political science favors this kind of explanation is not chiefly "moral"—to lend weight to the side of human freedom—but practical. The human motivation is the immediate or closest cause of action. Although it may be found to regularly co-vary with certain physical and economic factors, it usually has some independence or autonomy: no physical or economic cause is likely to produce a unique result in respect to any important human motivation, and no important human motivation will be found only under one set of physical or economic circumstances. As a result, no legislator could ever rest content with a explanation of the sort that substantial national wealth correlates highly with liberal democracy. The practical actor will want to know the human reason why this relationship holds in order to be able to make practical judgments in concrete cases about whether the case follows the rule or is an exception. No correlation can supply the basis for making this determination. Furthermore, because a legislator might not be able to change certain physical or economic facts, the most useful explanation is one expressed in terms of human motivation, for it alone can provide guidance about the possibility of attaining a political result in the absence of the usual physical conditions with which it is associated. The quality of explanation in political science is thus not solely a function of the amount of statistical variance accounted for, but of its potential utility in assisting practical deliberation. In the world of traditional political science, all variance is not equal.[7]

Because traditional political science is designed to serve as an aid to legislators, it gives, not more explanatory weight, but more systematic attention, to factors that lie within areas of human choice; and, within those areas, it gives more attention to the levers or instruments potentially available to legislators for structuring the character of society. The instruments of greatest interest in traditional political science have been law (constitutional and civil), institutions, and human formation (including education and socialization). The political scientist considers these instruments not only in terms of their immediate effect on the distribution of governmental power but also in terms of their influence on character, mores, and habits (culture), which are often more important than current constitutional law in fixing the real distribution of authority in society and in influencing the future course of regime development. Traditional political science has never been guilty of confining the study of politics to narrow legalities, or to governmental institutions, but has always insisted on a broad conception of the scope of the discipline.

The study of the character and properties of different forms of government constitutes traditional political science in its general aspect, as comparative politics on the level of general ideas. Still, most practical political inquiry focuses on particular societies, because the number of societies is relatively small and because people are usually concerned with particular cases. Traditional political science has therefore devoted much attention to the relationship that exists between knowledge on the level of general ideas and its application to specific cases. The analysis of specific cases involves a movement back and forth between general political science and a consideration of the conditions of each case. General political science can help in particular cases to throw light on the consequences of certain actions and can thus assist in devising strategies for maintaining or changing a form of government. But its applicability is indirect. Because each case has so many particular characteristics, the propositions of general political science must be translated into each specific context. The utility of general political science is therefore limited in consequence of the subject matter under consideration: complex entities that grow and develop in different places.

General political science is concerned with no one single case, but strives for knowledge that does not prove to be parochial and that is translatable into the widest variety of particular cases. Nevertheless, as one moves further away from particular cases or subsets of cases, less and less can be said about certain things that is helpful or significant. For example, important statements about the political institutions that support various regimes may be contingent on the level of economic development or on the size of the nation. General political science deals with this problem by developing lower-level theory in which the relationships posited hold only on certain assumptions (e.g., for small nations or for developed areas). Traditional political science is thus a never-ending enterprise, constantly exploring new hypotheses under different sets of conditions and assumptions.

Focusing on a subset of cases or on a specific case does not, however, alter the basic logic of political inquiry. The fundamental question remains the choice of the form of government, only now that question must be posed in a specific context, in terms of the possible alternatives in *this* place with the supports available *here*. This kind of inquiry is aided, as we have seen, by another part of political science, a knowledge of place. This knowledge aims to discover something about the characteristics or tendencies of development in a particular place. The pursuit of a knowledge of place has had many of the same epistemological and methodological problems that have troubled general political science. Disputes abound about whether it is best discovered positivistically by cause-effect laws, or by interpretive understanding; and there are disagreements about whether it consists of ad hoc insights into the peculiar character of each place, a systematic science of conditions that provides general categories for analyzing social entities, or discoverable laws of history that completely determine the process of development in each particular place.

Except under the last assumption of historical determinism in each context, a knowledge of place is not a substitute for, but a handmaiden of, general political science. It helps to determine what forms of government are within the realm of reasonable possibility, which alternatives are most in harmony with conditions, and what particular supports will serve to maintain different forms of government in a specific place. The options for a particular society are never, literally, general regime types (e.g., a liberal democracy or a theocracy), but a general type as it might be conceived in that setting, with the particular supports conceivable in that place.

Few problems have plagued social science more than the confusion caused by the use of the same terms for concepts in different parts of political science. A prime example is the term *culture*. It is used in one sense as a concept in general political science, as in efforts to establish relationships between a set of beliefs (e.g., the civic culture) and the support of a regime type (e.g., liberal democracy). It is used in another sense as a concept in the knowledge of place to refer to an existing set of beliefs and mores in a particular society (e.g., America's political culture or Tanzania's political culture). Only by distinguishing among the different parts of political science can we maintain clarity about the aims of the entire discipline. Acquisition of a knowledge of place, which is always helpful in understanding particular nations, is also an aid to the development of general political science. General political science is the higher or more theoretical kind of knowledge. It does not aim to explain what has happened, but to devise lawlike propositions (or probabilistic predictions) of what would happen in the pure case, unadulterated by contingent factors.[8] It exists as a body of analytic theory, to be consulted by legislators and applied to specific cases, in the full awareness that as each case is particular, general rules do not fully apply and therefore do not literally predict for that case.

Traditional Political Science and Reform

Traditional political science would be useless knowledge under either of two assumptions. First, it would be useless if each particular case or context were so different from every other one that there was nothing in common among them. Under this view, variously known as romanticism, traditionalism, or hermeneutics, it is difficult to derive anything from the study of a particular case that can be developed into a general idea, and more difficult still to imagine how any general idea can be translated back into a particular context. No significant kind of general political science is possible, but only an American, a Chinese, or a German political science. Traditional political science, as we have seen, rejects this view, even though it includes in its method a significant part of the practical insight or content of this position.

Second, traditional political science would be of no value if history were governed by deterministic laws, either on a worldwide scale or within each society. Social science could then have no other practical object than to understand those laws, and political science would be entirely subsumed under some kind of systematic knowledge of place. Traditional political science rejects this view as well. Although it does not minimize the constraints under which people act, it holds that there is a realm of free choice in politics. This means that there is room for people to make use of political science to alter and improve their condition. Political science is not, however, an ideology that takes sides between the proponents and opponents of reform; it is a body of knowledge that seeks to discover what actual possibilities for action are available.

Political science cannot, however, be simply neutral with respect to change or reform, even if it were to proclaim this as its intention. In the overall scheme of society, neutrality is impossible because there are only a certain number of ideas or doctrines that govern people's view of reform. By its very existence in society, political science displaces or modifies other views about change that in its absence would hold more influence. To the extent that political science manages to become operative in society, therefore, it has an impact on how people conceive of the prospects for change.

Historically, traditional political science has related to the cause of reform in different ways, depending in large part on the reigning prejudices it has had to confront in each epoch. The complex relationship of political science to society was evident from the moment political science was discovered in ancient Greece. The first political scientists reflected at length on what it meant for society to introduce political science into political life. The relationship of political science to reform was two-sided. On the one hand, political science lent partial support to the idea of change in society. On a theoretical plane, political science was a reforming, not a conservative, force. Prior to the discovery of political science, the dominant mode of thinking about politics derived from an adherence to custom or tradition. What was, or had been, provided the standard. By erecting another standard for judging society—human reason—political science operated to help free legislators from the simple prejudices of custom and to open their minds to the idea of choice and change by conscious means. On the other hand, in a more practical sense, political science played a cautionary or conservative role. At the time political science was discovered, adherence to custom and tradition was already coming under attack from another form of rationalism (sophistry) that deliberately encouraged political change and celebrated the direct application of reason to politics in each particular realm. Political science set itself up consciously to curb this radical doctrine, which it saw on balance as a dangerous threat to political improvement. Political science thus had a paradoxical quality to it. It was based on reason, but it was reason aimed in large part at showing the limits and dangers of human reason as a standard for politics, where human reason manifests itself as a logic that derived directly from ethics or from natural science.

After being overshadowed by religious dogmas, traditional political science reappeared in the late Middle Ages and early Renaissance. Once again it initially had the effect of lending weight to reform, this time by freeing legislators from the grip of religious standards and customs. Yet with Montesquieu in the mid-eighteenth century, we find political science fighting on a second flank—against a new prejudice, emerging out of the modern form of rationalism, that ignored the constraints of particular places and circumstances and encouraged legislators to an excess of reform. Political science now sought to temper the effects of this sort of human reason. It did so by introducing into social science a more systematic study of circumstance (a knowledge of place) that was designed to restrain universalism and bring back an element of prudence, through the notion of an equilibrium between regime choice and conditions. In a more general sense, traditional political science set itself against the modern scientific idea according to which political matter, like physical matter, was substance to be reordered by the will of the scientist-legislator or the despot. Political orders were—or for the sake of human good should be considered—as far less malleable than physical matter. Political orders were part of nature broadly understood, but they were distinct from physical matter and had to be understood on their own terms, by laws and relationships that applied to the sphere of sociological and political phenomena.

At the dawn of the modern era, Tocqueville proposed a different, and perhaps even more difficult, role for political science in society. Tocqueville saw that modern society was already so much influenced by the elementary idea of reason that political science now had no further social task to play in liberating people from blind prejudice or religious dogma. Instead, political science had to contend with two doctrines emanating from modern thought, both with dangerous potential effects on society. One was the rationalist project that had led up to the French Revolution and that encouraged people to think they could remake the world according to the dictates of reason. The other was a new philosophy, born of intensification of modern rationalism, that espoused historical determinism, whether local or universal, and that preached either fatalism or revolutionary fervor in the face of inevitable historical movement. Political science could check the excesses of both doctrines. It could serve as a restraining force against rationalism, whose despotic implications were now apparent from the French Revolution, and also against the various dogmas of determinism. Political science reminded people both of the limits they faced and of the measure of control they exercised over their own destiny. The fundamental political choice of liberty versus servitude remained within the province of free will. This view provides the opening for political science as a constructive social force and is fully in line with the American founders' cautious hope that people, under certain circumstances, can establish "good government from reflection and choice."

The role for traditional political science in contemporary society is surely no less complex than at the dawn of the modern era. It must continue to call attention to the dangers of a promethean rationalist project and of determinist theories under whatever guise. It is also faced, however, with combating two new dogmas: a positivist idea of social science, which imagines that a huge discipline charged with educating thousands of a nation's youth need not concern itself with the social consequences of its explanations; and a reaction to that positivism, in the form of an wandering normativism, that is often wedded to a progressive project to supplant liberal democracy. Political science will have to maintain the idea of an intellectual enterprise devoted to something more than mere academic theory, while at the same time dampening utopian notions that posit that all good things can be accomplished at once.

6

The New Normativism

NORMATIVE CONCERNS ARE once again a part of contemporary political analysis. According to Robert Dahl, "the normative orientation has become a rapidly expanding frontier of political science, just as empirical analysis had become earlier."[1] For those on the edge of this frontier, an empirical approach is regarded today as being quaintly, even embarrassingly, behind the times. Political science should concern itself with values—with instituting substantive justice, stimulating democratic participation, or freeing our consciousness from the grip of bourgeois capitalism.

Although the ascendancy of this normative orientation is celebrated as a return of political philosophy, it might be more accurately characterized as an application of ethics or psychology or purely academic philosophy to politics. Arguably, the term *political philosophy* should be reserved for systematic thought about politics itself. The new normativism, however, largely separates the activity of philosophizing from political analysis. It posits values or norms derived from abstract criteria and then applies them to the political realm without serious consideration of whether they could be incorporated into any workable political regime, let alone the societies for which they are being offered. Or, at the other extreme, it espouses values said already to be so much a part of a particular community that our only job is to seek out how to extend them. In either case, the current normative orientation ignores political science, in the sense of engaging in a systematic analysis of regime types and studying how different values relate to maintaining them.

The values making the rounds in contemporary normative analysis derive from a number of different, though overlapping, schools of thought. The most influential school is known as republicanism. It holds up egalitarian, participatory ideals drawn from an image of the classical republic and from certain strains of the thought of Rousseau. The foe of republicanism is liberalism, especially that part of it having anything to do with the assertion of the individual's acquisitive instinct. In the words of Benjamin Barber, author of *Strong Democracy*, "liberalism serves democracy badly if at all . . . the time may finally be ripe for a burgeoning of republican ideals that until this moment have been foreign to the American enterprise in its compromised form."[2] If liberal democracy is a compound (or "compromise"), the objective of the republican school appears to be to eliminate the liberal element in order to leave us a more thoroughly democratic order.

The republican school owes much of its current influence to work being done by scholars in American history, even though this whole line of thought seems to have been launched by the political theorists Hannah Arendt and J.G.A. Pocock.[3] This research claims to uncover an essentially republican core to American political thought. The key to this "essentially anti-capitalistic . . . republican synthesis," according to the historian Robert Shalhope, is the concept of "virtue," understood as the idea that "furthering the public good—the exclusive purpose of republican government—require[s] the constant sacrifice of individual interests to the greater needs of the whole, the people conceived as a homogeneous body."[4] This concept of virtue, curiously enough, has been attributed in modern scholarship to every major strand of thought in the founding period: the revolutionaries, the federalists, the antifederalists, and the Jeffersonians. The most recent scholarship, however, has connected this idea of virtue especially with the antifederalists, whose stock in trade has accordingly risen. The authors of the Constitution, in this view, began to deviate from a republican tradition and to rely more on a liberal—that is, Lockean—foundation.[5]

Historians working in this field make no claim to being proponents of any set of norms. The job of the academic historian is not to write history to promote one's own values, but to discover the actual elements of a tradition. Yet anyone acquainted with the effect of recent historical literature on general intellectual thought will know that more than just academic research is at stake. As Gordon Wood has written, "the stakes are high: nothing less than the real nature of America."[6] The overall result, if not the objective, of this research has been to build up republicanism as a value—*our* value—by establishing it as an integral part of America's tradition. In an age when the effort to derive values from any objective standard is, in certain circles, held to be impossible, one of the best ways to validate a norm is to find that it is embedded in the tradition.

The second school is known as communitarianism. This school accepts and celebrates the inwardness and warmth of community, proclaiming that values cannot be derived from any abstract or metaphysical standard, but must be found largely from within a community and its traditions. Norms are best established by a dialogue that attempts to bring out the best standards of a tradition. An old kind of conservatism has long made use of this approach, as in the southern traditionalism of M. E. Bradford. But most contemporary communitarians—those who self-consciously are attempting to lead a philosophic movement—have been partial to republican or social democratic norms. Typical of this approach is the work of Michael Walzer, whose thought for America culminates in a vision of equality. Walzer writes in his highly poetic *Spheres of Justice* that "a society of equals lies within our reach [and] is a practical possibility here and now, latent . . . in our shared understandings of social goods."[7]

The partiality of modern communitarians to democratic norms helps explain the link that has developed between this school and the republican historians. The republicans supply the historical interpretations from which the communitarians conveniently derive the best of our tradition. If, as Walzer writes, a "community's culture is the story its members tell so as to make sense of the different pieces of their social life," then historians would seem to have an important role as storytellers.[8] Nevertheless, in a strange exercise of deliberate self-deception designed to provide a cover of academic legitimacy, everyone is being asked to ignore the frantic hand-signaling going on between proponents of these two schools and to pretend that each is proceeding in holy isolation of the other.

A third school of contemporary normative literature is designated by the name *liberalism*—though the term should not be equated with the eighteenth-century meaning of limited government. The particular modern usage designates a mode of thinking, characteristic of scholars such as John Rawls, Robert Nozick, and Ronald Dworkin, that begins with the individual and some view of human nature and that reasons in general terms divorced from any particular historical context.[9] This individualistic ahistorical approach accounts for the use of the term *liberal*, as the mode of reasoning employed is reminiscent in some ways of liberal state of nature theorizing of Thomas Hobbes or John Locke.

The common formal method of these writers, however, should not lead one to neglect the different results of their inquiries and thus the different norms they adopt. At the political level, the contemporary liberal school splits into two factions. There is a libertarian camp, championed by Nozick and reflected in the principles of some rational-choice literature, and a more collectivist or social democratic camp, derivative from the thought of Rawls. The latter camp, which is the more dominant of the two in philosophic circles, is directly opposed to much of what is known as traditional liberalism. Beginning from a premise of individualism, Rawls nevertheless arrives at an idea of justice that supports redistributive governmental policies unfriendly to liberal notions of private property.[10] Thus, the economist Arthur Okun, after citing Rawls's difference principle ("all social values . . . are to be distributed equally unless an unequal distribution of any is to everyone's advantage"), concludes that Rawls's philosophy gives clear "priority to equality" and therefore can be used to support schemes for large-scale income redistribution.[11]

A fourth school, known as critical theory, aims to show how currently accepted meanings of central-value terms, such as liberty and property, have been foisted on us by groups or classes in the past that had an advantage to gain from a particular definition. "Language," according to Jurgen Habermas, "is a medium of domination and social power [and] serves to legitimate relations of organized force."[12] Critical theorists aim to deconstruct central-value terms and reveal their hidden ideological biases, thereby decoupling these terms from their historically determined meanings and opening the way to their constructive redefinition. Of course, any new meaning must be biased as well—there is no other possibility. Nevertheless, some critical theorists hold that in the realm of the biased certain meanings are more biased than others. The meanings that we impose today are potentially different than those in the past, because critical theory has made us aware of the instrumental use of language and because we can take steps, in Russell Hanson's words, "to reconstruct historical discourse [to avoid] distortions introduced by inequalities of power."[13]

Value terms can therefore now be redefined, as long as we somehow take into account the traditions that have formed language up to this point. These definitions could be on the Right or the Left—or conceivably even in the center. For the most part, however, those who have taken upon themselves the task of making up the meaning of modern words have to this point been inclined toward egalitarian ends. This tendency is especially evident in the study of jurisprudence and legal history, in which the critical legal-studies movement has sought to deconstruct bourgeois legal ideas and reconstruct key terms to promote more egalitarian standards.

The final school is the developmental Left, as it has been variously inspired by Marxist, socialist, and social democratic thought. The developmental Left looks to derive norms in large part from history, seeing in what is developing economically and technologically a reality that dictates or points to certain progressive, democratic values. In particular, it is assumed that history has taken us to the point that anything like a (classical) liberal foundation to a modern regime must give way—or at any rate should give way—to new and more collectivist foundations for modern society.

This line of thinking permeated a whole range of literature in political science that implicitly celebrated the need for "a strong state" or a "corporatist" orientation.[14] In a more explicit fashion, it worked its way in the later part of the seventies into calls for socialist programs or for a "third way" of Yugoslavian-style self-management society. In the study of American politics, Charles Lindblom has advocated the Yugoslavian model, while the strong state idea has been advanced over the years by Walter Dean Burnham. Writing in the early 1980s, Burnham noted that the "inability of capitalism to manage its affairs" created a situation that called for "a markedly higher degree of 'stateness' at the political center."[15] The rejection of more "stateness" in Great Britain and America in the last decade has led Burnham to modify his predictions, though he still maintains that the "neo-liberal" reaction to big government represents the last phase of an "interregnum state" and that "the crisis will move to a new and 'dialectically' higher plane of intensity."[16]

Representative works from each of these schools could be selected to illustrate the characteristics of this new normative orientation. But I have found one essay that brilliantly encapsulates the overall spirit of this approach, at least as it manifests itself as an argument on the contemporary Left. It is to a discussion of this essay that I turn in this chapter.

The Impediments to True Democracy

Dahl's "On Removing Certain Impediments to Democracy in the United States" is an essay of unusual scope and interest.[17] Written by one of America's most well-known and highly acclaimed political scientists, it addresses two of the most fundamental questions of American political life: What are the merits of the regime under which we live? Should that regime be retained, or should it be replaced by a new system? In answering these questions, Dahl provides a direct and succinct statement of his mature views on the foundations of the American republic.

Dahl's essay consists of three main arguments. First, Dahl contends that the historical choices Americans make are largely the result of national "consciousness," meaning the "inherited ways [we have] of thinking about ourselves." Thus, contrary to the view of Marxist interpreters of American history, Dahl holds that the movement of history is not predetermined by objective material conditions (at least not in the present historical moment), but depends mainly on subjective human factors, such as beliefs, ideas, and values.

The elements that make up our rational consciousness, according to Dahl, have been shaped by five basic historical "commitments" that "still dominate the way we think about ourselves and our future." These commitments are: (1) constitutional liberalism (deriving from the period of 1776–1800), (2) democracy (1800–1836), (3) corporate capitalism (from the latter part of the nineteenth century), (4) the welfare state (from the 1930s), and (5) world-power status (from the 1940s).

This statement of historical causality is followed by Dahl's second argument, in which he offers a diagnostic method for examining our mental health. The failure to realize our greatest potential—to "free up our consciousness for greater political creativity"—results from contradictions among the elements that form our consciousness and from our lack of awareness of these contradictions. Human choice may govern history, but Americans have not always made their choices rationally: "We fail not so much because our aspirations are too high but because they conflict . . . our consciousness, both individual and collective, distorts our understanding of ourselves and our possibilities."

The reasons why "we fail" suggest the formal properties of a cure. If we can become aware of our submerged conflicts and analyze them, we will be in a much better position to resolve our historical contradictions and "choose self-consciously rather than blindly among our political futures." Up to now, one might say, we have been unable to achieve full self-understanding. But with the therapeutic assistance of Professor Dahl's analysis, which brings to the surface the contradictions of our national (sub)consciousness, we may "at last be entering into our maturity." We have the chance to leave the realm of contradictions and to enter the realm of freedom. Dahl believes that political science should lead the way.

In his third argument, Dahl goes beyond this formal diagnosis and prescribes a remedy. He thus breaks with the behavioral or scientific approach, which can offer no guidance to its patients about ultimate standards or ends. For Dahl, there is a simple standard of health: democracy. Proposing changes of "great moment" in our society and politics, Dahl calls for nothing less than the substitution for the current order of a new regime he calls "procedural democracy." This new regime will replace the Constitution. Whereas Madison, the Father of the Constitution, beheld "a republican remedy for the diseases most incident to republican government," Dahl, as the would-be progenitor of our new constitution, beholds a democratic remedy for the diseases most incident to democratic government.[18] Or, to put the same point into contemporary language, Dahl's new founding will follow John Dewey's old maxim "The cure for the evils of democracy is more democracy."[19]

Procedural Democracy versus Liberal Democracy

Whereas logic demands an analysis in sequence of the three parts of the argument, curiosity bids us to steal a brief initial glance at Dahl's new regime. His choice of the name *procedural democracy* would almost appear misleading, because the changes he has in mind have as much to do with substance as with procedure. Dahl calls not only for a transformation of our political institutions to promote more formal control by popular majorities but also for a major restructuring of society to redistribute economic power and resources in a more egalitarian way. Dahl believes that procedure and substance are in this case complementary. Considerations of democratic procedure require that each citizen's preferences be "equally taken into account," which means that government may need to equalize those resources, such as wealth, that bear on the capacity of citizens to promote their preferences. At the same time, Dahl holds that redistributing economic resources promotes "substantive distributive justice," meaning what is just in itself, apart from considerations of effect on the distribution of political power.

The direction in which procedural democracy would take us is not especially original, nor does Dahl claim it to be. The core of his program is the ordinary staple of the left wing of most European socialist parties (especially when those parties have been out of power). The elements of that program are: (1) an assertion in principle of the public character (and hence the public's right to possess and control) of what are now considered private corporations; (2) a substantial redistribution of wealth and income to achieve greater equality; and (3) autogestion, or industrial democracy, meaning the control of the decision-making process of business firms by a democratic procedure involving all of a firm's workers.

To supplement this standard European socialist diet, Dahl blends in a few ingredients from the American Left of the sixties and seventies. These include: (1) a strong hostility to executive power as it is manifested in America's "imperial presidency" (to deal with this problem, Dahl suggests we consider a parliamentary arrangement consisting of a single house with a multiparty system and proportional representation); (2) a participatory ethic that casts suspicion on national representative institutions (Dahl urges consideration of citizen assemblies chosen by lot to advise congressional committees); (3) a centralist view of democracy in the political sphere (Dahl attacks "constitutional federalism" as a device contrary to "the majority principle"); and (4) a not-so-veiled indictment of America's role as a major power in world affairs for being "paranoidal," militaristic, and jingoistic (Dahl seems to lend his support to a kind of neo-isolationist foreign policy in order to help us to protect the world from America's excesses).

In view of the radical break Dahl seeks from the existing regime, one might think that he would present himself as a severe critic of the fundamental principles of the American political tradition. This is the position of many other intellectual critics of the American regime who propose some kind of socialist or democratic alternative. For these critics, the fundamental values of the American tradition—referred to variously as "bourgeois capitalism," "outmoded Lockean liberalism," and "purposelessness and privatism"—are the cause of our problems, not the source of a solution.[20] If America is to be saved, according to these critics, we must look to anchor our regime in a foundation from outside the American tradition.

On this issue Dahl refuses to follow any party line. The values that underlie his regime of procedural democracy, he claims, come from *within* the American tradition and represent the "best standards to which we are already committed by our national experience." Although Dahl can be as unstinting as his fellow critics in attacking the current regime, it is not because he rejects our tradition but rather because he sees the present regime as a negation of our own best standards. These standards derive from the commitments of the Jeffersonian-Jacksonian era (1800-1836) and, to a much lesser degree, the founding era. In Dahl's view, these commitments

> may be interpreted as an aspiration towards a society with a political system in which liberty, equality, and justice would jointly prosper, a society therefore requiring also a socioeconomic system that would foster these ends by supporting the kind of policy necessary to them. Thus interpreted, these two

commitments would give priority to political ends over economic ends, to liberty, equality, and justice over efficiency, prosperity and growth, a priority that the commitment to corporate capitalism reversed both in ideology and in practice, and which has remained reversed down to our own day.

It is in this reading of the American tradition, rather than in the familiar content of Dahl's socialist-type program, that we find the originality of the essay. Few have gone so far in arguing that a mixing of the principles of the founding and the Jeffersonian-Jacksonian eras yields support for a socialist program created by a powerful central authority unconstrained by any element of federalism. Dahl's striking interpretation seems to contradict what both friends and critics have long recognized as fundamental to those commitments. We know, for example, that the founders specifically rejected an equalization of property, arguing that "an inequality in property would exist as long as liberty existed, and that it would unavoidably result from that very liberty itself."[21] And we know that Jackson was an ardent foe of too vigorous a central government, contending in his famous veto message of 1832 that a National Bank threatened powers "scrupulously reserved to the states."[22]

How has Dahl managed to transform or transcend these traditional interpretations? Or has he? Dahl's objective in the essay, we should remember, is to extract the "aspiration" from each commitment, a purpose that presumably frees him from being bound to the particular form that an aspiration assumed under its original circumstances. Even so, there may be only so much poetic license that such an approach can afford. The looseness of Dahl's language ("may be interpreted as an aspiration") tempts one to think that he may have abandoned genuine historical interpretation in favor of a project of creative mythmaking in which standards from outside the American tradition are smuggled in and elevated to the highest status.

Setting aside all such considerations of historical veracity, however, it is quite clear that Dahl's interpretation offers a distinct rhetorical advantage over those of most of his fellow critics. In a nation that has enjoyed at least the modest success of America, a good many people, including even some intellectuals, feel a strong attachment to their tradition and an almost instinctive desire to stand up in its defense. Those who choose to attack the tradition at its core may risk provoking a spirited response. But Dahl's interpretation, by praising the aspirations of the oldest parts of the tradition, disarms this reaction. Whereas Dahl's fellow critics inveigh against the American tradition, Dahl wraps himself, selectively to be sure, in its mantle. In America, it is clearly preferable— if you can do it—to run with James Madison and Andrew Jackson than with Karl Marx and Herbert Marcuse.

Dahl's general argument is similar in its structure and potential appeal to the argument made earlier in this century by the influential historian Charles Beard.[23] It is similar as well to the new school of republicanism discussed above, which has not only reinterpreted the meaning of the antifederalists to make it accord with a semi-classical understanding of a popular republican order, but has also implicitly introduced this view as a kind of standard for America. Dahl, Beard, and the new republicans all use one part of the American tradition to call into question another, and all conjure up a Golden Age in American history that embodies pure democratic values. For Beard and the new republicans, the Golden Age was the period from the Revolution until the oligarchic reaction of the Constitution, whereas for Dahl it is the Jeffersonian-Jacksonian era. In either case, the history of America since its Golden Age has been one of reversal and decline. For Dahl, this reversal includes not only the oligarchic excesses of the corporate capitalist era at the turn of the twentieth century but also the subsequent reforms of the welfare-state era, which he views as sops designed to stabilize a system that today mocks our earlier commitments to liberty, equality, and justice. American history since the 1830s has thus been one of objective decline, although fortunately there seems to have been some progress in understanding made by a few enlightened intellectuals who can perhaps help lead us to "the best standards to which we are already committed by our national experience."

The Meaning of the American Tradition

Dahl's interpretation of the American tradition may allow some critics of the system to feel good about our heritage, even while they continue their efforts to destroy the present regime. But will Dahl be able to inspire a similar sense of euphoria among serious students of American history, or even satisfy them that he has not impoverished the very idea of a tradition?

Studying a tradition, if it is a great one, should be an experience that deepens and enriches one's understanding by presenting perspectives that may challenge the axioms of contemporary conventional wisdom. This does not mean that one should accept the tenets of the tradition being studied, any more than one should accept the shibboleths of conventional wisdom; what it does mean is taking the elements of that tradition seriously and remaining open to the possibility of learning from them. It is this possibility that makes a genuine encounter with a great tradition so rewarding and that, in the case of the American tradition, has drawn so many students to a study of our past thinkers and statesmen. The American tradition has proven so enlightening not only because it is ours but also because it has been found to have something worthwhile to say.

Yet it is hardly in this spirit that Dahl approaches our tradition. Rather than making an effort to assess the worth of different values discussed in the tradition, Dahl begins, a priori, with the supreme value of democracy, announcing that he shall explore "certain impediments to the realization of democracy in the United States [that] have resulted from the other historic commitments." To label as "impediments" the consequences of certain commitments clearly assumes that these consequences (and to some degree the commitments) are bad and should, as the title of his essay recommends, be "removed." But what if the very commitments that impede democracy (in Dahl's sense) are necessary for promoting things that are more worthwhile than democracy? In that case, would we not be wiser to embrace these impediments? Indeed, if we were to find that by adopting Dahl's standard we should destroy things we consider more desirable, then might it not be appropriate to regard expanding democracy as an impediment to maintaining a healthy regime?

Dahl's exploration of the American tradition is not so much false as it is unenlightening. To be sure, some might charge Dahl with belaboring and exaggerating the undemocratic aspects of American history while neglecting or belittling major democratic achievements. It is curious, for example, that an essay on American democracy never calls attention to the fact that America is becoming, in the words of the Mexican philosopher Octavio Paz, "the first multiracial democracy in human history."[24] But such claims, even if valid, do not controvert Dahl's main contention that some of our major commitments were not intended to maximize procedural democracy. If, after all, you begin by holding democracy to be the supreme value and then define it to encompass a large measure of egalitarianism, it is hardly surprising to learn that many American commitments stand as impediments to democracy. Some commitments were clearly never meant to promote Dahl's version of democracy, but to promote values other than democracy or to promote democracy in a quite different sense.

To determine whether we should prefer Dahl's democracy to his impediments or the impediments to his democracy, we can look at the same commitments Dahl identifies and remove those elements that create the impediment. Readers can then decide whether they prefer the impediments—with all that these entail—to the result that would obtain (or would have obtained) in their absence. We shall consider the commitments in reverse order, moving from the most recent to the earliest.

WORLD-POWER STATUS This commitment impedes democracy, Dahl argues, because it produces a concentration of power in hierarchical institutions, notably the president and the military (an establishment "more rigidly hierarchical than the rest"). The same objections, it may be observed, were voiced during the debate over the ratification of the Constitution. Opponents of the Constitution charged that the new government endangered democracy by establishing a strong executive and by allowing for the creation of a standing army. The founders' response was clear: though America might enjoy a more democratic form of government without these hierarchies, the nation would be unable to defend itself or protect its interests. Because providing for the common defense is one of the principal moral foundations of the republic, without which other moral attributes cannot be enjoyed, some degree of democracy must regrettably give way to the requirements of national defense. The antifederalists, according to the founders, were unable to make a choice. At one moment they conceded in principle the necessity for defense in a world in which America could not control the actions of other nations; at the next, they proposed measures, such as limiting the standing army to three thousand men, that would cripple the nation's capacity for defense. The antifederalists refused to think constitutionally—to realize that certain objectives, perhaps desirable in the abstract, could not be attained without producing other, more undesirable consequences; or that certain desirable objectives could not be achieved in full without sacrificing other, more desirable ends.

America's military establishment is clearly much larger than anyone in the 1780s could have imagined. The greater part of the growth dates from the 1930s, when the size of the army, smaller than that of Portugal, did nothing to help deter Hitler's aggressive designs. Yet the expansion of the American military in the past half century, far from being a simple result of a sentiment for militarism, reflected an adaptation to changed circumstances and new threats. Until this century, America was a secondary power, protected by the oceans and the British navy. The foreign powers with whom we dealt were not bent on total world domination. All this changed during World War II with the decline in the relative power of the European democracies and the emergence of new kinds of foes, exemplified by Nazi Germany and the Soviet Union, claiming a mission to rule the world in the name of unquestionable ideologies.

There is no disputing Dahl's claim that our role as a major world power has placed tremendous strains on our system of government. But this observation, while reminding us of a problem, offers us no instruction about how to deal with it. Either we can attempt to cope with the challenge, working to maintain a republican form of government in the face of these new difficulties, or we can seek to remove the impediments by weakening the presidency and disarming the military establishment. Say all that one will about what Dahl terms an "obsession with national security," it may not be so clear that we should prefer more procedural democracy to continued security. In urging a reassessment of our latest historical commitment, Dahl tells us that "experience suggests that when Americans, or anyone else for that matter, begin to talk about a national mission to save the world, it is time for everyone to run for cover." By reminding us, albeit in passing, that others have had designs for world domination, Dahl may inadvertently have offered the best justification for maintaining our military establishment, which in today's world affords slightly more protection than running for cover.

The American military hierarchy has also done a great deal to promote the cause of democracy in the world. Two of the world's leading democracies— West Germany and Japan—were forged under American military occupation, and the American military has served as the principal defensive shield for many democratic nations. Although the presence of American troops has not always promoted democracy, where American armies have been driven back in defeat— as in Southeast Asia and North Korea—there is today little prospect of democracy.

Finally, being a world power has imposed on America the responsibility for decisions that affect the fate of the world. This responsibility has brought with it a sense of vitality known mainly in nations powerful enough to influence the unfolding of world history. World-power status has imparted a seriousness to American national political life that has helped check against a politics focused solely on physical or psychic gratification. It is no longer possible to say that the nation's business is business. America's role in the world has lifted the focus above such concerns.

WELFARE-STATE CAPITALISM Let us turn next to a consideration of the commitments to corporate capitalism and to the welfare state. These may be treated together, for Dahl presents them as two phases in the development of the economic system beyond the simple agrarian-based order of the early nineteenth century. Dahl's objection to these commitments echoes his argument against our world-power status: they create hierarchies that stand as impediments to democracy. In the case of corporate capitalism, the hierarchy is the business enterprise itself. In the case of the welfare state, it is both the business enterprise, which the welfare state regulated but did not fundamentally alter, and the federal bureaucracy, which has accumulated vast new powers. "Far from diminishing hierarchies," Dahl writes, "the welfare state has multiplied the number, domain, and scope of hierarchies in American life."

Again, there is no disputing Dahl's premise that modern economic organization and its regulation have created certain impediments to democracy. But it is essential to ask whether we prefer the conditions that accompany the impediments to the situation that would obtain if we sought to remove them. The most direct approach for removing these impediments, analogous to the plan to disarm, would be to destroy our industrial base (or, viewing the matter historically, never to have developed it in the first place). We could be a nation of farmers and shepherds, with corn growing in New Haven and sheep grazing in Palo Alto. Yet in exchange for this condition of pastoral bliss, what would we have to sacrifice?

First, development beyond agrarianism is an essential component of economic and military power. America's edge in the world has long been tied to its technology and its conquest of nature. It is doubtful whether an agrarian nation could defend itself, even assuming the farmer to be the virtuous citizen-soldier that agrarian theorists imagined. Jefferson himself learned this lesson in the aftermath of his ill-fated embargo policy, when he conceded that a nation of free and independent husband-men could not be a free and independent nation. Hierarchies had to be accepted as the price of national independence.

Second, the process of economic development in America has been one of the major democratic events in modern history, and it remains so today. If by *democracy* one includes the notion of the chance to rise in life without regard to previous status, industrial capitalism has served as a vehicle of democracy for millions of the world's poor and oppressed, offering either to them or to their children a way up in life. (Meanwhile, many of the more socialist-minded states in Europe are requiring their immigrant workers to accept departure funds to go back to their countries of origin.) This democratic achievement could not have been attained in an agrarian society because of insufficient land to support so large a population. The antifederalists and agrarians often opposed immigration, whereas those favoring industrial development, such as Hamilton, sought "an increase of the . . . acquisitions to the population, arts, and industry of the country."[25] It is no secret that economic development produced hierarchies and inequalities—indeed, very often brought on outright exploitation; but it is not at all clear that this process taken as a whole has been a net loss for democracy. The American ideal of democracy and equality has traditionally placed a greater emphasis on opening new opportunities than on redistributing the existing stock of resources. To overlook this part of the story of development is to miss an essential element of the American experience.

Finally, economic development is the direct source of a certain quality of life. In choosing economic development, America has allowed for a way of life quite different from the peace and bliss of quiet rural existence—what Marx labeled the "idiocy of village life." Those who urged development did so not only because they wanted to advance material wealth but also because they believed that the differentiation characteristic of a complex economy provided an opportunity to satisfy the desires and talents of different individuals. In Hamilton's words, a complex economy would "furnish greater scope for the diversity of talents and dispositions which discriminate men from each other."[26] It would promote human development, not always in ways that foster egalitarian results, but in ways that lead to pluralism, diversity, and a striving for success and excellence.

Listing the benefits of economic development may seem slightly off-target, for Dahl never directly calls for the elimination of America's advanced economic infrastructure. Although he uses the supposed equality of America's agrarian era as his base for criticizing the subsequent undemocratic consequences of development, in the end he apparently accepts the inevitability, if not the desirability, of modern economic development. Yet by doing so, he would appear also to have to accept certain hierarchies of society in its present phase of development, for many of them, such as differences in skills and education, stem directly from the tasks that must be performed in a modern economy. The real alternative against which Dahl must measure welfare state capitalism, therefore, is not agrarianism but some other arrangement broadly consistent with advanced economic development. This could be the Soviet system (which is generally conceded to be more hierarchic than our own); some existing system with a great socialist component (only marginally different from our own in regard to private hierarchies, though generally having larger nonmilitary government bureaucracies); or a system that does not yet exist (which is the option Dahl selects).

It is in this connection that one must consider Dahl's attack on the welfare state component of the economic system. Modern-day liberals, who worked so hard to eliminate or mitigate the excesses of an unfettered capitalist system, will no doubt be dismayed by Dahl's criticisms. They are likely to discover, however, that Dahl's critique partly bypasses their own concerns. Dahl's first criticism of the welfare state—that it has "not much reduced the inequalities in the distribution of wealth and income"—creates a standard that is perhaps not central to its purposes. For many, the chief end of the welfare state has been to provide certain rights for workers, place a floor beneath people in society, and protect them against the vagaries of the business cycle. Moreover, even if it were true, as Dahl asserts, that income inequalities have not "much" been reduced since the advent of the welfare state, it surely does not follow that "relative political advantages and disadvantages" have been unaffected. When employers can no longer exclude workers from all security benefits or deprive them of livelihood in their old age, the power relationship between capital and labor has been fundamentally altered, regardless of whether the ratio of inequality in earnings remains the same.

Modern liberals are apt to find Dahl's other criticism of the welfare state—that it has led to the growth of "extensive government bureaucracies"—even more unfair, for these bureaucracies, in the absence of some other kind of solution, seem to be necessary to promote many of the ends Dahl espouses. Indeed, if one wants to observe "extensive government bureaucracies" in the world today, they can be found to a much greater degree in socialist societies than in our own welfare state system. For the most part, public bureaucratic hierarchies have grown to provide social services such as welfare and health care. Moreover, in contrast to socialist regimes that have state-supported business enterprises, only a small part of the public bureaucratic structure in America's welfare system is involved in running or policing business activities. It is therefore difficult to see how Dahl's plan for the economic system, under which "any large economic enterprise is in principle a public enterprise," would help in any way to shrink the public bureaucratic hierarchies that he deplores.

Modern liberals and democratic reformers probably cannot help feeling a certain frustration at being dismissed by one who speaks in the name of equality and democracy. Yet by now, perhaps, they have begun to realize that many of today's theoretical proponents of democracy will have nothing to do with their modest reforms, but will always be found leaping ahead to a position beyond any option under practical consideration. From this haven, these critics can easily disassociate themselves from the problems or failures of liberal reforms by denying that such reforms are "genuinely" democratic.

Oddly enough, Dahl seems to borrow many of his criticisms of these reforms from conservatives. Has the welfare state developed meddlesome bureaucracies, particularly as it has moved more to attempt to engineer an equality of results? For many years conservatives have said yes, and Dahl agrees—only for him it is not because of the movement to egalitarianism, but because the welfare state is not egalitarian enough. Has the presidency evidenced pathologies associated with its democratic character? For many years constitutionalists said yes, and Dahl agrees—only for him it is not because such changes were really democratic but because they were "pseudo-democratic." Whereas most have been literal-minded enough to accept the liberals' claim that their reforms are democratic (and, where there is disagreement, to point out that democratization can be a source of some of the problems), Dahl hurdles the whole dispute, disclaiming any connection between his democratic principles and those mundane democratic reforms that may have fallen short of realizing their initial expectations.

The obvious problem that modern liberals and ordinary reformers face in dealing with this kind of criticism is that no matter how far they go, it can never be far enough. There will always be a true democratic position beyond any in the real world from which all real world positions can be dismissed as paltry or pseudo. Earlier it was said that Dahl accepted the maxim that the cure for the evils of democracy is more democracy. That statement was inadequate. For Dahl the cure for the evils of democracy is his pure form of procedural democracy. Nothing less will do.

Despite Dahl's claim that welfare-state capitalism has moved us further away than ever before from the ideal of pure democracy, he is nonetheless confident that we can reverse our decline. This confidence rests on the premise that consciousness determines history and that America's consciousness is on the verge of a great leap forward. But Dahl's discussion of the origin of corporate capitalism, in which he acknowledges the inevitability of economic development, suggests that objective material conditions play a much larger role in his understanding of what moves history than he formally allows. If this is so, we may wonder what he considers to be the objective material conditions today that support the emergence of the new consciousness in favor of true procedural democracy. The answer at which Dahl hints near the beginning of his essay, and which for a time became a pervasive element in the thought of many critics of the American regime, is that we have entered an era of limits in which we can anticipate an end of economic growth and development.

The espousal of an era of limits by so many critics in the late 1970s has been one of the most interesting developments in modern social thought. Students of Marx will recall that he celebrated economic growth and never doubted that it must be continued until nature was fully conquered; indeed, the mature Marx proclaimed the necessity (or superiority) of communism in part on the grounds that capitalism would be unable to promote economic development. This theme was present in the thought of communist and socialist thinkers at least up through the 1950s. Until that time, socialists, in addition to proclaiming the superior justice of their system, also held that capitalism was inefficient and that socialist planning was a better method for assuring development. But in light of the performance of capitalist welfare economies in the thirty prosperous years from the end of World War II to the mid-seventies, this claim began to ring hollow.

In reaction to this success, many on the Left in the 1960s began to shift ground. No longer did they praise economic growth and the conquest of nature but turned instead to a celebration of more "humane" and pastoral values. Conceding that capitalist welfare systems might indeed be efficient engines of economic growth, they now argued that economic growth was itself undesirable. To use the popular expressions of the day, economic development in capitalist societies was "alienating" and "dehumanizing."[27] Yet as long as growth continued, this New Left, while enjoying a certain appeal to the overindulged and dissatisfied, could be dismissed by most as no more than a plaintive romantic reaction to the problems of modernity.

In the seventies, the Left attempted to break out of this romantic mold. The occasion was a slowdown in economic growth in Western societies and the predictions by many analysts that we had reached, in Dahl's words, the "limits that are imposed by nature's laws and the scarcity of resources." The Left seized on this theme of "limits" with obvious delight, for it could be used to show that capitalist systems, whatever their past achievements, had now lost their economic rationale and that it was therefore time to move beyond capitalism to a new and more just system. Moral progress became a genuine historical possibility in light of the paradoxical opportunity presented by the end of material progress. The Left's new and strange ally was now "nature's law," understood not as human nature but as environmentalism.

Once again the Left could claim to be on the cutting edge of history, only history was now said to be cutting in a different way than socialist thinkers had predicted. On this point, Benjamin Barber speaks more directly than Dahl:

> Faced with the prospect of limited growth, perhaps eventually even zero growth, [America] now has the chance to make a necessity of virtue and readapt its institutions to meet the demands of contraction and interdependence. The new pressures of ecology, transnationalism, and resource scarcity in combination with the apparent bankruptcy of privatism, materialism, and

economic individualism—the pathologies and the ambivalent promises of our modernity—create conditions more inviting to the generation of public purposes and a public spirit than any American has ever known.[28]

This criticism of welfare capitalist systems raises an important intellectual challenge. Defenders of liberal democracy have long celebrated as one of its virtues its capacity to stimulate growth. Does it follow, therefore, that the rationale for this system depends solely on its capacity to promote growth, and that if growth should cease, the rationale for liberal democracy would collapse? Posing this question has forced defenders of liberal democracy to seek a justification of the regime that grounds it in principles more fundamental than material well-being. Yet to say that the deepest moral foundation for liberal democracy does not consist in economic growth, and to admit that steady growth along the lines experienced from 1946 to 1976 may not be inevitable, is not to say that economic growth is bad or should be avoided. On the contrary, though material progress cannot be equated with moral progress, economic growth has brought more wealth for the average person, has eased tensions among social classes, and has helped stem pressures for redistribution. Modern liberal democracies therefore have a vested interest in promoting growth, and defenders of this system—unlike critics such as Benjamin Barber—have been able to greet the economic growth of the 1980s without undue disappointment.

What is clear is that the Left's realism of the 1970s, expressed in its constant evocation of limits, was not realistic at all, but pseudo-realistic. Its motive was not to assess the actual possibilities of economic growth but to use a period of limited growth as a pretense for changing the political system. No wonder, then, that the recent period of growth has led many such opponents of liberal democracy to shed their rhetoric of realism and crawl back into a warmer, romantic version of republicanism. A crisis will no doubt bring them out of this cocoon and back to the practice of speaking "realistically" of economic development. The Left's foundation constantly shifts—from history, to environmentalism, to the values of our community—but the political objective remains the same.

AGRARIAN DEMOCRACY Dahl's Golden Age of American history came in the Jeffersonian-Jacksonian era, when the nation made its commitment to democracy. Although an act of human choice must have been involved in making this commitment, Dahl gives little weight in this instance to the independent role of thought or ideas, emphasizing instead the influence of the objective socioeconomic order that "fostered a condition of equality among the citizens." Under the circumstances of this agrarian order, "white male citizens lived with fewer social, economic, and political inequalities than any larger number of persons in history had existed up to that time, and very likely since."

It may seem strange that Dahl uses the equality in this era as his standard, given its dependence on an economic circumstance that was a "historical rarity" that "had no future." If the conditions required to support procedural democracy are so particular, the effort to reproduce equality under different circumstances could prove as difficult as reinstituting paradise in a fallen world. Of greater interest is whether Dahl has correctly characterized the commitment of this era. That it was democratic is clear. But there are different senses of democracy. The era's most prominent figure, Andrew Jackson, declared in the national-bank veto message that "equality . . . of wealth cannot be produced by human institutions." What each person is entitled to is "the full enjoyment of the fruits of superior industry, economy, and virtue." The equality Jackson sought entailed above all putting an end to an active federal government, which operated to produce artificial advantages for the wealthy.[29]

Dahl might cite changes in circumstances as a way of explaining away such apparent differences as his own endorsement of the principle of public ownership of corporations and Jackson's opposition to public assistance for a national bank; his dismissal of federalism and Jackson's defense of the prerogatives of the state governments; and his acceptance of a vast extension of public authority over societal activities and Jackson's suspicion of a large government. But it is more difficult to see how Dahl might account for what seem to be very different underlying principles. Dahl's socialist vision of democracy is predicated on an equalization of results; Jackson's, on an end to artificial privilege. Dahl's emphasis is on sharing equally the product; Jackson's, on expanding opportunities. Are these aspirations really similar?

THE FOUNDING Let us now turn to Dahl's analysis of the Founding and the Constitution. Dahl gives the founders a mixed review, praising them for establishing liberty but criticizing them for not committing us to democracy. The founders' undemocratic legacy is found in the constitutional devices of federalism, separation of powers, and bicameralism, all of which are said to impede simple majority rule.

Dahl proposes to remove these anti-majoritarian devices by doing away with the Constitution and replacing it with a multiparty, unicameral parliamentary system. Although this system might not work quite as democratically as Dahl supposes (real majority sentiment sometimes gets lost in the bargaining process among parliamentary parties), it seems reasonable to assume that, at least by his standard of democracy, the new government would be more majoritarian than the Constitution. As in the case of the other commitments, the pertinent question is whether we prefer the impediments, with the values connected to them, to Dahl's form of democracy. Dahl confronts this question by mentioning another "laudable" objective the founders weighed when they constructed the Constitution: the protection of fundamental rights. But, Dahl goes on, we now know that the antimajoritarian elements of the Constitution were not really necessary for that purpose and that the founders "were guilty of overkill." The antimajoritarian devices serve—and probably were intended to serve—a different purpose of aiding the privileged: "Because they [the founders] succeeded in designing a system that makes it easier for privileged minorities to prevent changes they dislike than for majorities to bring about the changes they want, it is strongly tilted in favor of the status quo and against reform."

This account of the Constitution is striking in its reduction of the possible aims of government to the two goals of protecting individual rights and promoting majoritarianism. What this view overlooks are other goals built into the Constitution's complex governmental structure that help explain some of its antimajoritarian devices. Why, for example, does the Constitution support the antimajoritarian principle of federalism? Not only to protect individual rights, the founders tell us, but to assure a sphere of partial autonomy for governments below the national level. By including federalism, the founders were thus guilty of the antimajoritarian goal and of allowing local majorities to make decisions that might differ from those of national majorities.

Why did the founders provide for a separation of the executive from the legislature? Not only to secure individual rights but also to promote a vigorous executive, needed for "the protection of the community against foreign attacks . . . and [for] the security of liberty against the enterprises and assaults of ambition, of faction, and of anarchy."[30] The founders here were again guilty of an antimajoritarian device—this time to provide for a strong president, whose performance of the essential executive tasks would not depend on shifting majorities in the legislature. This view may be unfashionable at a time when so many political scientists stress the superiority of the parliamentary system. Yet parliamentary systems have succeeded in solving the problem of energy in the executive only where the governing party has a majority or a near-majority in the parliament. Where, as Dahl prefers, there is a multiparty system, and where no party approaches a majority, we often find dangerously weak governments, as in Israel and Italy today or in France during the Fourth Republic (1946–58).

Why, finally, do we have bicameralism and checks and balances? Not only to protect individual rights but also to reduce the likelihood of unwise choices by temporary majorities. The founders were not afraid to state openly that public opinion, pandered to by flatterers and encouraged by demagogues, can produce unstable policies and lead to unwise decisions. Requiring concurrence by more than one body was one of the founders' institutional arrangements to help cope with this problem. If this system sometimes blocks or retards policies sought by a majority that are not unwise or mistaken—as it surely has—this problem does not by itself discredit the arrangement, for there is no institutional solution that does not entail some costs in producing a benefit.

The foregoing discussion presupposes entertaining of at least the possibility that majorities may not always know what is best and that there may be a decision-making process that is able to improve a simple reliance on majority opinion. The founders referred to this filtering aspect of the governmental system by speaking of its "representative" or "republican" character, which they distinguished from a pure democratic system. Early in his article, when attacking the system of checks and balances and the presidential veto, Dahl comes close to denying the existence of any standard, except for the protection of individual rights, by which it might be said that majorities can err. Yet when it comes time to sketch his own regime, Dahl concedes that majorities can fail in making the correct choices if citizens do not meet what he calls the "criterion of enlightened understanding." Instead of relying, like the founders, on institutions of government to assist in dealing with the effects of something less than full enlightenment, Dahl puts his faith almost exclusively in an ambitious program of adult education. He would make available "quasi-expert intermediaries spread among the whole body of citizens," who could help the less-informed citizens "to gain an adequate understanding of their own basic rights, needs, and interests, and of the policies best designed to satisfy these needs." Although this proposal to put a policy analyst in every shopping mall might resolve the employment problem for doctoral candidates in the social sciences, it remains an open question how many citizens would avail themselves of this opportunity to be patronized and how many would actually leave these counseling sessions with their opinions measurably more enlightened.

When encountering the criticisms of someone who argues that the present-day American regime is not democratic, defenders of the regime may feel tempted to deny the charge and congratulate themselves on how democratic the nation is. The denial is largely in order, but the congratulations should be offered with care. Despite the deviations noted above, the American regime today is quite democratic in its procedures. Of all the world's democracies, or at least of those of considerable size, it is quite possibly the most democratic, though such comparisons are admittedly difficult and often meaningless. The American system is one of the few that gives most of the lawmaking power on a day-to-day basis to a popular legislature; biennial legislative elections provide an occasion for popular input at intervals more regular and frequent than that found in most democratic systems; and candidates for party nominations are selected for the most part in popular primaries (a unique arrangement). If there is one reason to hesitate proclaiming the democratic character of the American regime, it surely has to do with the role played by the judicial branch, which has ventured deeply into the policymaking process, in ways never intended by the founders, to make many decisions that have been opposed by local or national majorities. Curiously, however, though Dahl decries time and again the "pseudo-democratic imperial presidency," he never once takes issue with the policymaking authority of the judiciary, even though it would seem to present the most formidable impediment to procedural democracy. Perhaps his hands-off treatment of the judiciary owed something to the Supreme Court's understanding of "substantive justice" in the decade preceding the writing of his essay.

The fact that the American regime is so democratic, however, should not automatically be taken as a cause for rejoicing. Dahl readily concedes that pseudo-democratic developments do not always produce good government; perhaps the same could be said sometimes of real democratic developments. While there are certain facets of the American regime that might be improved by democratization, there may be other facets for which the opposite is true. Is it clear, for example, that we have bettered our system by every cause in recent decades that has marched under the banner of democratic reform? Has the performance of our political parties improved, and does Congress in every instance operate more effectively? These appear to be open questions on which students of American institutions may disagree. Even to begin to make judgments on such matters requires abandoning the modern prejudice that equates the good exclusively with the democratic. It requires instead a search for the principles of good government. A genuine encounter with the American tradition, and in particular with the founders, might not be a bad place to begin.

The New Democratic Order

What would it be like to live in Dahl's regime? Let us put aside further discussion of governmental institutions and turn to the principles that animate his society. Although the picture Dahl paints is sometimes fuzzy, his regime is intended to combine the aspirations of liberty and democracy (or equality). As between the two, however, Dahl's society would seem to promote, in Tocqueville's words, "a more enduring love for equality than for liberty," so much so that when the two conflict, as surely they must, preference is given to equality. Dahl's more enduring love for equality can be seen most clearly in his treatment of property.

The attack on the principle of liberty as it relates to property is introduced indirectly. Dahl tells us that procedural democracy requires giving equal weight to each citizen's preferences. The unequal distribution of wealth and income threatens this equality, because money is a political resource that gives an immense advantage to the rich. Although this advantage might conceivably be negated by placing limits on the use of money in politics, this approach has not worked adequately. Dahl therefore recommends the "other approach" of going to the root of the problem and attacking inequalities in wealth and income. To eliminate a source of inequality in promoting preferences in the political arena, Dahl proposes sacrificing the principle of economic liberty and private property.[31]

This "back-door" attack on economic liberty and property may leave one wondering about Dahl's real standard of judgment. There are other resources besides money, such as positions within organizations and access to media, that are as important in influencing the capacity of individuals to promote preferences in the political arena. Yet in these instances Dahl never suggests employing the "other approach" of attacking political inequalities by sacrificing rights. Dahl's objection is therefore not only simply to the political inequalities related to wealth but also to the existence of differences in wealth and property. His reason for singling out these differences has finally to do with enforcing his standard of "substantive justice." The accumulation of wealth in unequal amounts by different skills or effort is not, evidently, considered the stuff of which even a presumptive right is made.

Actually, Dahl's view seems to be that property once had a claim to being a right, but has one no longer. In the Golden Age of agrarianism, wealth was produced by the farmers' "labor, ingenuity, anguish, planning, forbearance, sacrifice, risk, and hope." The implication is that in a modern capitalist economy, the qualities referred to in this formidable string of adjectives no longer apply to the activity of generating wealth. Wealth is a product of collective social factors, with differentials in individual activity related to any worthwhile character attributes accounting for very little. Under this view, individual private property has no moral claim to protection. Because the economic product of society is collectively generated, it follows that it belongs to everyone and that the majority should be authorized to distribute it according to the tenets of "substantive justice." The implications of this general doctrine for the extension of public authority are fascinating for any socialist to consider. Even more exciting for the limits-minded socialist is the prospect that, under this new economic system, we may never have any economic growth to fear.

Many today who are not directly involved in producing wealth have little understanding of, let alone respect for, the activity of economic enterprise. The view that this activity might be necessary for the well-being of society and worthy of protection as a right is not an idea that is highly regarded in certain circles, where real rights are more apt to be associated with matters of expression or privacy. What sophisticated consumers of society's wealth may be able to appreciate, however, are the second-order consequences for liberty that might flow from the elimination of private property.

Liberty is valued in society in part for its fruits—for its diversity, for the treasures of civilization it helps preserve, and for the opportunities it provides to add to or embellish the store of human culture and knowledge. These fruits of liberty, though they cannot be bought, depend in some measure on the provision of physical resources (i.e., money). Money can be supplied by private sources, by public sources, or not at all. Money coming from private sources is linked to private property and to an inequality in wealth, as certain forms of patronage for culture are supplied chiefly by the better-off. If this private source of support were eliminated or diminished, part of the loss might be made up by increased public spending. Yet quite apart from the new bureaucratic hierarchies this would create, there are certain institutions and activities that democratic governments might find very difficult to support. One thinks, for example, of certain private elite universities in which the resources lavished on a small number of students and faculty might strike some as excessive. Indeed, in a regime committed to an egalitarian standard of distributive justice, it is difficult to see why the crucial resource of intellectual talent should not be redistributed on a more equal basis throughout the entire higher-education system. Whatever the problems attached to the unequal distribution of wealth—and these differ from one society to another—those who love liberty and appreciate its fruits will wish to think twice before adopting a simple regime principle that endorses the justice of economic equality.

Almost as important for liberty as the protection of a right to individual private property is some notion of private property for business corporations, a concept Dahl not only opposes but also ridicules. But the ridiculous here may have a touch of the sublime, even if one readily concedes that a right of property for corporations has a partly analogical and fictive character. Whoever speaks of liberty should speak in the same breath of the practical instruments in society that protect and maintain it; these are its guardians and fences. To define liberty in terms of rights and wave that definition around like a talisman is not enough to ensure its protection, for abstract principles are not self-executing. Nor is it sufficient to rely exclusively on courts, because a judicial branch powerful enough to be the chief guardian of liberty is also powerful enough to pose a threat to it. It is far better if the overall conditions in society provide a balance of power that renders liberty more secure. Those things that serve to protect liberties, even where they may create certain dubious privileges or entail certain regrettable costs, may be justifiable.

Liberty may be threatened, as we know, by the failure of the state to use its power against private sources in society that would deprive individuals of their rights. As these private sources become larger and more powerful, the authority of the state may need to be expanded to supply the necessary check. This was the rationale for curbing corporate power under the welfare state and for modifying certain absolute or excessive claims made on behalf of corporate private property. Yet the threat to liberty that comes from private entities, however dangerous it may be, is limited by these entities' lack of plenary power and full moral authority.

Far different is the threat to liberty posed by the state, which, because of its power and its moral authority, possesses the potential over time for a much greater assault on rights. Institutional arrangements that check or balance the active use of power by the state to intrude in society therefore work on balance to support liberty. Those today who devise doctrines that help to join the power of society's most formidable private entities—the business corporations—to the power of government are no friends of liberty; they are the modern counterparts of those in the Middle Ages who sought to fuse the power of church and state. By contrast, those who have helped devise a presumption of at least a partial right of property in the business corporation have been among the benefactors of liberty in modern times. And let it be added, to avoid any simplistic identification of this position with every injustice associated with economic development, that the principle of private property in the corporation does not preclude state protection of the worker's welfare. Neither does it prevent a variety of modes of ownership, among which is included the possession by employees of their own firms, or experimentation with different systems of industrial relations, such as worker participation or codetermination of production decisions.

Dahl has no end of poking fun at "the absurdities in extending Locke on private property to . . . the business corporation." Yet his interpretation of Locke as a mild-mannered, avuncular defender of a simple agrarian order is not without interest of its own. The Locke that Adam Smith and Karl Marx read provided the philosophic tools that undergirded modern economic development. Dahl's transformation of Locke is reminiscent of his transformation of "the best" in the American tradition. In his sanitized interpretations, both have been made to serve his peculiar vision of democracy. Here is an instance, however, in which the naked truth of the unexpurgated version may prove not only more exciting but more enlightening as well.

Political Science and Political Improvement

Dahl's essay is a direct invitation to overturn the existing liberal democratic regime in America and to institute a new arrangement of government and society. By discussing so bold a proposition without precondition—as I have done thus far—I have followed Dahl in a kind of abstract theorizing about political life in which choosing regimes is treated in much the same way as one would treat a policy question: the various policy options are outlined, and then, having decided on what appears to be the best one, an effort is made to put it into effect. But an intellectual exercise of this kind when applied to a choice of regimes has about it the air of children at play or madmen at work.

In the real world—where lives, fortunes, and beliefs are at stake—a change of regimes can never be considered so lightly, for the slate is never clean and there are huge "sunk investments." These investments in America today include a Constitution that has endured for two hundred years, a people that accepts the basic principles and framework of the current government, and many nations that depend on the stability of America for their defense against totalitarian domination. The sheer weight of these interests makes a mockery of seductive intellectual discussions that presuppose a clean slate. Real-world concerns call for a political science that incorporates an account of the circumstances under which it might make sense to pull down an existing regime and call on a science of politics to help construct a new one.

To ask political science to endorse the idea of urging a change of regimes might be reasonable under a circumstance in which the existing regime is precarious or destined soon to fall, for in that case little is being risked. Alternatively, it would make sense where the existing regime is deeply flawed, for in that case, even if the change fell far short of expectations, it might lead to an improvement. In other circumstances, advocating total change becomes a much more problematic venture. It should only take place after an assessment of what a science of politics can reasonably expect to teach us, of the likelihood that the counsels of that science would be followed, and of the risks and costs of change itself, including the possibility of catastrophe.

If Dahl engaged in this or any other explicit process of prudential theorizing about the circumstances for advocating total change, it is certainly not evident in "On Removing Certain Impediments to Democracy in the United States." If one were to attempt, however, to piece together his answer from his treatment of the American case, it might be the following. It is clear to begin with that Dahl does not think that the Constitution is precarious or destined soon to fall, for he marvels at its resiliency in surviving three decades of war and an imperial presidency. Next, although Dahl scarcely mentions the potential costs or risks involved in refounding the regime, he provides a mild surprise when he warns against inflated expectations for modern political science. We have no grounds, he tells us, for supposing that we possess "the knowledge and skills to excel the performance of the framers" in matching the correct means to achieve the desired ends. Because the founders, in Dahl's view, constructed a government that produced harmful and often unwanted consequences, it is likely that modern founders, in their attempt to establish procedural democracy, also will commit mistakes of a similar magnitude.

What, then, can justify the call for a change of regimes, even when we know of the likelihood of committing serious blunders? The answer helps account for Dahl's insistence on a continuing degeneration in the moral quality of the American regime is that liberal democracy today is so fundamentally flawed that we can reasonably discount fears that a change could work out for the worse. As long as we know that we are committed to a superior standard of political health—and this we know—the superior result of a new effort at constitution-making cannot be much in doubt.

This leads us back to our point of departure: Dahl's standard of political health. For Dahl, political health is marked by a progressive growth in consciousness to the point at which we can transcend conflict by embracing the warmer unity of a more egalitarian order. More even than his love of equality, it is Dahl's desire for an end to our being "conflicted" that characterizes his political science and that seems to distinguish it from the political science of the founders. What the founders teach is that the good things in politics themselves often conflict and that the object must be, in Madison's words, "mingling them in their due proportions."[32] Designing and maintaining a constitution is not an exercise in avoiding conflict, but an effort at discovering the institutional forms that achieve the best possible mingling" of the goods of political life.

Despite having presentiments of nuclear annihilation, Dahl trusts in a special kind of progress according to which we can look forward to a time when we transcend our psychological conflicts, collective and individual. Near the end of his essay, Dahl expresses his muted optimism: "When we turn toward the inner self and ask what we need in order to understand the needs and interests of the self, including those crucial aspects of oneself that are inextricably bound up with and require a sympathetic understanding of other selves, we confront a question to which the answer is inescapably open-ended. . . . The criterion of enlightened understanding beckons us forward but it cannot tell us what we shall discover."

These words are the key to Dahl's new liberation psychology, which serves in turn as the foundation for his new liberation political science. The new democratic "self," characterized by "sympathetic understanding" as well as "love, nurturance, pity, joy, compassion and hope," is the model both for Dahl's new world order, in which, with the elimination of America's will to dominate, peace will be more likely, and for his new American regime, in which a benevolent state will ensure a happier and more egalitarian society. This vision of the future, however benign it may appear, represents a flight from the realism of the greatest parts of our tradition and a rejection of the sterner qualities of the human spirit that have helped to build and sustain our constitutional republic.

7

Political Science and the Political Culture of Liberal Democracy

OF THE THREE BASIC CAUSES that traditional political science postulated for any regime—geography, political culture or mores, and law—political culture holds the central place. This, at any rate, was the view of Alexis de Tocqueville, who remarked that if the importance of these causes for maintaining a liberal democracy in America were ranked, "the contribution of physical causes is less than that of laws and that of laws less than mores."[1] Although Tocqueville was not the first to study what political scientists today call political culture, he applied that concept to the analysis of democratic states with greater rigor than any previous thinker. It is to Tocqueville's thought, therefore, that we turn in this chapter to study the relation of political culture to liberal democracy.

Tocqueville left America in 1832 with the intention not only of describing its political and social institutions but also of creating a "new political science for a world itself quite new." His object was to clarify the forces shaping the modern world and to provide "those who now direct society" with the knowledge of how to reconcile liberty and democracy (the social state of an "equality of conditions").[2]

Tocqueville addressed *Democracy in America* to the entire generation of modern readers, but his immediate audience was clearly European, not American. No narrow chauvinism was at work here, but instead a frank assessment of the status of philosophy in different nations of the world. Nineteenth-century America hardly needed and could scarcely digest a work such as *Democracy in America*: "The spirit of the Americans is averse to general ideas. . . . They pay very little attention to the rival European schools [of philosophy]. Indeed, they hardly know their names."[3]

America was at the intellectual periphery, but for the moment at least ignorance was bliss. Without either a taste for abstract political thinking or a large class of intellectuals, America alone had succeeded in reconciling democracy and liberty. Nor was this a mere coincidence: America, Tocqueville contended, had met the challenge of the modern age not despite, but in large measure because of, the minimal influence of contemporary doctrines of political thought and the absence of a class of intellectuals to spread them.

The role of political thought in Europe could hardly have been more different. Purveyed by a powerful intellectual elite, political ideas had a tremendous influence on European societies. Political philosophy at the time was divided between two basic schools that were openly competing for dominance of the public mind—philosophe rationalism (the more influential school) and traditionalism. Tocqueville believed that both of these schools tended ultimately to undermine liberty. Political thought had lost a constructive role as a guide to political action and was promoting the march toward despotism. This intellectual crisis demanded a theoretical response—"a new political science"—the rudiments of which Tocqueville discovered in his study of America's ostensibly unsophisticated political culture. Seldom has an anthropological expedition yielded so much for a philosophic debate.

Tocqueville defined mores *(moeurs)*, or what we call political culture, in very broad terms as "the sum of the moral and intellectual dispositions of men in society . . . the habits of heart . . . [and] the sum of ideas that shape mental habits." The importance Tocqueville ascribed to mores accounts both for the scope of his political science—which extends to what we today would consider to be sociological and cultural elements of society—and for its distinctive method of studying a political system, under which institutions are considered not only for their effect on governing efficiency but also for how they influence citizens' "mental habits" or ways of thinking and reasoning. Of all the aspects of the American regime, it was the people's mores that Tocqueville believed best accounted for America's success. America was characterized by less brilliance and possessed less efficient political institutions than some nations in Europe, but it had developed the mental habits that could sustain liberty.[4]

Following Montesquieu, Tocqueville traced the sources of political culture to such fundamental causes as past history and laws.[5] Because these factors are in some degree particular to the experience of each nation, it is more correct to speak in the plural of political cultures than of a single political culture. Yet what struck Tocqueville about the modern age was the emergence of certain factors that were influencing all developed nations along the same lines: "Democratic peoples . . . in the end come to be alike in almost all matters. . . . [T]he same ways of behaving, thinking and feeling are found in every corner of the world."[6] The two most important forces Tocqueville identified as causes of this common development were the spreading social condition of equality and the emergence of modern political thought as an active force capable of influencing the political cultures of all societies.

To understand the possibilities implicit in this path of development, Tocqueville abstracted from the particular nations and political cultures of his day in an effort to discover the picture of a common social state. This social state, which he originally referred to as "Democracy," consisted of a set of properties and tendencies that if left to their normal course of development would more likely eventuate in despotisms, whether of the usual or new tutelary variant, than liberal democracies. Although the tendencies of democracy operated to some degree on all modern societies, they were refracted by the special characteristics of each nation's political culture, with the result that different nations were more or less likely to establish liberty. Tocqueville chose America as the obvious place to study the properties of democracy, but it turned out that America was in many respects atypical of his general model, mainly because of the special intellectual foundation of its political culture.

Each nation, by definition, has a political culture. By studying the various regimes and political cultures, the political scientist seeks to discover the elements of a political culture that operate to support each regime type. The political scientist then proceeds to see how existing political cultures in specific cases might be adjusted in the direction of the political culture that best supports the maintenance of the chosen regime. This form of general regime analysis applied to specific cases is then supplemented by a purely local analysis, in which the political scientist considers specific aspects of political culture that have grown in that place, analyzing whether they work to strengthen or weaken the existing regime.

Tocqueville intended political science to be an alternative influence to rationalism and traditionalism in shaping the political culture of modern states. In light of the threat to liberty posed by these two schools, political science could not remain aloof or detached, but had to become an active force in history. Yet in no sense could it become a simple ideology, though from time to time it might have to avail itself of rhetorical features. Political science represents a complex approach that synthesizes certain epistemological elements of rationalism and traditionalism into a truer picture of reality. The factors shaping the development of modern times, though increasingly common to all nations, are not entirely beyond human control, either within each nation or within the developed world as a whole. The decisive choice between freedom and despotism is largely determined by the doctrines and ideas that guide people's thought.

I shall begin this analysis of political culture, accordingly, with a discussion of Tocqueville's account of the development of rationalism and traditionalism, as these were the two philosophies that most shaped the mental habits of modern society. Next, I shall sketch Tocqueville's political science and his stratagem for inserting it into society, indicating how he sought to mix rationalist and traditionalist elements to fashion a political culture that could sustain liberal democracy. Finally, I shall conclude by briefly surveying some of the threats to that political culture which exist in America today.

Rationalism and Traditionalism

Tocqueville's point of departure was the reaction of his contemporaries to democracy and to the shattering event that brought democracy to the center stage of European consciousness—the French Revolution. On one side, according to Tocqueville, stood the proponents of a radical version of rationalism, who saw themselves as the heirs of the French philosophes. For these thinkers, the French Revolution marked the dawn of a new era in which philosophy for the first time became an active force in transforming society. Philosophy stripped away the cloak of tradition that had supported superstition, injustice, and parochialism, offering instead universally valid principles, derived from reason, that could instruct the enlightened on how to remake society and construct new political orders.[7]

On the other side were the proponents of traditionalism, or organicism, who turned for their inspiration chiefly to the writings of Edmund Burke. This school, which emerged as a conscious reaction to philosophe ideas, attacked the abstract, speculatist character of rationalist thought, seeing in its universalism and its contempt for tradition a dangerous doctrine that threatened political stability, diversity, and the noblest elements of civilization. Only by a renunciation of this kind of metaphysical thought and a return to respect for tradition—meaning an appreciation for hierarchy, diversity, and transcendence—would the world be saved from the ambition of the philosophes, who, according to Burke, had ushered in "a barbarous philosophy," which "rudely tore off . . . all the decent drapery of life."[8] About all that both schools could agree on was that philosophe ideas had prepared the way for, if indeed they had not been the chief cause of, the French Revolution.[9]

Tocqueville distinguished four different stages in the development of rationalist thought. The first stage, which occurred in the sixteenth century, focused on the relationship of humanity to God. Religious reformers "subjected the dogmas of ancient faith to reason," while still maintaining a belief in the Deity. The second stage, in the seventeenth century, saw the application of this way of thinking by Francis Bacon and René Descartes to the respective realms of natural science and philosophy (metaphysics); these philosophers consciously defined the mode of thought known as "method" and launched a philosophic project that "destroyed the dominion of tradition and upset the authority of masters." The essence of method was a reliance on individual reason, in the light of experience, as the standard for evaluating truth, rather than prejudice, revelation, or tradition.[10]

It remained, however, for a third stage to extend the principles of method to the social and political spheres, turning the world upside down and spreading in the public mind a mode of thinking "by which all ancient things could be attacked and the way opened for everything new." This approach was popularized by the eighteenth-century thinkers and in particular by the French philosophes and economists. Its governing idea was to replace the complex of traditional customs with simple, elementary rules deriving from the exercise of human reason and natural law. Tocqueville was aware, of course, of other strands of rationalist political thought that were not as radical or abstract as the French school, and he was personally drawn to certain English rationalists, such as Hume. Yet it was French philosophe ideas that had the most profound influence on shaping the political cultures of his day and that had become "the common coin of thought" throughout much of Europe.[11]

Under the influence of the philosophes, French writers of the next generation extended their mode of thinking to "an unrestrained passion for generalizations." This marked yet a fourth stage in the evolution of rationalism, which occurred during Tocqueville's own time: "No writer . . . is satisfied with an essay revealing truths applicable to one great kingdom, and he remains dissatisfied with himself if his theme does not embrace the whole of mankind." French thought—which in contrast to English thought brought almost no practical experience to bear in writing on politics—was characterized by a literary spirit largely devoid of any contact with reality. It built abstract, utopian models, ignoring the real world and real constraints. In France at least, this "literary spirit" came to shape the public's intellectual dispositions: "It was this vision of the perfect state that fired the imagination of the masses. . . . Turning away from the real world around them, they indulged in dreams of a far better one and ended up by living, spiritually, in the ideal world thought up by these writers."[12]

By the end of the eighteenth century, therefore, what passed for rationalist thought was very different from the original rationalist method identified by Bacon and Descartes and later pursued by Hume and Montesquieu. Whereas rationalism had begun as an inductive or empirical approach characterized by the careful movement from the particulars of experience to generalizations, it evolved by the end of the eighteenth century into an abstract and deductive mode of thought in which authors fabricated their own systems and then sought to impose them on reality. Tocqueville regarded this shift from an empirical method to "a passion for generalization" as a perversion of the original spirit of rationalism.

Rationalism now increasingly displayed an a priori suspicion of tradition and an irrational prejudice against the old. It relied on a mode of reasoning that moved from general or abstract ideas to particulars, rather than from particulars to generals. Although Tocqueville clearly welcomed the dissemination of a few key general ideas that were foundations for society as a whole—natural rights were one—he deplored the spread of the mental habits that led people to reason from generals to particulars. He was convinced that this way of thinking would end by putting intellectual opinion in charge of society and destroy the cause of liberty. It was only in America that rationalism in its original, empirical form was practiced in daily politics: "America is the one country in which the precepts of Descartes are least studied and best followed."[13] There was less philosophy in America than in Europe, but America was paradoxically the nation most defined or affected by philosophy.

Tocqueville gave traditionalism a less systematic treatment, probably because of its more recent origin.[14] The traditionalists of Tocqueville's time ranged across a broad spectrum of opinion, but their diagnosis of the evils of philosophe rationalism reflected a common theoretical position that could be traced to Burke's writings. Traditionalists rejected a reliance in political life on what they took to be abstract, metaphysical thought. Burke called political science a "practical science" and emphasized the need to view political phenomena in terms of concrete circumstances and particulars. Traditionalism thus presented itself partly as a defense of the realm of prudence for the statesman against the misinformed intrusion of speculative philosophy. In this respect, traditionalism was consistent with the pragmatic character of original rationalist thought, which counseled making judgments on the basis of experience. But traditionalism went far beyond a reliance on this form of reason in its assault on rationalism.

First, traditionalists attacked metaphysical speculation, and sometimes reason itself, in the name of a veneration for the old and familiar. They upheld the "prejudices" of the community and glorified an "instinctive patriotism." For the traditionalist, Tocqueville explained, "the idea of evil is indissolubly linked with that of novelty."[15]

Second, and following from this depreciation of reason, traditionalists celebrated the heritage of each nation as it emerged as the product of the particular and accidental forces that shaped its development. According to traditionalists, historical bonds of union formed the only sound basis for community, not individual reason or the individual's calculation of interest. Each nation's constitution was the product of—and ought to be bounded by—its particular historical development. Beginning from this organic perspective on society, traditionalists viewed the homogenizing effects of universalistic ideas with profound suspicion. Universal ideas not only eroded the basis of community but also destroyed the charm of diversity in the world. Indeed, Joseph de Maistre went so far as to deny the "general idea" of man or mankind: "The [French] Constitution of 1795, like its predecessors, is made for *man*. Yet there is no such thing as *man* in this world. I have seen, in my life, French, Italians, Russians, etc . . . but as for *man*, I have never seen one in my life; if man exists, it is without my knowledge."[16]

Finally, traditionalists strongly supported religious faith, especially as it manifested itself in the particular religious institutions of each society. Traditionalists sought to make common cause with the faithful by contending that religion was one part of an integral world view being attacked by rationalist ideas.[17]

All of these elements of traditionalism can be found in Burke's writings, but they received a simpler, and far more extreme, expression in Maistre's works: "[Man's] cradle should be surrounded by dogmas; and when his reason awakes all his opinions should be given him. . . . Nothing is more vital to him than prejudices. . . . Religion and political dogmas, mingled and merged with each other, should together form a general or national mind sufficiently strong to repress the aberrations of the individual reason."[18]

After sketching the development of rationalist and traditionalist thought up to his day, Tocqueville turned to their likely evolution and to their potential consequences on the political culture of modern societies. Although each school claimed in its own way to support liberty, Tocqueville contended that they ultimately denied that individuals could control their own destiny and therefore eroded a fundamental belief necessary to support liberty. Maintaining liberty requires more than an acceptance of an idea of rights and a favorable set of institutional arrangements. It requires a metaphysical foundation in certain ideas respecting historical causality and free will. Liberty depends on people being able to choose and on believing that their choices can make a difference.[19] Without this belief in free will, people loose their own will to choose and see no reason to support the idea of rights and legal institutions designed to protect liberty.[20]

Yet it was precisely this belief in free will that rationalism and traditionalism called into question. Philosophe rationalism began with the seeming assertion of boundless human choice: "It has been said that the character of the philosophy of the eighteenth century was a sort of adoration of human intellect, an unlimited confidence in its power to transform at will laws, institutions, customs."[21] Human beings can remake the world according to the dictates of reason, overthrowing the tyranny of tradition and accident. Yet in its ever-expanding quest for universal principles of explanation, philosophe rationalism led paradoxically to the negation of the conditions for choice. The search for general and universal causes ended by positing the source of human activity not in the decisions of particular individuals, but in humanity as a whole or, beyond, in some immanent force in nature or history.

Tocqueville labeled this mode of thinking "philosophic pantheism." By tracing the springs of human activity to abstractions such as humanity or history, this doctrine made human choice appear meaningless. Tocqueville argued that choices for society can only be made by individuals on behalf of the species; the species itself cannot choose. Once one posits the power over human affairs in the species, that power lies with no one in particular and hence with an invisible system that operates on all: "Individuals are forgotten, and the species alone counts."[22] With vast, general causes controlling their destiny, people lose their will to assert themselves and become weak and phlegmatic.

If philosophe rationalism carried to the extreme leads to one form of denial of human choice, traditionalism carried to the extreme leads to another. The result is equally paradoxical in light of the traditionalist goal of preserving a realm of discretion for the statesman. Yet by depreciating reason and making the heritage of each society both the cause and standard for its regime, traditionalists implied that there were no fundamental choices; all was as it had to be, or nearly so. The protection traditionalists sought to gain for the statesman in the realm of prudential decision-making was thus bought at the cost of denying human choice on fundamental questions. "Each nation," in the traditionalist view, "is inexorably bound by its position, origin, antecedents, and nature to a fixed destiny which no effort can change . . . [it is] the product of preexisting facts of race, or soil, or climate."[23] Mill provides a classic formulation of the traditionalist position (which he of course rejected): "[Governments] are a sort of organic growth from the nature and life of that people: a product of their habits, instincts and unconscious wants and desires, scarcely at all of their deliberate purposes."[24]

Traditionalist thought represented a radicalization of Montesquieu's idea of "the general spirit." As indicated in chapter three, Montesquieu was the most influential precursor of the traditionalist school, and the thinker whom Burke most admired.[25] Still, it is the transformation of Montesquieu's ideas that is most striking in traditionalist thought, if not by Burke himself then certainly by his followers on the Continent. Traditionalists elevated the idea of the "general spirit" from its status in Montesquieu's thought as a powerful *constraint* on human choice to that of an absolute *determinant* of a nation's historical development. They also expanded the concept's normative implications from that of a powerful analytic tool which assisted in avoiding extreme action to that of a near-absolute standard. That standard is now referred to by traditionalists as "nature," which is understood in the human context as the product of the organic development of history in a given place.

Traditionalism, then, leads to a doctrine of historical inevitability, though not of the sort with which we are most familiar today. Ever since Hegel, and especially Marx, doctrines of historical inevitability have usually assumed the form of *universalistic* theories in which the forces at work in history are said to be worldwide. Post-Hegelian historicism folds the general ideas inaugurated by the philosophes into an inevitable movement of *world* history, in which the decisive moments that form the world follow a pattern that flows either from the movement of Mind or material forces. The original doctrines of historical inevitability, however, were an outgrowth of traditionalism, and they sought to demonstrate that the cause of human societies lay with the particular and accidental forces that operate on each nation (or *Volk*).[26] Although Tocqueville glimpsed the possibility of a universalistic historicism and advanced one such mild variant of his own, he identified the historicism of his day mainly with those who sought to explain the fate of *particular* nations or peoples.

Notwithstanding the traditionalists' defense of rank and hierarchy, Tocqueville considered their doctrines of historical inevitability to represent a democratic mode of thought, in the sense that peoples, races, or climates, but not individuals, control historical development. (An aristocratic view of history puts the fate of the world into the hands of individuals whose actions account for the movement of history.) Although Tocqueville granted that the traditionalist variant of historicism might preserve a certain diversity in the world among nations or races, in the end it was hardly less hostile than the pantheistic variant to supporting a belief in free will and human choice. Traditionalist historicism left people with the idea that their actions could make no difference and that "societies unconsciously obey some superior dominating force," which is the view that prepares the way for despotism.[27] By extending Tocqueville's analysis, one can glimpse in this traditionalist variant of historicism as transformed by the atheism of Nietzsche the seeds of the radical "democratic" Right (fascism), just as it is possible to see in rationalism as modified by Marx the grounds of the radical "democratic" Left (communism).

Thus rationalism, by leading to philosophic pantheism, and traditionalism, by leading to historicism, deny free will. To promote the beliefs that sustain liberty, Tocqueville sought to free modern society from the exclusive influence of these schools. His alternative, the new political science, presupposed a significant, though not unlimited, degree of choice: "One may say that it depends on us whether in the end republics will be established everywhere, or everywhere abolished."[28] Political science was designed to help people choose well, which demanded knowledge of the historical situation and the capacity to face reality, avoiding the mistakes of exaggerating or underestimating the available possibilities.

Against the philosophe's excessive pride that all societies could be remade according to simple principles of reason, Tocqueville countered with the claim that regimes were still bound by the particular experiences of each nation. Despite the homogenizing forces set in motion by growing equality and the spread of modern thought, the political culture of each nation retained certain distinct characteristics. Tocqueville certainly had no wish to impose uniformity for its own sake. Insofar as political science might assist those who directed society, it was not by prescribing precise models that should be adopted in the same fashion in every nation, but by illustrating general principles to apply as far as circumstances within each nation would permit.[29]

Against the traditionalists, Tocqueville countered with a twofold argument to meet their two very different (and conflicting) assumptions. On the one hand, traditionalists virtually denied there could be a general science of politics to assist legislators. As the world in their view is governed by contingencies and accident, and as institutions are the product of particular cultures, the best the legislator can do is modify a constitution according to standards that emerge from understanding a nation's particular genius. According to Tocqueville, this view underestimates the degree of choice and the role that a general science of politics might play in informing the tasks of legislating and constitution-making.

On the other hand, traditionalists assumed that the movement toward equality of conditions and away from a respect for hierarchy and forms could be thwarted by the development of a counterideology. Tocqueville believed this option was effectively closed and could be pursued only at the cost of repression and destruction: "Burke did not see . . . that there could be no question of putting the clock back."[30] Although traditionalists purported to look at facts, they refused to acknowledge that the movement toward the social state of democracy and the penetration of society by some form of rationalism were historical facts in their own right that could not be denied or reversed. In his introduction to *Democracy in America,* Tocqueville attempts to force traditionalists to see that the real choice was not between the old order and democracy, but between democratic despotisms and liberal democracies. Given the traditionalists' expressed concern for liberty, they might, when faced with this choice, be persuaded to become adherents of the new political science.

The Philosophic Foundation of the New Political Science

Tocqueville's new political science combines generals and particulars to form a body of knowledge designed to promote the cause of liberty in modern times. It can thus be characterized not only by its normative goal—which makes it quite different from much modern political science—but also by its distinctive epistemological foundation. It falls into a middle ground between rationalism, which extended general ideas to the point of eliminating any prudential consideration of specific circumstances, and traditionalism, which denied the existence of general ideas that could inform or instruct prudential judgment. But it is much easier, Tocqueville tells us, to imagine the existence and utility of such a middle ground than to put it into practice.

The central problem for a science of politics concerns the epistemological status of general ideas, which distort reality in some degree by comprehending the distinctness of different objects under the same concept. Human thought creates a world of partially fictitious wholes that accord greater similarity to things than actually exists: "General ideas do not bear witness to the power of human intelligence but rather to its inadequacy, for there are no beings exactly alike in nature." It was this difficulty, among other concerns, that led Burke and other traditionalists to doubt the worth of a theoretical political science. For Tocqueville, however, the proper response to the inherent problem of general ideas was not to deny their value, but rather to recognize their limitations and avoid using them in an extreme or abstract fashion. Without recourse to general ideas, no science—indeed no advancement in human understanding—would be possible, for people "would soon be lost in a wilderness of detail and not be able to see anything at all."[31]

Political science is the careful construction of knowledge in which general ideas are founded not on abstract principles from self-contained intellectual systems, but on the painstaking study of particular cases and the "slow, detailed, and conscientious labor of the mind." "One man notices a fact and another conceives an idea; one man finds a means and another discovers a formula." It seems that political science is a collective enterprise—a profession, if you like—that is charged over time with acquiring and refining political knowledge. Yet even this knowledge, because it makes use of general ideas, is imperfect and partly distorts a true understanding of particular circumstances. This difficulty creates an inevitable gap between the statesman and the political scientist, "for while it is sometimes necessary to brush rules of logic aside in action, one cannot do so in the same way in treatises, and man finds it almost as difficult to be inconsistent in his words as he generally finds it to be consistent in his actions."[32]

A perfectly accurate understanding of reality is therefore unattainable, because it would require a humanly impossible method that could reap all the benefits of generalizing while avoiding all of its defects. Only God can employ such a method, for he alone "can survey distinctly and simultaneously" all mankind and each single individual.[33] Science does the best it can using the limited tools of human intelligence to emulate this God-like standard.

The thought of philosophe intellectuals, by contrast, subsumes more and more of reality into abstract general ideas without regard to the existence of particulars. Instead of minimizing the defects inherent in the structure of human thought, philosophe thought exacerbates it. If all that were involved in this activity was a few isolated individuals interpreting the world, the danger would be slight. But philosophe thought was part of a program or project, the aim of which was to eliminate complex customs and traditions and to reshape reality in accord with the "rules of logic and a preconceived system." In line with this program, rationalists of Tocqueville's day supported the powers of the largest unit of authority, the central government, no matter whether it was a strong monarchy or a centralized republic. Philosophe intellectuals saw the central government with its administrative apparatus as the chief instrument for "recasting [a nation] in a given mold, of shaping the mentality of the population as a whole and instilling the ideas and sentiments [of the intellectuals] into the minds of all."[34]

Even more important than the program of the philosophes for change was the impact of their thought on people's mental habits and way of thinking. By their inattentiveness to particulars, philosophes instilled a partiality for uniformity and a disregard for diversity. This result stood in marked contrast to the aim of political science, which in its concern for facts and practice encourages a respect for particulars and diversity. In his most revealing statement of the consequences of rationalist general ideas, Tocqueville wrote:

> To force all men to march in step toward the same goal—that is a human idea. To encourage endless variety of actions but to bring them about so that in a thousand different ways all tend toward the fulfillment of one great design—that is a God-given idea. The human idea of unity is almost always sterile, but that of God is immensely fruitful. Men think they prove their greatness by simplifying the means. God's object is simple but His means infinitely various.[35]

Rationalist intellectuals were either ignorant of the distortion of reality in their thought or else chose from ambition to disregard it. Yet this defect did not decrease their influence, for "what is merit in the writer may well be a vice in the statesman, and the same things that often make beautiful books can lead to great revolutions."[36] Here Tocqueville suggested a central problem of the intellectual in politics; theoretical constructs that are a false reflection of reality are apt to have a much greater impact on the public mind than ideas that present a true picture of reality. The products of a "literary spirit" result in "beautiful" works, whereas the products of a scientific spirit must sacrifice beauty for accuracy; they therefore result in works that are less compelling and appealing.

The discrepancy Tocqueville observed between accuracy and influence points up a deeper theoretical problem about what constitutes truth in political thought. If the philosophes' literary constructs are influential, can they be dismissed as false? If, as some imply, truth in social thought is a function of a capacity to control events—if the point of social science is not to interpret the world, but to change it—

then it would seem contradictory to complain of the inaccuracy of philosophe thought yet concede its power. Tocqueville's response to this line of reasoning was first to deny the premise that truth can be equated with the power to change reality. Social science has a standard different from that of propaganda. But he went on to contend, like Montesquieu, that the falseness of social thought is not inconsequential in regard to its capacity to achieve its effects in the real world. The world is not simply malleable in such a way that it can be constructed at will to accord to the dictates of mind or thought. There is a nature and structure to humanity and society. Accordingly, false ideas, though they may have a great impact, cannot achieve what they promise. By ignoring parts of reality, they lead to unintended consequences and promote grave dysfunctions. The centralizing and homogenizing influence of philosophe thought on modern regimes was not bringing them closer to the promised goal of equality in liberty, but was instead promoting a new form of despotism.

Traditionalists had led the way in identifying and exposing the homogenizing and despotic tendencies of modern philosophe thought. Tocqueville accepted their critique, but he rejected their ultimate standards and doubted the efficacy of their methods for combating philosophe ideas. Unlike the traditionalists, Tocqueville upheld theoretical reason at the same time that he attacked the reason of his contemporaries, and he defended the intellect at the same time that he attacked the modern intellectual. His critique of rationalism was thus carried out in a different spirit and with a different aim than that found in traditionalist thought.

Political Science as an Active Force in the World

Given the complicated character of his new political science, one immediately wonders how Tocqueville hoped to make it an active force in modern society. Although the goal of political science—promoting a regime that could reconcile liberty and democracy—was not hostile to the spirit of modern times, the complexity of political science meant it would have no mass appeal. It might, of course, be taught directly to those who pursued higher education, but Tocqueville was under no illusions that it could become a popular ideology that could, like philosophe thought, "fire the imagination of the masses." "Generally speaking, simple conceptions take hold of people's minds. A false but clear and precise idea always has more power in the world than one which is true but complex."[37]

Because political science could not win a public war of ideas against philosophe ideology, Tocqueville relied on an indirect strategy for inserting it into the political culture of a modern liberal democracy. This strategy was based on encouraging certain mental habits that would produce results compatible with, if not always exactly the same as, the lessons taught by political science. Tocqueville's approach follows from his broad conception of political culture, according to which culture is defined not only as the major opinions or beliefs in society but also as the predominant mental habits and way of thinking. Political culture, in other words, consists of more than content; it refers also, and perhaps even primarily, to mental processes—to the way in which people see reality, sift information, and go about the task of thinking and reasoning.

Conceiving of political culture in large part as the mental habits or way of thinking of people in society is a key insight for political science. The reason is not only the importance of the way of thinking to any notion of culture but also that political structures and institutions do far less in the way of embodying specific ideas or beliefs than they do in forming mental habits. For the founder or legislator, accordingly, it is essential to consider the way of thinking that promotes different regime types, for this is the most helpful knowledge respecting political culture for designing institutions. Political institutions and structures, in Tocqueville's view, are to be judged by a twofold criteria: the quality of the decisions they promote, and their impact on the political culture that sustains the regime. The key element of political culture affected by institutional arrangements is the character of the way of thinking that prevails in society.

A liberal democratic system for Tocqueville depends heavily on a way of thinking in which citizens reason from particulars to generals rather than from generals to particulars. The institutions of society, especially those having an important role in influencing opinion, are judged healthy in large part as they limit the influence of modern intellectuals and promote this empirical or pragmatic way of thinking. Tocqueville did not seek to fight philosophe ideology with ideology, not only because such a battle would have been futile but also because a society directed by ideology (and intellectuals) could not, in his view, remain a free regime. It would be an intellectualocracy. A free regime is one in which the people play an important role in governing, and to perform this task the people must be equipped with certain mental habits.

Under Tocqueville's strategy, public opinion would form more along the lines of the American than the French model. The influence of ideas produced by intellectuals at the top would diminish, whereas the influence of other sources of authority (e.g., political leaders and lawyers) and of opinion generated from the bottom would increase. Opinion generated from the bottom reflected democratic sentiments and concrete interests as these were modified by the knowledge and experience gained by citizens involved in the task of self-government. Political science would help show how this kind of opinion could prevail in society.

In this section, I shall examine Tocqueville's application of the practical aspects of the new political science to the press, the legal system, and local government, noting how he analyzes institutions in part by their effect on mental habits. In each case, Tocqueville illustrates how American institutions, especially when compared with French ones, serve to limit the influence of general ideas and to promote reasoning from particulars to generals. The way Tocqueville uses America and France in this context may be surprising, given his starting point of studying America as the "picture of democracy." Yet Tocqueville discovered that American political culture did not always follow the most likely path of democratic development, but instead had often succeeded in meeting the difficult challenge of reconciling democracy and liberty. In the instances discussed below, France forms the picture for certain democratic tendencies in their pure (and dangerous) form, whereas America becomes the (partial) model for how these tendencies can be managed in a framework that is consistent with democracy.

The Press

Tocqueville's discussion of the press is the most striking case of his effort to limit the influence of intellectuals. Along with most philosophe thinkers, Tocqueville was an advocate of a free press, arguing that citizens in free regimes need a free flow of information to govern themselves and that a governmental power to regulate the press could lead by stages to despotism. Yet unlike the philosophe thinkers, who saw the press as a perfect vehicle for spreading their version of enlightenment to the public, Tocqueville preferred an arrangement of the press that limited the intellectual's influence.[38]

As an independent source of power over public opinion, the French press had no equal. The "vital part" of its newspapers was devoted to political discussion, and the "spirit" of French journalism demanded a "lofty and eloquent way of arguing about the great interests of state." French journalists were highly esteemed, as the relatively small number of newspapers was concentrated in Paris and attracted talented and cosmopolitan writers. It was with the aid of the press that intellectuals were able to spread their thought from the center to the peripheries and to enlighten the provinces with the latest and most advanced ideas.[39]

The American press could hardly have been more different. Newspapers were filled with advertisements, and the presentation of the news lacked the kind of "burning argument" and lofty commentary that was commonplace in France. There was an extraordinarily large number of newspapers in America, which were widely dispersed throughout the nation. The effect of this arrangement was to divide and limit the influence of the American press in comparison with that of the French press. In addition, American journalists were generally of low educational status and possessed only modest talents. When they expressed political viewpoints, they did so not by adopting an intellectual perspective, but by making crude appeals to lower passions, often "attacking people [and] revealing their private lives and vices." American journalists won a wide audience by these techniques, but the more enlightened part of the public sensed the narrow spirit of their inquiry and had little respect for journalists as a group.[40]

Even though the press in America was less powerful than in France, its influence was still very great: "After the people, the press is nonetheless the first of powers." It was not, however, journalists as independent opinion-makers who held most of this power; rather, it derived from the newspapers' role in communicating ideas among groups in society, such as political parties and associations. In the early nineteenth century, American newspapers were the instruments of parties and associations and were explicitly committed to their patrons. The American press therefore contributed to the formation of public opinion by political associations rather than by intellectuals, allowing opinion to build from the bottom to the top, rather than from the top to the bottom.[41]

By any criterion of literary or journalistic excellence, the American press was inferior to that in France. Tocqueville never doubted that the "deplorable abuse of thought" that took place in the American press adversely affected "the taste and morality" of the American people.[42] But the harm done in this respect was more than offset by the benefit derived from blocking a portal of access for the intellectuals' general ideas. Tocqueville was quite willing to sacrifice sophistication as the price for protecting citizens from the thinkers who sought to run their lives.

The Legal Profession

Tocqueville's discussion of the legal profession provides a second example of his effort to limit the power of intellectuals and general ideas. Tocqueville sought to promote the legal spirit in society to serve as counterweights to the literary one, and lawyers as a counterweight to intellectuals.[43] The legal way of thinking has much in common with the empirical strain of early rationalist thought: "It pronounces on particular cases and not on general principles."[44] Judges and lawyers are trained to reason from particulars to generals and therefore develop an affinity for order and forms that leads them as a rule to shun momentary popular passions. To the extent that the legal profession influences the thinking of society as a whole, it imbues the citizenry with some part of its mental habits. Tocqueville, for example, considered the institution of the jury as much in terms of its impact on mental habits as on its efficiency as an instrument of justice.

After sketching the general spirit of the legal profession, Tocqueville turned to the particular spirit of French and Anglo-Saxon lawyers. Although lawyers in both nations deal with particulars, French lawyers, following continental theories of jurisprudence, analyze particulars in the light of general principles, whereas Anglo-Saxon lawyers, working in the common-law tradition, consult "the law of precedents" and consider particulars in light of "the legal judgments of their fathers." "The first thing an English or American lawyer looks for is what has been done whereas a French one inquires what one should wish to do." The spirit of French law is more abstract, as it is based on a "whole system of ideas," whereas that of English and American law is more historical.[45]

The spirit on which Anglo-Saxon law rested antedated not only philosophe thought but also the emergence of rationalism. Although it incorporated along the way many ideas of rationalism, its spirit or way of proceeding was characteristic of traditionalism. Tocqueville's discussion of English and American law virtually reads as a commentary on traditionalist thought. English and American lawyers proceed with "a superstitious respect for all that is old" and value laws "not because they are good but because they are old." With their expertise resting on an "obscure" tradition, they relate to the public "somewhat like the Egyptian priests, being, as they were, the only interpreter of an occult science." English lawyers will introduce change, but only by hiding the fact and going to "absurd lengths" to avoid admitting to the "crime" of being an "innovator." The character of English law is decidedly organic—a point Tocqueville emphasizes by employing the metaphor of a "trunk of an old tree," on which lawyers continually graft "the strangest shoots."[46]

Tocqueville appreciated much in the traditionalist character of Anglo-Saxon law. But his tone, which is almost ironic, and his admission that this system of legal thought was filled with "defects" leave no doubt that he considered traditionalism to be unsuitable as the first principle for the entire government. Its merits aside, the Anglo-Saxon legal spirit could not serve openly as the foundation for a modern society, because its premises were out of step with rationalist standards of legitimacy. Anglo-Saxon lawyers could "raise no banner of their own" and won a measure of influence not by openly defending their principles but by insinuating their spirit into society, "penetrating each class and constantly working in secret upon its unconscious patient."[47]

Despite these reservations, however, Tocqueville thought that the Anglo-Saxon legal spirit provided a salutary corrective to the excesses of certain democratic tendencies, moderating the citizenry's fascination with novelty and limiting its susceptibility to the appeal of general ideas. The legal spirit in America served in its context to promote the political culture of liberty, even though it was grounded in mental habits and a mode of reasoning slightly different from that of early rationalist thought.[48]

Communal Government

Tocqueville's discussion of communal liberty and citizen participation in local governments is the best-known example of his application of the principles of the new political science to practical affairs. It is important, however, to avoid confusing his ideas on citizen participation with an endorsement of populism in national politics. Tocqueville was a staunch opponent of direct democracy in national politics and a strong defender of the American founders' goal of establishing representative institutions that preserved broad discretion for deliberation and statesmanship. Populism or direct majority rule in national politics embodied the worst tendencies of democracy without producing any of the corresponding benefits. Tocqueville's idea of direct citizen participation emphasized activities in matters falling within the sphere of the citizens' own experience, not in affairs of state, such as foreign policymaking. The importance of participation was based as much on the mental habits promoted by the activity of deciding as on the content of what people decided.[49]

By taking part in political affairs, citizens learn and practice the mode of reasoning of the pragmatic strain of rationalism. These habits reduce the influence of general ideas and increase the weight of experience in the formation of public opinion: "If, then, there is a subject concerning which a democracy is particularly liable to commit itself blindly and extravagantly to general ideas, the best possible corrective is to make citizens pay daily practical attention to it." For citizens to become enlightened in more than a cosmetic sense depends on their being able to complete their literary education by participating in the practical task of governing: "True enlightenment is in the main born of experience, and if the Americans had not gradually grown accustomed to rule themselves, their literary attainments would not help them much toward success."[50]

Local government also functions for Tocqueville as a major secondary power that stands between the individual and the central state. Tocqueville seldom discussed liberty without also discussing the concrete means by which it could be secured; these means included possession by citizens of a sense of their *power* to defend their rights. Secondary powers serve as rallying points for citizens to resist the overwhelming weight of central authority. Yet secondary powers are threatened in democratic times by forces tending to concentrate authority in central governments, and it is only by great effort and intelligence that they can be maintained: "In the dawning centuries of democracy individual liberty and local liberties will always be products of art; centralized government will be the natural thing."[51]

Of the secondary powers Tocqueville identified—civic associations, political associations, and business enterprises—the commune was the most durable, for it alone rested on a "natural" foundation (although it, too, could be maintained only by "art"). The commune is natural in the sense of being a form of social organization that grows organically rather than being consciously constructed: "[It] is the only association so well rooted in nature that wherever men assemble it forms itself. . . . [M]an creates kingdoms and republics, but communes seem to spring directly from the hand of God."[52] The organic growth of the commune is not, however, merely a historical creation; rather, the historical pattern reflects or grows out of a natural inclination.

Tocqueville introduces here a key distinction between the natural (in the sense of the organic) and the conventional (that which people make by the application of their own intelligence). His final standard is not the natural in the organic sense, but rather nature or natural right as discovered by human reflection on the world and its possibilities.[53] In contrast, however, to the fabricated human ideas propagated by philosophe intellectuals, Tocqueville's understanding of natural right does not depart entirely from the organic idea of nature. A satisfactory modern regime must combine a rationally constructed principle of rule with a respect for the natural foundations of community that are found in the communes.

The conflict Tocqueville identified between the standards of philosophe rationalists and the standard of the natural is played out on the plane of practical politics in the conflict over the role of local governments in the modern state. The commune develops outside the sphere of human contrivance and derives much of its operating spirit not from abstract theory or ideology, but from custom and practical experience. Philosophe intellectuals, who rely for their power on units of central opinion formation and on centralized administration, regard communal liberty as an enemy of their designs. They want to impose their enlightened standards on the commune and thus run roughshod over communal custom and local experience: "A very civilized society finds it hard to tolerate attempts at freedom in a local community; it is disgusted by its numerous blunders and is apt to despair of success before the experiment is finished."[54] Here Tocqueville depicts the characteristic vice of modern intellect, which is an absence of forbearance in relationship to many existing local customs and an impatient impulse to do things for people rather than to let them act for themselves. Philosophe rationalists prefer to impose right opinion in every case, rather than inculcate the mental habits that would allow people to decide for themselves—and therefore inevitably to make mistakes.

The question of where to draw the line between central and communal authority was for Tocqueville a complicated matter that depended on considerations of national security, the stage of economic development, and the degree of enlightenment in the communes. Although not a dogmatic opponent of all intrusions of the central authority in local affairs, Tocqueville nonetheless expressed a strong preference, all other things being equal, for respecting communal self-government. In the northern states of America Tocqueville found his practical ideal of the modern commune. Free of feudal customs, localities had developed a new tradition based on equality and the exercise of pragmatic rationalism in politics. These communes were enlightened, but they were still far from being the centers of sophistication adored by philosophe intellectuals. Tocqueville had no hesitation, however, in defending them, as his goal was not a society directed by the most advanced ideas of modern thinkers, but one that allows free citizens to practice the art of self-government.

Tocqueville's comparison of opinion formation in France and America risks slipping at times into an ideal-type analysis in which

America, in order to be contrasted with a nation influenced by philosophe rationalist thought, is presented as devoid of intellectual reflection and successful only because of the unconscious operation of geographical and historical advantages. Although Tocqueville pointed to many of the fortunate circumstances that contributed to America's success, his analysis makes clear that the establishment of the Constitution in the 1780s was a remarkable achievement of political sagacity. America was adverse to "general ideas," if by general ideas one means the sort of ideas generated by the philosophes and their opponents. But the American founders were certainly not adverse to the study of the first principles of politics, and important elements of the American public grasped the principles of science on which they had based their work.[55]

Although Tocqueville had nothing but praise for the intelligence of America's founders, he did not consider any American to have been a "great writer on politics." The understanding of what made America work was only partly contained in the thought of *The Federalist*, which, because it focused on the principles for establishing a national government, provided an incomplete account of state and local governments and the fundamentals of American political culture.[56] By contrast, Tocqueville's account concentrates far more on the state and local governments and on the people's mores.

Tocqueville's analysis in effect combined the concerns of the federalist and the antifederalist (and Jeffersonian) traditions in American political thought by blending certain attributes of the small republic—or at any rate worthy facsimiles thereof—with the qualities needed to sustain a large modern commercial regime. Tocqueville showed that a modern liberal democracy depends on elements that are both liberal and republican. Significantly, however, his republican element is based on and is designed to promote, not an antiquated classical republican ideal of virtue, but a modern idea that relies in large part on encouraging a particular kind of *rational* citizen. Many of the republican elements Tocqueville defends—and the same was true for many of the antifederalists and certainly for Jefferson—were not fundamentally at odds with the modern project, even though they would have to be modified to fit into a larger liberal democratic state.

Public Opinion Formation

All of the specific institutional arrangements discussed involve an attempt to control and regulate the character of public opinion. To admit the importance of public opinion, however, points up a limitation of rationalism as the foundation of society. The original rationalist position as it filtered into society held that each person could make up his or her own mind, using a personal assessment of reality as the standard of truth. But this position is finally untenable, if held literally, for it is impossible for individuals to decide all things on their own. Given the limitations of time, inclination, and capacity, "man has to accept as certain a whole heap of facts and opinions which he has neither leisure nor power to examine and verify for himself . . . [s]omewhere and somehow authority is always bound to play a part in intellectual and moral life."[57]

Aristocratic societies were arranged implicitly in acknowledgment of these limitations, and people experienced no great problem in receiving opinions from tradition or from those considered wiser. In democratic societies, however, individuals are imbued with the idea that they can make up their own minds. As their pride demands that they consider themselves fully equal with everyone else, they resist openly accepting the intellectual authority of any other individual. Nevertheless, sensing their own weakness and needing to resolve many matters, they must turn somewhere for answers. They turn to public opinion. By bowing to no one in particular, they flatter themselves that they have not sacrificed their independent judgment. With their minds thus at ease, they accept a source of intellectual authority that is potentially more powerful than those found in aristocratic societies. Rationalism, which begins from the supposition that each person can make up his or her own mind, may paradoxically end with a state of affairs in which few think for themselves and in which "public opinion becomes more and more mistress of the world."[58]

There is no avoiding a great moral as well as political power for public opinion in democratic society. But there is a good deal of choice in determining who or what forms it and what is its precise scope. In regard to who forms public opinion, there are two basic possibilities: either public opinion is formed by intellectuals, who insinuate their ideas into the public mind, or it emerges from the interests and sentiments of the people. Both sources of opinion are likely to be democratic, but the differences are more notable than the similarities. Opinion formed by intellectuals calls for equality and uniformity, dressing these claims in systematic language and mapping out clear programs for action. Intellectuals create ideas that move people beyond a common-sense calculation of their interest to conjure up exciting but fictitious visions. Opinion deriving from the people is coarser and reflects untutored desires for material gratification and for some kind of equality.[59]

This difference helps explain why Tocqueville advocated institutional arrangements designed to limit the intellectuals' influence. Intellectual opinion tends to be rigid and dogmatic, whereas opinion emerging from the bottom is more amenable to modification by political experience and to direction by political leaders. It leaves more space in society to the exercise of the mental habits conducive to liberal democracy and maximizes the citizens' capacity to reason on matters under their competence.

The Limits of Rationalism and the Political Culture of Liberal Democracy

Tocqueville's strategy to reduce the intellectual's influence on society and instill in citizens the mental habits of the early rationalist method was designed to rescue the original core of rationalism from its later distortions. A rationalist standard by itself, however, could never serve as an adequate foundation for society. The distortions that rationalism had undergone in the eighteenth and nineteenth centuries derived logically from its deficiencies as a political doctrine; thus even to save rationalism's original core, its political principles had to be supplemented and modified.

Tocqueville turned here to insights from republicanism and traditionalism. Beginning with the basic rationalist concepts of individual rights and self-interest rightly understood, he mixed in republican ideas of participation and traditionalist themes of religiosity, community, and spiritedness, blending these elements in a way that might allow them to form a workable practical whole. A perfect theoretical consistency among the principles of these different schools was not attainable, and thus to insist on one principle as the sole foundation of liberal democratic society becomes an act of political imprudence. Liberal democracy is a complex regime that can survive only by combining elements of republicanism and traditionalism with rationalist liberalism.

Tocqueville's most notable qualification of a rationalist foundation for society is found in his insistence on the importance of religious beliefs. He is one of the few genuine supporters of traditional religion among the great liberal democratic thinkers. In matters of religious beliefs, as on the question of natural right, he encourages the authority of "general ideas": "General ideas respecting God and human nature are . . . the ideas above all others which ought to be withdrawn from the habitual action of human judgment."[60] If the scope of critical inquiry in these areas is not limited, people will be placed into an intellectual vacuum that leads either to despair and paralysis or to the spread of dangerous pseudo-religions.

Many liberal political thinkers argued that people could live without a religious dimension. According to Tocqueville, however, people possess a "taste for the infinite," which if repressed in its healthy form must eventually surface in an unhealthy one. Although it is possible in a secularized society for most to abandon religion and immerse themselves in the pursuit of material gratification, some individuals will inevitably experience a gnawing sense of emptiness, causing them to turn to fanatical religious sects or mysticism. Alternatively, certain people may displace religious sentiments onto politics and create political religions, as had occurred during the French Revolution, which "though ostensibly political in origin . . . assumed many of the aspects of a religious revolution." Tocqueville here identified the mind-set of the modern intellectual revolutionary, a "hitherto unknown breed," who infused politics with repressed spiritual feelings.[61]

While sharing the traditionalists' view of people's incapacity to support total intellectual doubt, Tocqueville did not extend this principle to a reliance on what Burke called "prejudice" in political affairs. Tocqueville's model for the intellectual foundation for modern society had citizens combining a belief in God with a pragmatic rationalist approach to truth in the political sphere. Religion and rationalism, although resting on different foundations, could be joined together into a workable doctrinal system as long as the tenets of each view were not pushed to their ultimate extreme. Religion could not only coexist with rationalism, but could actually enhance its position in practical affairs. Limiting rationalist inquiry on a few vexing metaphysical questions enabled people to exercise their reason more effectively in the domain of politics: "I am led to think that if [man] has no faith he must obey, and if he is free he must believe."[62]

Tocqueville also saw the need to supplement liberal rationalist theory to promote a sense of community in modern societies. Liberal rationalism threatens to destroy the bonds of community because of its premise that each individual separately judges truth on the basis of his or her own reason and experience: "[E]ach man is narrowly shut up in himself and from this basis makes the pretension to judge the world." This starting point leads to a malady that Tocqueville called "individualism," but which, given the modern connotation of that term, might better be called apathy or privatism. Privatism causes individuals to ignore political and social concerns and withdraw into a life preoccupied with the well-being of self and family.

This tendency can be strong enough to overcome natural inclinations for community and pave the way for despotism, which "sees the isolation of man as the best guarantee of its own permanence."[63]

To integrate the individual into the community in a modern liberal democracy requires adding traditionalist elements to basic rationalist principles. Rationalism can promote obligation to the community up to a certain point by having individuals calculate the obvious benefits they gain from the community. From participating in politics, citizens can also learn to appreciate other, less evident ways in which their private interest is served by furthering the public interest. Finally, from the habits acquired in applying the rational principle of "self-interest rightly understood," some citizens develop a concern for the community as such; where opportunities for participation are extensive, the ambitions of a large number of individuals are attached to the political process and enlisted in behalf of maintaining the regime. In the end, however, the full inclusion of the individual into the community must also rest on building affective ties based on people's sentiments. A political community is an affair of the heart as well as the head: "Every citizen of the United States may be said to transfer the concern inspired in him by his little republic to love of the common motherland."[64] A modern state cannot be viewed as a purely organic unit, but neither can it be regarded entirely as a human convention, artificially created by asocial individuals who join together by contract. Both conceptions are required: a rational view that asks individuals to assess their interest and a traditional view that recognizes and encourages the sentiments of patriotism.

Finally, liberal rationalism is inadequate in accounting for and sustaining the fundamental goal of liberal democracy: liberty. Liberty for Tocqueville is a multi-dimensional concept. It refers first to individual rights—to a sphere of private activity that is protected from governmental interference and shielded, in some measure, from the coercive effects of social opinion. Second, it refers to the right of citizens to govern themselves. Liberty in this sense is formally recognized by the principle of majority rule, but its practical significance grows dimmer as the unit of government grows larger. Hence liberty as self-government in a large modern state acquires much of its real meaning at the local level, where citizens can feel the import of their own actions and satisfy their own pride in governing themselves. Tocqueville was perfectly aware that these two senses of liberty were in some tension. Liberty as self-government can threaten liberty as individual rights, as Tocqueville shows when discussing the "tyrannical" character of many of the laws of the New England Puritan republics.[65] Yet it also serves to protect individual rights by preventing the accumulation of too much power in a central government.

Third, liberty implies the obligation to respect the dictates of law and a duty, sanctioned by religious teaching, to do what is good. Tocqueville cites John Winthrop's "beautiful definition of liberty," which included the injunction to do "without fear that which is just and right." Tocqueville knew this conception was at odds with modern principles, but he also thought it could serve as a valuable restraint against the excesses of modern individualism. It is a measure of his prudence that he would not undermine this older notion of liberty as long as he knew it maintained a certain resonance in society.[66]

These different senses of liberty go well beyond pure rationalist conceptions. Rationalism can help people see their interest in liberty and, through the principle of self-interest rightly understood, lead them to appreciate its utility in promoting wealth and power. Ultimately, however, liberty must be maintained by appealing to each person's will and pride, which is rooted in the traditionalist idea of spiritedness. Tocqueville urges those who direct democratic society to exhort citizens to have a "higher idea of themselves and of humanity":

> What has made so many men, since untold ages, stake their all on liberty is its intrinsic glamour, a fascination it has in itself, apart from all "practical" considerations. . . . The man who asks of freedom anything other than itself is born to be a slave. [The love of liberty] is something one must *feel* and logic has no part in it. It is a privilege of noble minds which God has fitted to receive it, and it inspires them with a generous fervor. But to meaner souls, untouched by the sacred flame, it may well seem incomprehensible.[67]

The Contemporary Challenge

In considering the work of any major political theorist, it is necessary to attempt to understand the world in the same terms as that theorist. To stop at this point in Tocqueville's case, however, does not do justice to his enterprise. His political science points to an ongoing project for reconciling liberty and democracy by engaging in concrete analysis of the specific conditions of each era: "Different times make different demands; the goal alone is fixed . . . the means of getting there ever change."[68] Vast changes have occurred since Tocqueville's time in the factors affecting Americans' mental habits. In this concluding section, we shall look briefly at the specific areas discussed earlier in this chapter.

The most striking change in the factors shaping mental habits lies in the greatly expanded role of intellectual thought in American society. America has emerged as a leading center of intellectual life, with some of the world's most prestigious research institutes and universities. America's intellectual elite, once shut off from the latest ideas and fashions, now often sets the trend for Western intellectual development. America can therefore no longer rely on its insulation to escape the consequences of the propagation of general ideas. Like the European nations Tocqueville addressed in the nineteenth century, contemporary America needs a deliberate strategy to combat the potential dangers of intellectual thought to liberal democracy.

The growing power of the intelligentsia, not only in the United States but also in all developed countries, has been a major theme in the recent analysis of what sociologists call "postindustrial society." This literature depicts the rise of a new service class of educated professionals concentrating in public-service jobs or occupations related to the production of information and culture. Members of this class, who pride themselves on being free of ordinary political self-interest, have become voracious consumers of general ideas and are thus strongly influenced by prevailing intellectual opinion.[69] A measure of the growing weight of the intelligentsia is reflected in the common meaning of the term *establishment,* which once referred to a business or social elite, but which by the 1970s regularly was used to include intellectual elites in major universities and research foundations.

For all the prominence of intellectuals in America today, there is still a great deal in American political culture that continues to resist the immediate influence of deductive intellectual thought. In no Western society does mass culture have more organs for expressing itself, often in opposition to intellectual opinion. Since the 1970s, moreover, a substantial part of the intelligentsia has become conscious of the antitraditional character of prevailing intellectual opinion. This development, in combination with a growing conservative political movement, temporarily mobilized public suspicion against highbrow opinion and bolstered the prejudice that intellectuals do the least damage to society when they remain safely confined to their own journals and their academic settings. Finally, intellectuals in the social sciences were forced to acknowledge the failure of many of their cherished nostrums for solving social problems.[70]

The United States today might therefore be described as the nation in which general ideas often enjoy the most influence but also provoke the greatest resistance. Political science should look for strategies to bolster that resistance in ways that foster liberal democratic mental habits. This task is admittedly complicated by the political scientists' membership in the general intellectual community, which naturally makes them wish to join rank with their colleagues in promoting the authority of intellectual opinion. But political scientists have a unique charge within the intellectual community; they cannot be content with merely considering the content of ideas, but also must assess the consequences for society of relying on the authority of intellectual ideas. If this authority is harmful to liberal democracy, then political scientists must be prepared to break with other intellectuals and look for ways to limit their influence, even if this means countenancing an instinctive popular skepticism to certain academic approaches.

A second notable change since Tocqueville's time has occurred in the institutions of communication. The nineteenth-century press acted as a counterweight to the rapid dissemination of the intellectuals' ideas in society, largely because of the dispersion of media influence among a large number of newspapers. In this century, the influence of local newspapers has diminished in relationship to that of national news agencies, particularly those of the major television networks. The result is a centralization in the sources from which the public receives much of its political information. Moreover, television journalists and writers for major national newspapers now enjoy a very high status in society and are widely considered to be experts. Through academic programs and conferences, the journalistic community has developed close ties to universities and research institutes. Intellectuals and journalists court each other in a kind of easy commerce that was virtually unknown a half-century ago.

The penetration of intellectual ideas into society through the major media should not, however, be exaggerated. Modern journalists view their task as the search for news, not the propagation of general ideas. Their concern for news means that much of their energy is devoted to finding a story, uncovering the new, and emphasizing the deviation of today's occurrence from yesterday's expectation. The preoccupation with this evanescent gloss on reality represents a very different kind of journalism from the broad, interpretive essays of the French press of Tocqueville's time. Even with their high status, American journalists today deal far more with personalities, scandals, and events than with general ideas.

Journalists do rely on intellectual opinion, however, to define the broad context in which they interpret events. And it is therefore true that the modern communications system has indirectly opened the door to greater intellectual authority in society. Strategies for reducing the influence of centralized news agencies on public opinion are thus still important for protecting liberal democratic mental habits, and the objective should remain a system of communication that blocks a top-down formation of opinion directly influenced by intellectuals. In the short term, this objective can be promoted by a strategy that encourages popular suspicion of the major centers of influence in the mass media. For the longer term, an institutional approach is likely to produce better results. This approach would look to foster a greater dispersion of media power by strategies that reduce the audiences of the major networks, increase the number of networks, and vary the geographical bases of centers of media influence. This approach might produce less sophistication in the character of the news, but it would have the compensating advantage of diminishing the prestige of journalists, which in turn would lower their value to intellectuals.

A third important change since Tocqueville's time has occurred in the character of jurisprudential thought. Nineteenth-century jurisprudence was a largely autonomous body of thought with traditionalists roots; it could thus serve to counterbalance philosophe thought. Today, jurisprudence has lost its autonomy and become a battlefield on which various philosophical schools contend, be they modern moral philosophy (deontology), rational choice (law and economics), or critical theory (critical legal studies). Jurisprudence is a carrier for these ideas and is filled with discussions of efficiency, abstract justice, and theories of literary interpretation. The method and structure of contemporary American jurisprudence, accordingly, resembles more the French model of a movement from general ideas to particulars than the old Anglo-Saxon model of building up from particulars to generals.

It is impossible yet to say which school will eventually triumph. At this point, the school of law and economics seems to be gaining the upper hand in the jurisprudence of civil law, while moral philosophy, in the form of a new theory of rights, holds sway in the field of constitutional interpretation. The new conception of rights, understood expansively as a right of each individual to equal concern and respect, has been employed on the one hand to limit the role of government on matters of community values, while on the other hand to justify a greater role for government in economic and welfare matters in order to insure a more equal distribution of material goods. The idea of rights has supported bold claims for the prerogatives of courts, which are asked to enforce these rights if need be by requiring government to undertake active social policies. It is in the name of promoting rights that government today often exercises its most far-reaching authority in society.[71]

The influence of legal thinking today is certainly no less great than it was in the nineteenth century. In addition to the direct authority that courts exercise in policymaking, the nation's major law schools are enormously wealthy and powerful institutions that help shape legal as well as political thinking. The effect of the contemporary legal spirit on the mental habits of society, however, is quite different than in the nineteenth century. Tocqueville had hoped to limit the influence of intellectual opinion by defending substantial prerogatives for lawyers and the courts, whereas today these prerogatives tend to expand the influence of general ideas. Political science accordingly needs to consider a different stance toward the legal spirit in order to promote liberal democratic mental habits. The strategies must, of course, be carefully devised. Because legal forms help foster the rule of law, any new stance must reject populist reactions that attack the legal spirit in its entirety. It is possible, however, to avoid these extreme positions while still working to limit the influence of legal thinking and to deflate presumptuous jurisprudential claims to vast new authority for jurists and courts. If possible, too, political science should explore new jurisprudential approaches that combat general ideas and that reestablish a basis for the jurisprudence that introduces more inductive mental habits in society.

A fourth important change since Tocqueville's time has been the far greater centralization of power in American politics. Many matters that previously were decided at local levels by political means are now decided at higher levels, very often by administrative or judicial bodies. Much of this shift represents an inevitable response to the greater interrelatedness of a modern economy and modern communications. Centralization has also increased, however, because of the collapse of any meaningful constitutional doctrine of federalism. Federalism as a constitutional doctrine became discredited after it was used as the chief instrument in the attempt to block the civil-rights movement in the 1950s and 1960s. But the legal doctrines that have subsequently emerged go beyond the objectives of the civil-rights movement and embrace the agenda of the new rights. Much of the growth of power of centralized decision-making bodies proceeds, as just noted, from courts employing this new interpretation of constitutional rights.

The general movement toward greater centralization has been halted by a countertrend toward decentralization since 1980. The emergence of a conservative public philosophy in national politics led to more state and local control in certain areas of public policy; and severe budgetary constraints during the 1980s at the federal level forced states and localities to assume more responsibility. For the long term, however, reviving local decision-making cannot rest on the accidental effects of budgetary politics but will require a strategy to put in place institutional arrangements that connect people's interests and politicians' ambitions to protecting spheres of local authority. The constitutional doctrine of federalism has an important role to play in this strategy. Given the size of the states today, however, it is evident that federalism is only the first line of support in a genuine conception of local authority. Instruction in the practical art of political reasoning requires empowering people in local decisions, even where this process initially entails sacrifices in administrative efficiency. This movement can only hope to succeed, however, if it eschews a romantic fringe that defines local democracy as a republican movement hostile to general principles of bourgeois liberal democracy.

The final change to note since Tocqueville's time has been in historical and philosophical interpretations of the general prospect for liberal democracy in the world. The clear danger today is that liberal democracy will lose its spirit from within at the very moment it appears to be achieving ascendancy. And it will lose the spirit in part because of general ideas that now attempt to account for its success. From its inception, liberal democracy faced openly avowed enemies on the international scene. In the nineteenth century, the enemy was the "old regime" (under whatever guise), whereas in this century it has been the ideologically based regimes of fascism and communism. The conflict with these last regimes has had one important salutary effect: it has fortified liberal democratic political leaders in their opposition to theories of historical inevitability. Because fascism and communism were based on ideas of historical inevitability, liberal democracy more easily defined itself against historicism and gained in spiritedness as a consequence of that opposition. Liberal democracy had its own sustaining faith in the idea of progress, but this was quite distinct from fatalistic doctrines of inevitability.

The sudden collapse of communism in the 1980s in the East and in the West has discredited historicism in its principal form. How curious, therefore, that this same mode of thought should suddenly reappear in the argument in behalf of liberal democracy. Frank Fukuyama, in the article "The End of History?" is one of the first serious thinkers to attach the idea of historical inevitability to liberal democracy.[72] The great attention his thesis received, both in academia and the popular press, suggests the attraction his new historicism holds for intellectuals in liberal democracies. Modeling his argument on an interpretation of the structure of Hegel's thought, Fukuyama asserts that there is only one idea of political legitimacy that can lay claim to being viable in the contemporary world: "liberalism." Because, per Hegel, ideas are the essential driving force of history, liberalism's victory as a doctrine must means its victory sooner or later on the plane of actual history. Every other principle today, be it communism, fundamentalism, or nationalism, is merely a temporary or backward force fighting a losing battle. The final victory of liberalism means that no basis remains for serious conflict in the world, which is what allows Fukuyama to pronounce history, as we know it, to be at an end. Notwithstanding the fact that Hegel, the greatest German philosopher of the nineteenth century, was mistaken in claiming that history was over with Napoleon's victory at Jena in 1806, Fukuyama is quite confident in affirming that history ended sometime around George Bush's inauguration in 1989.

Although this argument has been called original, its central thesis is not, after all, very different from Tocqueville's claim that equality would be the sole source of legitimacy in the modern world. Yet Tocqueville was more prescient in his analysis. What Fukuyama calls "liberalism" is far from being the perfect unity he imagines; the liberal principle, as he uses this term, is broad enough to embrace regimes that are liberal in a traditional sense of respecting private rights of property and regimes committed to "substantive equality" in which wealth is in principle fully socialized. Fukuyama thus ignores or obscures the fundamental choice for modern times that Tocqueville presented between a regime of political liberty and a new kind of regime (a soft despotism) in which people might believe themselves free, but in which in reality they would have abandoned the conditions in society that could promote significant human action. From the distant heights of the end of history, the struggle of human beings over the kind of society worthy of being called free appears as inconsequential and lacking in meaning or dignity.

Far more serious, however, is the potential effect of the character of Fukuyama's argument on the way of thinking in a liberal democracy. Tocqueville's qualified argument about the path of historical development points to the place of political science as one of the most important intellectual disciplines in modern times. Fukuyama's historicism leaves no room for political science, but replaces it with a world-weary mode of thought he calls philosophy. His argument leads straight to fatalism—a view that things can only be one way, regardless of human effort. Fatalism erodes liberal democracy's foundation in the view that human actions can make a difference.

Fukuyama seems uncomfortable with the moral implications of his own historicism. Noting that life in the posthistorical age lacks any opportunity for heroic action, he slips from fatalism into decadence and looks for some kind of relief from his own existential boredom. Having made the kind of modest claim that history is at an end, Fukuyama concludes with the no less modest proposal to start history up over again, which of course could only come from some sort of attack on liberalism. Tocqueville, of course, had rejected this heady kind of abstract thinking in the name of a constructive public project of political science. He proposed two tests of the worth of any political argument: whether it is true and whether it has a salutary effect and thus serves the cause of truth. Whatever the accuracy of Fukuyama's discussion of the current historical situation, there is nothing in his metaphysical position that even pretends to be helpful. If history is really over, and the *Geist* is with us, no important choices of any kind are required and no sacrifices can be demanded.

Political science as an active enterprise in society is rightfully concerned with strategies that seek to influence the character of intellectual doctrines in society, including those that purport to proceed from the highest reaches of theory. Political science cannot answer all theoretical questions, but it can offer counsel, based on an analysis of the effects of theoretical ideas on the mental habits of the people in society, of the kind of public theorizing that is helpful. Before philosophizing about politics, those who claim to be political theorists should consider what political philosophy can reasonably hope to accomplish, as there may be limits to what speculative thought can explain. It is better to avoid endowing any analysis of existing trends, however prescient it might be, with the dubious status of a metatheory of historical inevitability, especially when the forces that move human history are so elusive and seem as varied as human experience itself. Political theory may prefer to deal constructively with the challenges with which history presents us than to invent theories that imagine that we can foresee the movement of history, let alone its demise.

Tocqueville's analysis of the connection between political thought and political culture—and between changes in the one and transformations in the other—points to the need to transcend the artificial modern division between political theory and practical political science. If one follows Tocqueville's approach, political culture must be understood ultimately by reference to the ideas that govern how people see the world and formulate their opinions. The task of maintaining a political culture of liberty requires the search for a set of philosophic ideas, capable of being embodied in the mental habits of citizens, that can provide people with the means and the will to maintain their freedom.

8

The Constitution and Its Critics

It is with infinite caution that any man ought to venture upon pulling down an edifice which has answered in any tolerable degree for ages the common purposes of society
EDMUND BURKE

A NATION'S POLITICAL REGIME, according to traditional political science, is a product of its physical circumstances, its mores or political culture, and its laws. The laws subdivide into the categories of the civil law (laws relating to such things as contracts, torts, and inheritance) and the all-important political law, meaning the legal rules and practices that determine who rules and that fix the arrangement of the major political offices. The political law in the United States today is made up of the Constitution, of long-accepted statutes and practices that have grown up around it (e.g., the Judiciary Act, political parties, and the practice of judicial review), and of the state constitutions.

For over a century, ever since the young political scientist Woodrow Wilson proclaimed the priority of the "life" or "spirit" of democratic government over its legal forms, the American political science profession has supplied a steady stream of authors who have criticized the fundamental principle that undergirds the Constitution's arrangement of offices. This attack on the doctrine known as the separation of powers has recently gained a renewed momentum, even though today's critics often prefer to hide their outright opposition to the Constitution and speak only of a need for reform. In this chapter I examine the case for a change of the Constitution. The analysis falls into the third and final part of traditional political science, which considers the political regime in a specific nation and asks how its "excellencies may be retained and its imperfections lessened or avoided."[1] The chapter therefore constitutes a fitting conclusion to a study of liberal democracy and political science.

Zero-based Constitutional Thinking

Only once in recent history has a major democratic regime changed its basic institutional structure with the clear aim of remaining a democracy. That change occurred in France in 1958, when Parliament could not form an effective government in the face of the Algerian crisis and the imminent threat of a military coup. While Parliament fiddled, Paris nearly burned. France had lost the *sine qua non* of any functioning government: the power—let us call it, with Locke, the "executive power"—to act with energy and discretion to save the nation from conquest or disintegration. To remedy this fatal flaw, the founders of the Fifth Republic, drawing heavily on the American presidential model of government, instituted a unitary and independent executive elected outside Parliament and endowed by the Constitution with a broad grant of power. The new office was designed to ensure that there would always be a force to act for the state, even in the event of a stalemate among the political parties on the usual policies of governing. The nation's heart would never cease to beat.[2]

Today in America, a group of prominent people, joined together under the name of the Committee on the Constitutional System, is urging the American people to undertake a similar act of constitution-making. Oddly enough, however, while at least some in this group proclaim a desire to strengthen the executive office, they are recommending the opposite course from that taken in France in 1958; they are calling for a change from a presidential (or separation-of-powers) system to something akin to a parliamentary system. They propose this change not because America faces an immediate crisis but because the government does not function as well as it might—because, in Lloyd Cutler's words, we are unable to "'form a Government' [that can] propose, legislate, and administer a balanced program for governing."[3]

Although members of this group acknowledge possible risks in changing basic institutions, they can scarcely be accused of operating with a sense of the fragility of constitutional forms. Self-proclaimed "children of the Enlightenment," they judge political life not from the cautious perspective of what can go wrong but from the sunny perspective of what can be improved.[4] Early leaders urged an "act of constitutional surgery at least as severe as that of 1787."[5] In their plan to wipe the Constitutional slate clean and begin again, the proponents of change seem intent on applying a recent theory of policy science to constitutional forms; they are advocates of zero-based constitution-making.

Zero-based constitution-makers possess certain advantages over defenders of the existing system. The activity of writing about politics entails, even at its best, an abstraction from reality and a simplification of its complexity. Inevitably, therefore, those who build neat, logical systems on paper will appear more persuasive than those who rely heavily on circumstance and prudence. Zero-based constitution-makers are also likely to find a receptive audience for their proposals among commentators and intellectuals, many of whom delight in dismissing tradition and celebrate any new plan that challenges fundamental beliefs. Nor is financial support for such an enterprise likely to be wanting; it is not difficult today to find foundation backing for weighty commissions that promise to resolve pressing problems of the day by bold schemes of institutional change.

Of course, the most renowned of founders have been zero-based. One thinks of Lycurgus, who remodeled the Spartan constitution; of our own founders, who discarded the Articles of Confederation; and even of Plato's Socrates, who built a city ("in speech," as he says in *The Republic*) from the ground up. Yet the situation in these cases was entirely different from that in America today. In Sparta, as Plutarch tells us, "anarchy and confusion had long prevailed," justifying a bold new departure.[6] And even then, as Publius observes in *Federalist 38*, Lycurgus had to rely on the "expedients . . . of mixing a portion of violence with the authority of superstition." In the United States in 1787, Madison compared the nation to a patient whose "disorder daily [is] growing worse" and whose "remedy can no longer be delayed without extreme danger."[7] As hard as they try, our modern-day Lycurguses and Publiuses cannot quite conjure up the same kind of full-scale crisis—not even in the large federal budget deficit or in the inconvenience of the presidency being in the hands of a different party than the legislature. Moreover, in contrast to Plato's Socrates, today's reformers offer their proposals not merely "in speech," but as a genuine plan of action. (Their proposals do, nevertheless, admirably serve teaching purposes in introductory American government courses.)

It is true, of course, that in the last few years the more practical-minded in this reform movement have grown more circumspect in their criticism of the Constitution. Just as zero-based budgeting lost much of its luster among policy analysts in the early eighties, so too, it seems, zero-based constitution making has fallen into a certain disfavor among political scientists. Spokesmen for the Committee on the Constitutional System profess to be advancing only a modest agenda. One of its committee's co-chairs allows that there are "many virtues in our 200-year-old Constitutional structure" and that there is "no reason to reverse . . . the basic constitutional framework," adding that "in any event it is not feasible to do so."[8]

According to the committee, the main problem with our political system today is not so much the original plan as the "recent decline in the cohesion of the political parties." To deal with this problem, however, it turns out that we shall need a few, small constitutional amendments, which would provide among other things for four-year House and eight-year Senate terms (arranged to eliminate midterm elections), straight party-ticket voting for the president and members of Congress, and participation of members of Congress in the Cabinet. By the time one tallies up all these little remedies, it becomes clear that the complaint about the "decline in the cohesion of parties" is merely the Trojan Horse for eliminating the separation of powers and for moving the Constitution toward a parliamentary-type system.[9]

What is most extraordinary, however, about these proposals for change is that they rely on a method of study that political scientists have for some time recognized as outmoded. Under this method zero-based constitution-makers take the formal mechanisms of a regime to define its essence and then proceed to compare alternative mechanisms on the assumption that a best form can be discovered and implanted in any system. But if there is one lesson that the study of comparative politics can teach us, it is that the formal mechanisms of government constitute only part of what defines a regime. Modern behavioral political science has joined traditional political science in extending the study of regimes beyond their formal mechanisms to such other factors as informal structures (e.g., parties and interest groups), social structure (e.g., class and ethnic composition), and political culture (e.g., animating beliefs and ways of thinking about the political world). It is to these other factors, no less than to the formal mechanisms, that we must look to understand how any system works. Yet in none of these calls for change do we find even the slightest mention of the influence of the Constitution on America's political culture or the likely impact that a new arrangement might have on it.

Within the industrialized world today are some twenty-three liberal democracies, so classified because they share certain characteristics, such as governments that reflect the preferences of broad segments of the citizenry, the protection of individual rights, and the protection of the right to associate and to compete for political power. Although these regimes also possess certain institutional similarities—all of them, for example, have independent judiciaries and checks of some kind on the remaining political power—there is a great deal of diversity in their institutional forms.[10] This diversity should make it clear that in discussing the differences among the mechanical systems of liberal democracies, we are not dealing with a first-order question. Different kinds of institutional systems work to promote liberal democracy in different regimes. There is, accordingly, no practical necessity for resolving which institutional form of liberal democracy is best but, on the contrary, every reason to make such choices on prudential grounds in light of the circumstances in each case. American statesmen have therefore acted wisely in emphasizing the virtues of the general regime form of liberal democracy while avoiding efforts to proselytize on behalf of Articles I, II, and III of the Constitution.

Of course, no one would deny that if a regime ceased to function or lost its legitimacy, legislators should weigh the respective merits of different constitutional arrangements, as they did in America in 1787 or in France in 1958. No one, moreover, would deny that, within a functioning regime, legislators should consider aspects of other systems to find possible ideas for improving their own. (For example, some in Great Britain, worried that the regime has been sliding gradually into an elective dictatorship, have looked to the committee system of Congress with the aim of adopting certain of its features to strengthen Parliament.)[11] Yet a reliance on the study of comparative institutions in these instances offers no support for its wider applicability. It is used in the first case (where the regime has ceased to function) because of the necessity of relying on theory where practice cannot provide a guide, and in the second case (to improve a functioning system) only to the extent of supplying possible suggestions for change, which must then be fitted to the character of the system in place. No reasonable interpretation of what political science can teach us would suggest that it is prudent to make any broader claims for the use of the study of comparative institutions.

Political regimes as they exist in specific contexts grow and assume their character from a combination of formal mechanism, informal structure, and political culture. The weight of each of these factors in any regime is something that political scientists can only roughly gauge. The notion that one should tear down and rebuild constitutions on the basis of a study of different formal mechanisms is thus not only radical but also lacking in all scientific foundation. The impulse for remodeling is all the more ill-advised when one considers that the bonds that tie a people to a government rest in large part on a belief in the government's legitimacy. Where this belief is strong—as it assuredly is in the United States—its protection may be worth more to the well-being of a regime than any marginal gains that might be realized from a better mechanical system.

The search for a best formal model for liberal democracy is thus an abstract exercise having only limited practical application. If one must engage in such an exercise, however, the theoretical foundation of the American presidential system is arguably the soundest. The presidential system is the only one that, by virtue of its formal mechanism alone, provides a workable solution to the great problem of modern government: ensuring the existence of a unitary force needed to act for the nation in extraordinary circumstances while providing the means for taming and even humbling that force under normal conditions. The American system establishes the executive power in its primary or essential sense while reducing to a minimum the threat of despotism.

In making this claim about the possible superiority of the American system, I am referring for the moment to formal mechanical properties, not to the operation of any actual regime as modified by informal factors. The formal properties of the presidential and parliamentary systems are fairly clear. Under a presidential system, the essential executive force is never extinguished or in doubt; under a parliamentary system, the executive force cannot be guaranteed (and in practice has not been). As one moves from the level of the essential executive power to what is commonly called policymaking or sometimes leadership—that is, the force that proposes, legislates, and administers a general program for governing—the comparison between the two systems yields a different result. Under the American system, a policymaking structure must be created in a context that divides power and thus precludes the establishment of a unitary and extremely energetic force. The parliamentary form admits of more variation: it can allow for stalemate (from which, incidentally, derives the term *immobilisme*, which critics now apply to the American system) or for a formidable concentration of power in an executive (usually collective) that far exceeds anything possible under the American system.

What this analysis suggests is that the parliamentary system leaves much more to chance or circumstance than the American system. Informal properties play a much greater role in a parliamentary system than in the American system in defining the actual character of a regime. Given a certain set of circumstances (notably two large, disciplined parties), a parliamentary system may produce an executive force nearly as strong as that in the American system on the level of the primary executive power and a policymaking force in the executive far more powerful than that in the American presidency. Given a different set of circumstances (such as a large number of small and undisciplined parties), a parliamentary system may produce an executive force that is stalemated on the level of the primary executive power and weaker as a policymaking instrument than the American presidency. The American system purchases the security of the essential executive power at the cost—if it is a cost—of a highly energetic and unitary policymaking system.

Up to this point I have sketched the properties of the American and parliamentary systems chiefly from a mechanical perspective. Suppose, however, one goes beyond mechanical forms to real constitutions as they are molded by their informal as well as their formal properties. This, it seems, is what most of America's zero-based constitution-makers unconsciously have in mind; for when they speak of adopting a parliamentary model, they conceive of how that system operates (or, actually, how they imagine it to operate) in Great Britain but not, let us say, in Italy. But the system that operates in Great Britain functions as it does less because it is parliamentary than because it is British. It relies on the "accident" of a party system in which one of the parties normally wins a majority of seats in the Parliament and does not have to govern in a coalition. This situation is not guaranteed under a parliamentary system. Indeed, the understanding of the fundamental characteristics of a parliamentary system on much of the Continent is the opposite of what American reformers have in mind. Parliamentary government is equated with a weak and unstable government, whereas the presidential system is thought of as being strong and energetic.

Herein lies the point: how can one expect, through a formal mechanical change, to replicate in America the particular, informal properties that make (today) for a strong executive in a country such as Great Britain? For Great Britain, which has had a predominantly two-party system consisting of disciplined parties, a parliamentary system is one thing; for America, which possesses some of the most undisciplined parties in the world, it might be something quite different. It is true that America has a longer history of two-party competition than Great Britain. But this stability may be due to the lack of discipline of American national parties, which, except in their heyday at the turn of the century, have been far less cohesive than most parties in parliamentary systems. Change the system and there is no guarantee that American parties would become disciplined or, if they did, that there would be only two of them.[12]

If one were to suppose, however, that constitutions could be put on and taken off as easily as articles of clothing, would it be wise for America to adopt the British system? The answer to such a question is not easy. The British system, for all its undoubted virtues, has certain defects: it frequently gives almost complete power to a party enjoying the support of well less than a majority; it has an executive force, increasingly embodied in a single individual (the prime minister) that some fear is too powerful; it has a civil service that exerts an extraordinary degree of influence; and it greatly exaggerates the pressure for change, forcing swings from one extreme to another with shifts in government.[13]

The American system also, of course, has important defects, which its critics never tire of pointing out. No doubt in both nations certain defects might be partially remedied by reforms that would not touch the basic character of the system. But some of the defects in each regime, one can be certain, are inseparable from the system itself and thus could not be remedied without also destroying the entire system, its virtues included. No political system is perfect. The question whether the American or the British system is superior is certainly one on which sensible people can disagree but on which no practical person in either nation should probably spend much time. What counts for any system in place that "has answered in any tolerable degree the common purposes of society" is how it can be maintained and improved, not how it can serve as a plaything to satisfy the curiosity of self-styled "children of the Enlightenment."

The American Political System

The contemporary attack on separation of powers is not the first of its kind. Criticism of the basic system enjoys a long tradition. Regrettably, however, this tradition of criticism has served more to obscure than to clarify the fundamental character of our political system. With few exceptions, critics have ignored the problem of the essential executive power and focused on the secondary question of the character of the policymaking function. Their main complaint is that the American system lacks a strong, unitary policymaking system headed by an executive officer. Yet, by attacking our system for having a weak executive (when it was designed to be strong on the essential point), they have skewed the entire debate and have defined their version of the strong executive *against* the theory that underlies the Constitution. By so doing, they have torn the presidency from its constitutional moorings, leaving it vulnerable to attacks that have weakened the office in its essential properties.

Although it is impossible here to present a complete picture of the American system, we need at least a rough sketch of its basic outline. The American system must be viewed as operating on three levels, each successive level being influenced, but not fully determined, by the level(s) that precede it. These three levels are fundamental sovereignty, the exercise of primary powers, and the policymaking process.

LEVEL 1: FUNDAMENTAL SOVEREIGNTY The first level consists of the power to form and modify the basic character of the government, determining its powers and structure. This power lies, in a primitive sense, with the body of the people in the right of revolution, recognized in the Declaration of Independence. In its legalized form, sovereignty lies in the Constitution, and thus with those empowered to ratify and amend it (as spelled out in Articles V and VII). It is this sovereign power, and this power alone, that in theory can alter the basic governmental structure.

At this level there is no sharing of power among the different branches of the government. Neither the president nor the Supreme Court plays any formal role in the amending process. The power to ratify and amend the Constitution, which is the sovereign legislative power, is reserved exclusively to representative assemblies. It lies with legislators (in the state legislatures and in Congress) or specially selected delegates to conventions. (The amending process requires extraordinary majorities and is arranged to give some weight to state concerns.) The close connection between legislatures or conventions and the people justifies Madison's claim that the sovereign authority under the Constitution derives from "the people . . . the only legitimate fountain of power."

LEVEL 2: THE EXERCISE OF PRIMARY POWERS The second level consists of the arrangement of the primary powers of the federal government. The Constitution divides the three primary powers (legislative, executive, and judicial) among three branches (the Congress, the president, and the federal judiciary). Each of these branches is given respectively the major part of each of the three powers. But in certain instances the powers are shared by more than one branch.

This statement of the distribution of power in the Constitution requires one to think of the fundamental powers (legislative, executive, judicial) apart from their embodiment in particular institutions. The major founders shared this way of thinking, even while they sometimes disagreed on the character of these powers. In the most general sense, however, they thought of the legislative power as the power to make laws; the executive, as the power to carry out those laws and attend to matters requiring general discretion; and the judicial, as the power to punish and decide civil penalties and, under a written Constitution, to review the constitutionality of statutes.[14]

One of the most important questions the founders faced was deciding how these three powers should be allocated among the different branches of government. Should each power be vested exclusively in a distinct institution, or could there be some mixing of powers among the institutions? It is difficult for us today to think about this question in these terms. We have grown so used to our system that we tend to reason in reverse and define the doctrine of separation of powers according to the existing allocation of powers—to say that the powers given to Congress constitute the legislative power, the powers given to the president the executive power, and the powers given to the courts the judicial power. But to understand how the Constitution was informed by the doctrine of separation of powers, one must go behind the Constitution to the doctrine itself, which existed well before the Constitution was written.

There was widespread agreement during the Constitutional Convention to at least the following general principles respecting the doctrine of the separation of powers. The structure of the government should be based broadly on a recognition of the distinct powers, so that, at a minimum, the major powers (legislative, executive, and judicial) would be lodged chiefly in three distinct branches or institutions. The reasons for favoring this arrangement (i.e., a separation of powers) were twofold. First, assigning the greater part of each power to a distinct institution was seen as the best structural check against tyranny. The nature of the powers is such that, when each is placed largely in different hands, the resulting division makes despotism highly unlikely. It is not just a question of dispersing the mass of governmental authority among three potent institutions, but of dividing that authority on the basis of the distinct character of the different powers. The systematic dispersal of power provides a special security. When, in particular, the institution that punishes (the judiciary) is in different hands from the institution that makes the law or enforces it, the people feel safer in their liberty. Second, a separation of powers promotes governmental efficacy, at least in one very important respect. Because each power involves a different task, having different institutions makes it possible to design each one to perform its own speciality. Thus the executive function, which often requires speed and secrecy, can be vested in an institution with a single head, whereas the legislative function, which is best promoted by deliberation and the weighing of different interests, can be centered in representative assemblies. The founders understood, however, that on matters requiring constant coordination of two or more functions, this arrangement would suffer from certain difficulties. Greater efficacy in performing particular functions did not always mean greater efficacy in all phases of governing.

If there was agreement among members of the founding generation on these general points, there was disagreement on whether each power should be vested *exclusively* in one and only one institution. Some antifederalists attacked the Constitution on the grounds that the separation was not pure enough, a charge that surfaced particularly where antifederalists considered a mix to be prejudicial to the power of the Congress. (This criticism of the Constitution, it should be observed, is the opposite of the attack made by contemporary reformers, who argue that the Constitution goes *too* far in separating the powers.) The leading authors of the Constitution had clear reasons, however, for not instituting a pure separation. Indeed, they never considered a complete separation to be a requisite of the doctrine of separation of powers. As Madison showed in *The Federalist*, classical spokesmen of the doctrine, such as Montesquieu, had never insisted on such a standard. The basic objectives of constitutional government were to protect liberty and to ensure effective government. Placing distinct powers in different institutions was a means to those ends, not an end in itself.

While separating powers was the starting point and principal criterion for the allocation of powers, the founders never felt beholden to any formalistic dogma. They noted two general reasons to justify a mixing of certain powers. First, it can be helpful for maintaining a basic division of powers over the long run. The practical problem of the separation of powers is not how to separate the powers on paper, but how to keep them separate in fact. This problem translates into how to prevent one institution from overwhelming and controlling the others. Separation of powers on paper can turn out to be ineffective in practice, as many founders learned from observing the legislative despotisms that grew up under certain state constitutions. Second, mixing powers can promote a better performance of particular functions. Thus the founders argued that legislation would be improved if the president possessed a qualified veto; that treaties would receive more scrutiny if the Senate provided its advice and consent; and that the solemn act of declaring war must have the support of the popular branch in a republican regime. In short, where there is a genuine benefit from sharing a power or putting part of it elsewhere than its expected base, a deviation from a strict separation is justifiable.

The founders' readiness to accept less than a pure separation has led some contemporary interpreters to deny that the allocation of powers in the Constitution reflects a coherent theory of the nature of different powers. In this view, the Constitution does not rest on a preliminary allocation of the fundamental powers, but instead mixes and blends them at will to achieve some kind of institutional equilibrium. The separation of powers is the same thing as the checks and balances. This understanding of the Constitution is often summed up by citing Richard Neustadt's famous claim that ours is a government of "separated institutions sharing power." This statement, though not false, is misleading if it is taken to represent the deepest truth about the constitutional allocation of powers. It is more correct to say that ours is a government of separate institutions, each vested with a distinct fundamental power, which is then qualified by explicit exceptions that are noted in the Constitution.[15]

The disagreement among the founders over how strict a separation there should be was mixed up with a deeper disagreement about the nature of each of the three powers. Americans of the founding era were divided between two basic interpretations: a Whig, or prolegislative, view and a federalist, or proexecutive, view. Each side to this controversy understood differently the nature of the powers and the correct relationship or hierarchy that should exist among them (and hence among the three institutions). Very often it was this controversy that was at issue, with the purity of separation invoked only for rhetorical reasons. Most advocates of a pure separation during the Ratification debate were Whigs who attempting to limit the scope of the executive power.

To use the term *Whig* rather than *antifederalist* might seem to read into the founding period the controversies of the 1830s. Yet some antifederalists referred to themselves as "old Whigs," and many scholars have noted the great influence of British Whig theory on colonial thought.[16] According to American Whigs, the legislative was the supreme power and should hold most of the discretionary authority of the government. This view reflected not only a deep fear of the executive inherited from opposing the British monarchy but also a conviction that nearly all the important tasks of governing could be dealt with by law. The role of the executive should be limited to the modest task of carrying out the will of the legislative power expressed in laws. In addition, certain Whigs had a populist streak that favored the concentration of power in the most popular of the branches—an elected assembly. Because Whigs regarded the executive power as inherently monarchic—regardless of how the executive might be selected—the question of who should rule was for them intimately bound up with the allocation of powers. Seeking more democracy (or more protection for state powers), they could not countenance a strong executive.

The leading founders differed from the Whigs both about the wisdom of concentrating all the legislative power in the Congress (in particular, in the popular branch) and about the possibility of conducting all of the affairs of state by law. Commentators on the founders' thought often emphasize the first point, asserting that the allocation of powers was an antidemocratic device designed chiefly to prevent the popular will as expressed in the House from having its way. Yet this check on the House, important as it was, was secondary to protecting the executive power. For many of the founders, the principal concern was to establish the presidency as a distinct and separate institution in order to carve out a place for the effective operation of the *executive* power in its primary sense. It was the need for an office endowed with the capacity to exercise broad discretion, especially (but not only) in the conduct of foreign affairs, that led many founders to the doctrine of the separation of powers.

The doctrine of separation of powers was devised by Locke and Montesquieu to solve a fundamental problem in the thought of Thomas Hobbes. Hobbes, perhaps the first modern thinker to limit the purpose of government to the protection of fundamental rights, argued that to secure those rights required—paradoxically—an immense and unchecked political authority. This authority, called the sovereign, must have unlimited discretion—the sum of the powers we know as law-making, executing, and adjudicating. Hobbes argued that this awesome concentration of power was needed because the possible threats to the community, from both within and without, were such that nothing less than a potentially absolute power—free, if need be, of the constraints of written rules—could meet them. The frightful dilemma created by Hobbes's solution was that the sovereign's power was now so great that it jeopardized the very rights that government was instituted to protect. No wonder many found this to be less a solution than an intensification of the problem.

Locke and Montesquieu, the originators of modern constitutionalism, elaborated certain qualifications or checks on the Hobbesian sovereign. These included a right of revolution, general limitations on governmental authority, and the doctrine of separation of powers. But in regard to providing government with an executive power to act with discretion under threatening circumstances, Locke and Montesquieu were hardly less forthcoming than Hobbes. For Locke no less than for Hobbes, there are challenges to the existence of society that do not admit of resolution by law, in the precise sense of a clear rule that is known in advance. Although the legislative power may pass "laws" that grant broad discretion to the executive, such as general emergency powers, these instances only confirm that law, in its strict sense, is not sufficient to meet all circumstances; moreover, even such unlawlike laws do not solve the entire problem, because the executive may have to act in certain circumstances without a specific grant of discretion or even in contravention of an existing law. This extraordinary power, reminiscent of the power of Hobbes's sovereign, was known by Locke as "prerogative," which he defined as "the power of doing public good without a rule."[17]

The establishment of constitutionalism, however, marked a change from Hobbes's understanding of the executive power in three very important respects. First, Locke and Montesquieu (along with the founders) began with a different presumption about the need for prerogative. If the state has need of such power, it is needed only infrequently; and the exception or extreme case should not define the rule. Most government actions can be defined by law, or at any rate be sanctioned by revocable grants of authority made by the legislative power. Second, the executive power, though it cannot always be subject to precise limitations, can still be watched, checked, and supervised by other institutions possessing an equal or greater regard among the people. The existence of these other institutions, one exercising the greater part of the legislative power and the other the judicial power, stand as a check against prerogative being carried over into normal governance. Third, there is a sense in which the founders made the legislature supreme—not so much by giving it the law-making power as by giving it, when acting and organized in an extraordinary quasi-judicial form, the power to impeach and convict the president. By this means the legislature can dismiss the person exercising the executive power, even though it can never exercise that power itself. Impeachment checks prerogative. This division is the realistic bedrock of the constitutional balance between the Congress and president.[18]

Not all of the founders, of course, analyzed the powers in such theoretical terms; and even among those who did, it was recognized, in Madison's words, that "no skill in the science of government has yet been able to discriminate and define with sufficient certainty" their exact provinces.[19] An acceptance of the doctrine of separation of powers did not always yield the same conclusion about which specific tasks were part of which fundamental power. Yet the impossibility of being precise about boundaries did not mean general theory was unhelpful. In regard to the dangerous but necessary executive power, the leading founders understood it first to include the function of acting with the force of the community during moments of threat or crisis. This power is contained in the Constitution in the grant of the executive power to the president, as well as in such specific grants as the pardoning power, the "take care" clause, and the commander-in-chief role. Presidents have often relied on this reservoir of executive power in an effort to justify actions that have gone beyond the usual scope of presidential authority.

Second, the executive power for many of the founders included a general power to conduct foreign affairs. They took their cue here from the theory of separation of powers as spelled by Locke and Montesquieu. Locke originally identified, in addition to the executive, legislative, and judicial powers, a fourth primary power, which he called the "federative" (i.e., the foreign-policymaking) power. Although Locke considered this power to be analytically distinct from the executive power, he recognized that it was akin in nature to the executive power. Because the conduct of foreign affairs takes place in an arena in which law cannot usually prevail, in which discretion is required, and in which decisive and swift action is often needed, it falls in the province of the executive power. Montesquieu makes this power into the central function of the executive.

It was experience no less than theory, however, that instructed the founders on the need for a vigorous head to conduct foreign policy. America's leading diplomats during the period of the Articles lamented the weakness in foreign policymaking, which flowed not only from an ineffective national government but also from the absence of an institution charged with exercising the executive power. Adams, Morris, Jay, Franklin, and Jefferson welcomed the Constitution for its promise to strengthen the conduct of foreign affairs. It gave the government, in the office of the president, the capacity "to discern and to profit by . . . tides in national affairs . . . [and] occasions when days, nay even when hours, are precious."[20]

Following Locke and Montesquieu, many founders regarded the foreign-policymaking power to be essentially executive in nature. They nevertheless deviated from Locke and Montesquieu in not granting all of this power to the executive officer. Instead, the Constitution divides this power up, giving part to the Congress alone (e.g., declaring war), part to the president and one or both houses of Congress (e.g., the making of treaties), and part explicitly to the president (e.g., receiving ambassadors). This complex apportionment of power was made in the clear recognition that a liberal democratic form of government would not allow vesting all the federative power—especially the act of declaring war—in a single individual, and further that certain aspects of the federative power might benefit from the assistance of the Senate. Even this arrangement, however, left many Whigs to complain of an excessive concentration of foreign-policymaking power in the president.

Even though the founders assigned parts of the foreign-policymaking power to the legislature, the theory of separation of powers still informed the founders's logic and helps us interpret the Constitution. In conjunction with Locke and Montesquieu, the founders assigned the greater part of the conduct of foreign affairs to the president, and presidents have generally asserted—and have been accorded—a wide range of discretion in this area. General aspects of the foreign-policymaking power not explicitly assigned to Congress by the Constitution may be claimed by the president as a natural part of the executive power under Article II. This line of reasoning follows the interpretation that guided President Washington in issuing his proclamation of neutrality in the war between France and England, in one of the first great controversies over the president's role in the conduct of foreign affairs.[21] Of course, in saying that the president may claim a general discretion in this area, it does not follow that Congress must yield all claims to its own authority. A certain degree of conflict between the two institutions is a product of the separation of powers at points where claims of executive discretion and the authority of lawmaking overlap.

LEVEL 3: THE POLICYMAKING PROCESS The third level of our political system refers to the policymaking process. In the fullest sense, policymaking includes not only the tasks of legislating and carrying out (executing) but also planning, initiating, and mobilizing support on all matters other than questions of sovereignty or the exercise of executive power. The problem of establishing an efficient policymaking process—especially in relationship to the management of ongoing issues such as energy, trade, or welfare—has been the main concern of critics of the Constitution, who complain that there is no "government" in America.

It is important, accordingly, to ask about the status of the policymaking process under the Constitution and about its relationship to the doctrine of separation of powers. The Constitution does not itself define governing by reference to policymaking. Of the various tasks that form the stream of the policymaking process—planning, initiating, mobilizing support, legislating, and carrying out—only the last two are fully covered by the doctrine of the separation of powers or fixed in any detail by the Constitution. Some of the other tasks, though implicitly a part of legislating and executing, are either not clearly defined by the Constitution or are not uniquely assigned to one institution.

Who, then, is supposed to perform these unspecified tasks of policymaking? If we look at where they are performed today, a number of institutions are involved. Planning, initiating, and mobilizing for policies are done by the political parties, the bureaucracy, Congress, presidential candidates, and—especially in recent times—by presidents. Of course, describing present-day mechanisms does not necessarily determine what is consistent with the Constitution, for practice in many cases may have evolved in violation of the original doctrine. But in the case of the performance of much of the activity of planning, initiating, and mobilizing, the various mechanisms in existence seem to pose no problems of constitutionality, even though—or rather because—these tasks are not precisely assigned by the Constitution.

The separation of powers, it should now be clear, was designed chiefly to allocate the primary powers of government (executive, legislative, and judicial) on what we have defined above as the second level of governance. It was not meant to apply to the first level (sovereignty), in which power is given to the people, legislatures, and conventions. Nor was it intended to define fully the exact character of the policymaking process or to establish any one particular form for it (the third level). To be sure, separation of powers has implications for the policymaking process because, however it is constructed, it must be consistent with the basic structure imposed by the allocation of the primary powers. The founders welcomed some of these implications, such as slowing down the pace of policymaking; others caused them some concern, such as an absence of full responsibility or accountability.

The Constitution does, of course, go beyond an allocation of the primary powers to assign certain policymaking powers or duties to the president and Congress. The Constitution not only gives the president part of the legislative power in the form of the veto (which can be converted into a positive currency for planning) but also grants him specific powers of initiation. The president is to provide Congress "information of the state of the Union," make recommendations to Congress of "such measures as he shall judge necessary and expedient," and "on extraordinary occasions, convene both Houses, or either of them" (Article II, section III). These powers are suggestive of the founders's objective of encouraging active presidential leadership in policymaking. This kind of leadership was evident from the beginning, during the Washington administration.

Suggestive as these powers may be, they do not establish a specific design for the policymaking process that *requires* the president to be the policy initiator. At the most, they create a presumption for that role.[22] In the final analysis, therefore, there is not one single model for the policymaking function that is outlined in the Constitution, but rather constitutional limits within which policymaking models must be constructed. These limits derive from the allocation of the primary powers of legislating and executing, plus the assignment of a few other functions related more directly to policymaking. The Constitution leaves open the precise character and structure of the policymaking process, allowing it to be determined by subconstitutional arrangements, which might or might not become institutionalized for a time into the unwritten constitution.

One can speculate on why the founders did not prescribe a precise policymaking model in the Constitution. Five possible explanations come to mind: (1) they did not understand the policymaking function; (2) they disagreed on how it should be performed and decided not to decide; (3) they did not regard the policymaking function to be quite as important as we do today, because they envisaged (or perhaps deliberately sought to maintain) a limited role for the federal government; (4) they did not believe that the precise character of the policymaking process could be settled by fundamental law; and (5) they thought it best to allow the precise character of the policymaking process to change with time and circumstances.

Not all these possible explanations are in conflict; indeed, many at some level are compatible. If one looks closely, evidence can be found to support all five possibilities, depending on which founder one looks to and in what context. Yet the most compelling explanations involve the final two, which emphasize that the founders did not think that the Constitution should determine the regime at this level of specificity. It is not the function of a constitution, according to this logic, to define the exact arrangement for the policymaking process. The degree of hierarchy required in the policymaking process may change from one era to another. And within any era, given the variations in the political situation and in the abilities of different officeholders, the arrangement of the policymaking process is better left to the subconstitutional level so that it can be adapted to fit particular circumstances without creating a constitutional crisis.

The view that the Constitution does not specify a particular policymaking model is supported not only by an analysis of the doctrine of separation of powers but also by practice and precedent. For the two hundred years during which the government has operated under the Constitution, there have been a number of policymaking systems, ranging from the dominant congressional model of the nineteenth century to the strong presidential model of most of the postwar period. In addition, the party system was engrafted onto the regime in the 1820s, in part to resolve certain difficulties in the policymaking process. Given the existence of different policymaking models under the same Constitution, only two interpretations are possible: either the Constitution and the doctrine of separation of powers allow for significant variation in the structure of policymaking, or we have abandoned a separation-of-powers system for long periods of our history. Because almost no one has been willing to adopt the second position, it seems more reasonable to assume that the major historical systems for policymaking have been constitutionally permissible. Some systems may have been better conceived than others, or better adapted to the particular needs of their time, but these are not considerations that bear on their constitutionality.

Some Implications of the Theory of Levels

This analysis of the different levels of the American political system helps uncover some of the hidden difficulties in the current institutional debate. First, critics of separation of powers often mistakenly equate governing with policymaking. This error is explained in part by the origins of the modern critique of the separation-of-powers system. It was first articulated by Wilson in the latter part of the nineteenth century, when Congress was the dominant power in the policymaking structure and when the nation lacked a unitary initiating instrument to clarify policy options. In an effort to create such an instrument, Wilson eventually settled on advocating a powerful executive with a formidable rhetorical capacity able to focus the nation's attention on important policy questions. As a consequence, the executive power came to be associated with the policymaking function and with popular persuasion. Forgotten in this analysis was the tougher side of the executive's role—the exercise of the executive power where the president acts within his own realm and where rhetoric may consist more of explaining actions taken rather than mobilizing support for future proposals.

Although policymaking is the most common task of governing, the issues of governance addressed by an analysis of the primary powers, and especially the executive power, are no less important today than in 1787. Today, as in the 1780s and 1790s, international affairs constitute the dominant preoccupation of the executive branch. Commentators may fill all the pages they please about health policy, industrial policy, or urban policy, but these concerns in no way diminish either the need to use political power with energy and discretion at critical moments or the necessity of watching and checking that same power. A preoccupation with policymaking obscures these fundamental questions and falsely equates the task of governing with problem-solving or large-scale management.

Second, critics of separation of powers have engaged in an overinterpretation of the Constitution. Throughout their century-long history of criticism, they have sought to attribute to the founders and the Constitution a specific model of the policymaking process, which has usually been the model in existence at the time. Dissatisfied with the status quo, they have held the founders responsible for it. For all their hostility toward the founders, they demonstrate a curious dependence on them by constantly searching for an original constitutional intention for policymaking. They have been unwilling to assume responsibility for a task that the founders left to subsequent generations: establishing the theories and institutional mechanisms, within the limits of the Constitution's allocation of powers, for constructing a policymaking structure.

Third, critics of separation of powers have made the Constitution an enemy of what many of them want—a strong executive. Although the Constitution does not allow anything like a full concentration of the policymaking power in the executive, nothing in it precludes—and much supports—the notion of the so-called modern presidency, whose task, according to Arthur Maass, is "leadership . . . to initiate and impel."[23] Critics either have not seen the foundation of the modern presidency in the Constitution or else, demanding the whole loaf and being unwilling to settle for one slice less, they have deliberately chosen to make little of it. They can, of course, claim some credit in adding to the president's policymaking power. But they have done so by insisting that this authority rests on an extraconstitutional source. They have therefore severed the connection between the president's power and the Constitution. The paradoxical consequence of this view is that when some critics switched sides and found it expedient to attack presidential power after the Vietnam War and Watergate, they had great success. A generation of the intelligentsia, educated on a nonconstitutional understanding of the foundation of executive power, has helped prepare the way for a return of the Whig view, at least in the conduct of foreign affairs. At the same time, by assigning to the president more policymaking responsibility than our system will allow, critics of separation of powers have saddled the presidency with unnecessary burdens and created expectations for the office that it cannot meet.

Fourth, an understanding of the different levels of our political system enables us to avoid the false dilemma of having either to reject the principle of separation of powers or defend the current policymaking structure. If the current structure has problems—as I believe it does—our constitutional framework leaves a great deal of room for criticism and for modification within the existing framework. Opponents of separation of powers possess no monopoly on the right of criticism. Indeed, their frequent complaints today about the weakness of political parties and excessive fragmentation in the policymaking process only echo warnings of many analysts in the 1970s who cautioned against various schemes of reform enacted in the parties and in the Congress. In a remarkable display, many advocates of reform now indict the political system for its fragmentation and demand a fundamental change in the Constitution. Like river-boat gamblers, they keep doubling their bets to cover their losses. Having helped undermine the party system that supported the constitutional system, they now propose to undermine the constitutional system to help restore the parties.

Finally, much the same line of reasoning applies to the problem of divided government decried today by constitutional reformers. Divided government, meaning a split between the party controlling the presidency and the party controlling one or both houses of the Congress, was once the exception in the American history, but in the past twenty-five years it has become the norm. More specifically, it occurs today whenever a Republican is chosen as president, because, with the ability of incumbents in the House to secure reelection at an extraordinarily high rate, the House seems locked for the moment into a Democratic majority. Divided government, as the period from 1980 to 1982 showed, need not result in deadlock, and the coalitional patterns beneath the surface of party labels allow for far more variation than critics of the Constitution admit. Still, divided government as a norm does present certain difficulties.

There is no reason, however, why defenders of the Constitution must embrace this characteristic of the current policymaking process. To be sure, if the rate of reelection of incumbents is the result of a natural desire of voters, then divided government for the present would be a necessary concomitant of the basic constitutional arrangement. But if it is a product of certain artificial advantages for incumbents, attributable to subconstitutional factors such as the financing system or methods of congressional districting, then the problem could be addressed at a subconstitutional level. Not every problem with the current system reflects on the constitutional arrangement.

Comparison of the Critics' System and the Constitutional System

The level of thought about institutions in much of our public discourse has fallen to a deplorable condition. How often, for example, do we hear a chain of reasoning that argues that because we face serious problems which politicians have been unable to resolve, there must therefore be profound institutional, even constitutional, flaws in the system. The notion that there is an institutional solution for every problem ignores the fact that institutions do not solve problems; they only establish the structures within which fallible human beings attempt to solve them. Institutions in this respect may be considered good to the degree that they lessen the probability that decision-makers commit serious errors and increase the probability they may make good decisions. Yet because many political problems are unsolvable, especially in relation to expectations, and because political leaders are bound to make mistakes, even the best institutions will always leave some feeling dissatisfied.

Another common error in institutional analysis today is the practice of judging institutions not by their general capacities (e.g., energy or deliberation) but by their predicted effect in the short term on specific issues of public policy. Thus, depending on what position they think a president will take, commentators will shift from being supporters to being foes of presidential power, all the while proclaiming that they are offering detached institutional analysis. This kind of instrumental perspective on institutions is seldom admitted to in public, but is privately justified by the higher policy objective it serves. Tinkering with institutions to suit policy aims, however, is often self-defeating and dangerous. Institutional changes usually outlast the period for which they serve a specific policy purpose, after which they may serve other purposes. Instrumentalists are then in the awkward position of scrambling to explain how they can attack what they once defended and defend what they once attacked. Institutional arrangements also embody fundamental capacities and values that almost always outweigh in importance the achievement of any particular policy objectives.

The study of institutional reform requires a method that avoids these defects. A first step is to be clear about the meaning of *institution*, which I define here as a structure designed to endure for a relatively long time that, through grants and limitations of powers and structural incentives and disincentives, provides or denies authority to decision-makers and influences their behavior in patterned ways. The quality of alternative institutional arrangements should be judged by how well they help maintain the regime, which is a function of their efficacy in decision-making and of their effect on sustaining the appropriate political culture. A second step is to assess the performance of an existing institution against the expected performance of the proposed alternatives. The assessment must be made in light of the full range of functions affected by the institution. To isolate one or two items on which an alternative is superior proves nothing, because no institutional arrangement can simultaneously maximize all values. Institutions must also be judged as wholes, meaning that any assessment must take into account the practical things needed to maintain them. The final step is to consider the costs entailed by the process of change itself. Proponents of reform cannot be certain that their plan will function as they expect, for the unanticipated consequences of change often outweigh in number and significance the anticipated consequences. Moreover, the example of change may lead to calls for more changes in the future, which in the case of constitutional arrangements may open the door to constant meddling.

This three-step method cannot be applied in full here, but we can say how the system proposed by critics of the separation of powers compares with the system now in place. Let us begin with the case for constitutional reform. Proponents of constitutional reform seek to concentrate all policymaking authority in a hierarchic arrangement that is democratically selected. To guarantee against the abuse of power, they rely on electoral rather than institutional checks. In the words of James MacGregor Burns, "a popular majority, like democratic politics in general, furnishes its own checks and balances."[24] To avoid rule by a minority, advocates of a parliamentary model hope for two nationally oriented parties, either of which could then claim a national mandate. Because political power in this system is concentrated and democratic, proponents insist that it provides greater accountability than a separation-of-powers system, because the public knows which party is in charge and can hold it responsible.

Advocates of constitutional reform in America have based their case on ideological and institutional arguments. Ideological concerns were prominent before the 1970s, when critics of the separation of powers stressed the importance of extending the scope of activity of the federal government to build a modern welfare state. The multiple checks of the so-called Madisonian system, particularly the behavior of a retrograde Congress, was said to prevent government exercising greater control over society. Active government required the concentration of power at one point. This plan was openly liberal (i.e., pro-welfare state) in its assumptions that liberty in the modern world was threatened more by the forces of society than by government and that a concentrated national policymaking instrument, especially when the Democratic party had the majority, was needed to regulate society. But this justification for constitutional reform lost much of its appeal for liberals by the end of the 1960s, because a welfare state had been enacted *under* a separation-of-powers system and because the Democratic party had lost its national majority. By the 1970s, many liberals made their peace with the separation of powers and have since been happily entrenched in one subcommittee or another of Congress, singing the praises of that retrograde institution.

There still remains an ideological dimension, however, to the argument against the separation of powers. This position has moved further to the Left and dismisses the welfare state as part of the old regime. The new argument calls for a more powerful state to enact comprehensive economic planning and to change the relation of government to society. According to Walter Dean Burnham, "the problems of the Madisonian state are bound to be at the center of any serious effort to reconstruct the well-being of the American capitalist political economy."[25]

For the most part, however, the case against separation of powers today rests more on institutional than on ideological grounds. Advocates of change emphasize the complexity of modern government and argue that this new situation requires greater hierarchy and coordination in formulating and implementing public policy. These critics may be praised for their greater neutrality, which they proudly proclaim by emphasizing that the new governmental system might be used either for liberal or conservative ends. But the creation of a powerful policymaking instrument that can cut neatly into society hardly seems consistent with a conservative objective of promoting a limited government. As a constitutional principle, this system is more favorable not just to a strong state but to a large one.

Characteristics of the Constitutional System

In comparing the parliamentary model with the American system, we should recall that the separation of powers does not specifically determine, but only sets the outer limits for, the policymaking structure. We can only speak, therefore, of its general properties. One characteristic of the American system is the division of policymaking authority among different institutions. Critics claim that this arrangement necessarily leads to stalemate. Yet much policymaking is not a zero-sum game. The existence of policymaking authority in more than one institution allows each to initiate policies that the others may initially have ignored or opposed. Once one institution begins to deal with an issue, the others may be compelled to address it. In the modern policy process, we have not only ambition counteracting and thwarting ambition but also ambition prodding ambition. The vice of the American system's policymaking structure is not always stalemate, but sometimes too much policymaking.

A second characteristic of the separation-of-powers system is its peculiar way of calculating the public interest. Although all the institutions claim legitimacy because they represent the people, presidents promote the idea that they speak for the whole nation, whereas Congress often represents the nation in its various parts and specific interests.[26] It is in the dialogue between these two perspectives—between generalities (which are often too vague) and particulars (which are often too specific)—that the policymaking system attempts to discover the public interest. A third characteristic of the American system is its effect on how citizens think of national priorities. Americans have learned to live comfortably with the idea that at any time there may be no mandate on policy matters. This assumption—so different from how people think in many other liberal democratic regimes—is central to the operation of our scheme of representative government. The American system entails no theory of a "general will" on policy matters above the decisions reached by constituted authorities. Presidents, of course, claim mandates for themselves and their parties, and these mandates receive more or less credence according to such factors as the size of a president's majority and the number of seats gained by his party in Congress. But these claims are known to be assertions only, because congressional elections turn on other considerations besides national political issues.

A fourth characteristic is the effect of the American system on the nation's political culture. Institutional arrangements are important not only for how they affect decision-making but also for how they influence the way people think about the political world. America has been immune to broad programmatic ideologies because the separation-of-powers system contributes to thinking that retards the propagation of general political ideas. Two key elements of the electoral system are the separation of congressional from presidential elections in the presidential election year and the independent congressional elections at the presidential midterm—both features that constitutional reformers wish to modify or eliminate. Congressional elections function as repeated seminars in which the way the candidates mobilize support helps structure how Americans view the political world. Congressional elections work from the bottom up, giving heavy emphasis to concrete interests and emphasizing particulars. These inculcate a way of thinking that favors pragmatic considerations over broader ideological patterns of thinking.[27]

The final characteristic of the American system relates to its practices of administration. The Constitution bans members of the legislature from serving simultaneously as members of the executive branch; moreover, the independence of the executive allows presidents to choose cabinet officers from among those who have not served in Congress. The patterns of recruitment for cabinet officers give the American bureaucracy a distinctive cast of mind when compared with a parliamentary system, where almost all cabinet officials come from Parliament. In addition, in a separation-of-powers system all administrative entities serve two masters. While this gives them some room for maneuvering, it subjects them overall to greater political control. Administrative agencies have incentives (or can be compelled) to divulge a great deal of information, providing political leaders the opportunity to make decisions that in parliamentary systems often come under the de facto control of administrators.

Comparing the Two Systems

Now that we have surveyed the characteristics of these two systems, let us briefly consider their basic attributes in light of some general criteria of judgment that have been raised in the course of the controversy.

SECURITY A separation-of-powers system better meets the objective of assuring security, because it guarantees, no matter what the general political situation, the integrity of the essential executive power. There is always a power to act and act decisively in a critical circumstance, whereas in a parliamentary system this power is potentially in jeopardy whenever a majority is not secure. A reasonably stable parliamentary system, however, is more effective in conducting diplomacy and engaging in strategic and defense planning, because it avoids the constant struggles between the executive and legislative branches, which have become characteristic of American foreign policymaking in recent years.

EFFICIENCY The concept of efficiency as it relates to government decisions has two dimensions: the capacity to act energetically to put a program or idea into effect, and the ability to make decisions that take account of as much of the relevant information at hand as possible. A parliamentary system operating with a majority party or a firm coalition possesses greater efficiency in the first sense than the American system. In the second sense, however, the opposite is true. The growth of complexity in government in recent years, involving more interests and more trade-offs in most decisions, means that important information often escapes someone studying the facts from on high. This information can best be made known under a system of multiple checks and diverse points of entry, where the effects of any proposed policy can be gauged in a political process. The existence of greater complexity in policymaking today thus cuts two ways: it creates a need for both more and for less hierarchy. Given these conflicting tendencies, it is not clear that the separation-of-powers system is on balance less efficient than the parliamentary one.

ACCOUNTABILITY Critics of the American system claim that a parliamentary regime provides greater democratic accountability. Yet this accountability is fictitious when a government is formed by a party that has the support of less than a majority. Furthermore, except in rare cases in which governments in stable parliamentary systems fall, citizens may be compelled to live with mandates for up to five years. In America, a new sounding is taken every two years, and a president can lose influence in policy matters if his party suffers a severe setback in the midterm election. In a sense, then, the American system is more accountable than parliamentary systems, or at least accountable in a different way. A stable parliamentary system is biased to extract a concentration of political power from electoral decisions. The American system, by contrast, allows more of the ambiguities of electoral decisions to reflect themselves in the policymaking process.

SATISFACTION OF AMBITION A political system is more than a mechanism that processes inputs and outputs. It is made up of human beings, some of whom seek the honor and recognition of serving as political figures. Under a parliamentary system power is held by a relatively small number of officials; members of the legislature are virtual unknowns who exercise little power in their own right. In America, by contrast, an independent legislature provides an institution that can satisfy the desire for political honor of a much larger number of persons. Representatives and senators are powerful individuals who can receive national recognition. As the world's second largest democracy, the number of politicians in America yearning for a place in the sun is greater than in Great Britain, France, or Denmark. To limit recognition in America to a handful of individuals might too greatly restrict the opportunities to display political talent.

CAPACITY FOR CHANGE Proponents of a parliamentary model have attacked the American system for its inability to produce effective policy changes. But they have altered the exact grounds of their criticism over the years. Critics argued that the natural condition of American politics was one of deadlock and stalemate. But with the discovery in the 1960s of the historical phenomenon of critical realignments, it became clear that strong presidents, backed by relatively coherent parties and impressive electoral victories, had been able to achieve important transformations in the direction of public policy. Critics than shifted their position, arguing that while basic change can take place in conjunction with realignments, this institutional mechanism is inadequate and dangerous. Pressure builds up during stalemate periods, only to be relieved during realignment periods. American policymaking moves in fits and starts.

Contemporary critics have altered the argument yet again. They concede that the system was able to handle change reasonably well in the past, because most of the time the same party held power in both the White House and Congress. Today, however, we have entered a new era in which divided government is the rule. Under these circumstances, according to James Sundquist, a separation of powers is "characterized by conflict, delay and indecision, and leads frequently to deadlock, inadequate and ineffective policies, or no policies at all."[28] The only way out is through a revision of the constitutional system.

The attack by the critics has shifted positions so often that it makes one wonder whether they are clear about the alleged flaws in the Constitution. Every system would clearly benefit from avoiding deadlock in policy matters, but a system that responds too quickly to proposed changes or initiates unnecessary changes is also defective. Although a separation-of-powers system imposes a higher threshold for instituting comprehensive programmatic changes than a stable parliamentary regime, critics have never established that this bias is undesirable or worse than the bias of parliamentary systems. Parliamentary systems in which a single party controls the government can allow too much policy change. Each party enacts its maximal position, unhindered by institutional constraints. The result can be mutability on fundamental questions, such as the structure of the economy. Avoiding "the mischievous effects of a mutable government" was one of the founders' chief objectives when framing the Constitution and one for which they were willing, if necessary, to sacrifice a degree of responsiveness.[29] It is one thing to say that the American system has defects when measured against the criterion of an ideal capacity for change; it is quite another to show that it suffers from failures that a parliamentary system could correct without introducing more serious problems.

LIBERTY Critics and defenders of the separation-of-powers system have for years raised the question of protecting liberty. Unfortunately, this debate has suffered from major distortions and misunderstandings. To avoid getting lost in these difficulties, let us state the conclusion at the outset: both the separation-of-powers and parliamentary systems have proven capable of providing for nondespotic liberal democracies and of protecting liberty.

What, then, have been the disputes about liberty? One of them, raised by the proponents of parliamentary government, holds that the American system cannot promote liberty because of its bias against positive governmental action. Liberty today, in this view, is threatened less by government than by the free operation of the economic forces of civil society. It is now clear, however, that this line of argument exaggerated the link between political structure and output. The historical record demonstrates that the American system is not bound to a strict laissez-faire understanding of liberty and is compatible with the welfare state. (Indeed, Ronald Reagan came to power in 1980 partly because he ran against the size of the federal government.) Those concerned with protecting liberty may, nevertheless, find some advantage in the arrangements of the American system. Although the choice between the American system and a parliamentary system does not determine the degree of state intervention in society, the American system has clearly worked to retard bold schemes for centralized economic planning.

The second argument, raised again by proponents of a parliamentary system, puts into the mouths of the originators of the theory of a separation of powers a claim they never made and that is unnecessary for their case. The argument was popularized by Robert Dahl in his well-known *A Preface to Democratic Theory*. Dahl contends that the classic spokesmen of the doctrine of separation of powers were obviously mistaken in their central claim. His argument unfolds with what seems to be the inexorable logic of a syllogism: (a) separation-of-powers advocates such as Madison claim that a separation of powers is essential for maintaining liberty; (b) but we find liberty protected not only in America (a separation-of-powers system) but also in parliamentary systems; (c) accordingly, the classic argument of separation of powers as a protector of liberty is exaggerated, not to say absurd. According to Dahl, Madison's statement that the accumulation of all powers in the same hands results in tyranny is "demonstrably false, for it is pretty clearly not necessary to every non-tyrannical republic, as an examination of parliamentary, but certainly non-tyrannical, democratic systems like that of Great Britain readily prove."[30]

The flaw in Dahl's argument is that, after equating the American system with a separation-of-powers system, he concludes that a parliamentary system must be devoid of a separation of powers. This conclusion may be understandable in view of the common practice of labeling America a separation-of-powers system and then contrasting it with a parliamentary regime, which leaves the impression that a parliamentary system must be something entirely different. Yet if we are to be precise—and precision is called for at this point—saying that the American system is a separation-of-powers system does not entail asserting that parliamentary systems are devoid of all features of separation or that they are characterized, in Madison's words, by "the accumulation of all powers, legislative, executive and judicial, in the same hands."[31]

On the contrary, it is obvious that parliamentary systems do incorporate important aspects of a separation of powers. In the first place, all power is not in the same hands. The judicial power is separated from the legislative and executive powers. As Montesquieu argued, and as both Madison and Hamilton repeated in *The Federalist*, the most important element of separation for preventing tyranny is not the separation of the executive from the legislative, but the separation of either or both of these from the judicial power.[32] Second, in parliamentary systems there is a degree of separation of the legislative body from the executive, because the legislature can still separate itself from the executive and force a change in the government. The potential is always present and has a continual influence, even if it is seldom, if ever, employed. A parliamentary system, as William Gwyn has convincingly demonstrated, embodies important elements of the separation of powers: "Both the presidential and the parliamentary forms of government theoretically satisfy the requirements of the doctrine."[33]

The American founders never knew of a modern parliamentary system and, therefore, never asserted that it could not protect liberty. What they did claim, on the basis of their observations of the state governments, was that legislative-dominated regimes devoid of a strong and independent executive had proven incapable of protecting certain liberties. They made use of the doctrine of the separation of powers in structuring the new government, and the system they established clearly provides a fuller and more elaborate form of separation than is found under the parliamentary system. Not only does this system separate the judicial function from the legislative and executive ones, but also, unlike parliamentary systems, it establishes an ongoing, continuous separation between the president and the Congress. If the fuller separation of powers afforded by the American system is not essential for maintaining liberty—as it is not—it may, nevertheless, provide an added guarantee, especially in modern welfare-state systems, where administrative agencies are already so powerful.

The Causes of Contemporary Fragmentation

In the late 1970s a number of observers of American politics began to speak of a "new American political system."[34] By this term they meant to identify a fundamental change in the operation of the government from the norm of previous decades. The new system was characterized by an extreme fragmentation of the policymaking process, beyond the usual degree characteristic of American politics. This fragmentation led either to policy stalemate (the incapacity to implement broad new initiatives) or to policy hypersensitivity and incoherence (the enactment of many new initiatives, but in piecemeal fashion and without adequate attention to the full scope of governmental activity).

The first two years of the Reagan presidency called this assessment into question. The "Reagan revolution" temporarily demonstrated that the system was not so new or different that a strong president leading a unified party could not pursue a relatively coherent program of governance. Still, the structural changes identified by these observers seemed real enough, and after 1982 the tendencies toward fragmentation in the policymaking structure again became manifest. Yet what produced this "new" system, to the extent it exists, was certainly not the separation of powers alone, which, after all, has been in effect since 1789. Rather, it has been produced by four "isms"—reformism, collectivism, Whiggism, and judicial activism—that are in some degree still with us today.

REFORMISM The modern reform movement, launched at the 1968 Democratic National Convention, promoted a populist political philosophy opposed to hierarchic structures of authority. Reformers favored measures to substitute popular decision-making for decision-making by representative assemblies and to open deliberations of representative assemblies to public scrutiny. Major changes were made both in the party system and in Congress. The presidential nominating process was transformed into a plebiscitary contest, eliminating the need for presidential candidates to forge links with other party leaders and encouraging populist strategies of appeal. In Congress, institutional arrangements that had promoted some degree of coherence were either eroded or eliminated, and power was divided into smaller pieces and dispersed more widely to the subcommittees.

Although the full consequences of reformism are still being evaluated, one important change has been a deinstitutionalizing of the policymaking structure. Procedures that produced predictable and patterned behavior were eliminated in favor of procedures that opened the process to short-term and evanescent influences. In the rush to destroy the evils of hierarchy, reformers undermined subtle institutional mechanisms that had channeled the ambition of members of Congress in ways that tended to promote the public interest. In the aftermath of reform, politicians have become increasingly entrapped in the dilemma of being able to help themselves only by compromising the public interest.

COLLECTIVISM Throughout the 1960s and 1970s, even when Republicans controlled the presidency, policymaking took place in a context largely dominated by the public philosophy of modern liberalism. Under this public philosophy, more and more people came to depend on the federal government for their livelihood or well-being. Governing came to be identified with programmatic policymaking, understood as the activity of devising comprehensive plans to deal with major sectors of American society, from housing to families. This new role for the federal government brought it closer than ever before to the responsibilities assumed by certain Western European governments. The result was a series of dysfunctions that Samuel Beer called the "subsidy and benefits scramble" of the collectivist state: "Because so many are making claims, the claim of no single group can make much difference to the level of public expenditure. Self-restraint by a particular group, therefore, would bring no discernible benefit to it or to any other group."[35] The paradoxical result of this scramble, especially in the era of diminished economic growth of the 1970s, was government that did more but was weaker. Government not only yielded to unrealistic demands but also stimulated those demands by bidding up entitlements to win electoral support.

The problems of ungovernability charged against America's political system were not unique to America. Indeed, Beer's description was originally devised for Great Britain during the 1960s and 1970s. It is, accordingly, sheer parochialism to ascribe all the stresses and strains of governing in America to the separation-of-powers system. Whether the problems of managing the conduct of politics under the philosophy of collectivism are magnified by a separation-of-powers system is difficult to say. The corruption of a separation-of-powers system has assumed the form of piecemeal advantages won by interests that the general public may hardly see; the corruption of parliamentary systems has assumed the form of a more blatant bidding for group support by the parties. Between these two alternative paths to degradation, there may be little from which to choose.

A solution to the problems attendant to collectivism may lie less with any institutional changes than with a change in the public philosophy of collectivism. The ungovernability crisis in Great Britain was resolved only by a sustained and painful attack on collectivism by Prime Minister Thatcher, and the same might be said for the effects of President Reagan's halt to the expansion of collectivism in America. In the case of America, moreover, even if a public philosophy of collectivism were somehow defensible on its own terms, it would clearly be difficult to implement under America's form of government. Yet it does not follow that we should then alter our system of government, for this would give priority to a programmatic public philosophy over the values connected to the Constitution. One test of any public philosophy should be not only its desirability in the abstract but also its compatibility with the existing constitutional structure.

WHIGGISM Frustrations with the Vietnam War and Watergate led in the 1970s to a powerful attack on the presidency. This animus was sustained well beyond its original impulse by a new scholarly interpretation of the presidency that rivals the Whigs of the 1780s in its jealousy of executive power. The new Whiggism has made especially great inroads within the academic community, once the champion of presidentialism. Erstwhile supporters of the presidency became born-again proponents of congressional government. For a brief time in 1974, many began to beat the drums for a fundamental shift in the existing policymaking structure under which Congress would replace the president as the usual initiating force in domestic policy and would become an equal partner with the president in making foreign policy.

In the sphere of domestic policymaking, this view posed no serious constitutional problems, as Congress would only have been reasserting a role it had played throughout much of the nineteenth century. The constitutional permissibility of this plan, however, could not obviate its practical implausibility. The complexity of modern policymaking calls for at least some effort to view policy comprehensively so that trade-offs can be identified and priorities assessed. The decentralized power structure within Congress—made more incoherent by the reforms of the 1970s—left Congress even less equipped to assume this role. After 1975, talk of full-fledged congressional government politely began to die out. Congress today is surely as powerful in domestic affairs as it was before the 1970s, but it has become no more capable than before—indeed, probably less so—of taking on primary responsibility for planning and initiating.

In the sphere of foreign affairs, the new assertiveness of Congress has raised serious constitutional questions, not only in regard to the letter of the Constitution but also in regard to its underlying theory. In taking steps to fulfill the objective of becoming an equal partner, Congress has busied itself devising constraints on presidential discretion. In the House no less than in the Senate, foreign policy issues that would formerly have been considered primarily executive in nature have become matters for routine congressional attention and action. This assertiveness includes the use of the spending power to introduce restrictions on the conduct of diplomacy. Encouraged by contemporary Whig scholarship, many in Congress act as if that institution performs its proper duty in a separation-of-powers system when it ties the executive's hands and attempts to guide much of the nation's foreign policy through the instrument of law.

JUDICIAL ACTIVISM Contemporary critics of separation of powers complain that we suffer not only from an absence of centralized leadership but also from a lack of democratic accountability. On the latter point, at least, their contention is unassailable. Yet the source of this problem is not chiefly with the branches these critics identify—the presidency and the Congress—but with the branch they never seem to mention: the judiciary. The judiciary, for better or worse, has become a policymaking institution not only incidentally, in consequence of the performance of judicial duties, but also by deliberate design.

Perhaps because most critics of the separation of powers have favored a growth in federal responsibilities, they have chosen for instrumental reasons to treat the courts' policymaking role with benign neglect. Meanwhile, allies of the positions taken by the courts have adopted theories of constitutional interpretation that extend the judicial power beyond anything contemplated by the founders. These theories, backed by a powerful legal establishment, have served successfully to deter the other branches from summoning the political will to check the judiciary.

The four "isms" discussed here, much more than the doctrine of separation of powers, help explain the problems that seem (to some) to make American government unworkable. If there are changes needed, we ought to begin by realizing that the separation-of-powers doctrine imposes on us the responsibility of constructing, within certain constitutional limits, alternative policymaking structures. Before attacking the constitutional limits, we would do well to accept this responsibility and examine elements of the system that may require modification. Change there must always be, but let us approach it prudently, with a disposition to preserve and a willingness to improve.

Notes

CHAPTER 1. What Is Liberal Democracy?

1. *Federalist 10,* in *The Federalist Papers,* ed. Clinton Rossiter (New York: New American Library, 1961), pp. 81–82. In stating a more elaborate definition of a republic in *Federalist 39,* Madison concedes that his is a new usage: "we may define a republic to be, *or at least bestow that name on*" (emphasis added, p. 241). Madison expanded the word *republic* from its original meaning so as to allow it to include an indirect government, and then he attempted to reserve the word *exclusively* for the latter regime, probably because of the positive connotation *republic* carried at the time. See Gordon Wood, *The Creation of the American Republic, 1776–1787* (Chapel Hill: University of North Carolina Press, 1969), pp. 222–24 and 594–96.

2. See, for example, *Federalist 70,* p. 423. Madison himself falls back to this usage in *Federalist 63,* p. 386.

3. Thomas Jefferson to John Taylor, 28 May 1816, in *The Writings of Thomas Jefferson,* ed. Albert Ellery Bergh, 20 vols. (Washington, D.C.: Thomas Jefferson Memorial Association of the United States, 1907), 15:19.

4. The term *democratic republic* was used as a book title by a leading scholar of the American founding, Martin Diamond. Diamond writes: "We view the American system as seeking to reconcile the advantages of democracy with the sobering qualities of republicanism." Martin Diamond, *The Democratic Republic* (Chicago: Rand McNally, 1970), p. 10. The use of "republican" to suggest restraint is found especially in *Federalist 71,* where Hamilton notes that the "republican principle demands that the deliberate sense of the community should govern the conduct of those to whom they intrust the management of their affairs" (p. 432).

As far as I have been able to tell, the term *democratic republic* was first used in the United States by Nathaniel Chipman, *Sketches of the Principles of Government* (Rutland, Vt., 1793), p. 102 (Wood, *Creation of the American Republic,* p. 596). It was also Tocqueville's preferred term for the government of the United States. See especially his famous chapter, "The Main Causes Tending to Maintain a Democratic Republic in the United States," in *Democracy in America,* trans. George Lawrence (Garden City, N.Y.: Doubleday, 1969).

5. Some of the modern historians associated with this republican argument are Gordon Wood, Joyce Appleby, Lance Banning, and Richard Shalhope. It is interest-

ing to note, however, that these authors discover republican sentiments in different parts of the American tradition. Some identify republicanism with the revolutionaries, others with the antifederalists, and still others with the Jeffersonians. For a critical analysis of much of this literature, see Thomas Pangle's *The Spirit of Modern Republicanism* (Chicago: University of Chicago Press, 1988).

The word *republican* has been partly misappropriated in scholarly usage today to refer exclusively to a popular or democratic form of a government. The "classical republicans," Plato and Aristotle, were proponents of an aristocratic government. The republicanism referred to by contemporary historians is the one that originated in the seventeenth century by British republicans (Harrington, Milton, Sidney) and in the eighteenth century by Whig pamphleteers. These republicans are distinguished from the classical republicans by their acceptance of the doctrine of popular sovereignty. The British republicans were also influenced by the Roman tradition, especially as interpreted by Machiavelli, and by the commercial republics, especially Venice. See Zera Fink, *The Classical Republicans* (Evanston: Northwestern University Press, 1945).

6. *Federalist 10*, p. 81. For a general discussion of this issue, see Joseph Bessette, "Deliberative Democracy: The Majority Principle in Republican Government," in *How Democratic Is the Constitution?* (Washington, D.C.: American Enterprise Institute, 1981).

7. Robert Dahl, *A Preface to Democratic Theory* (Chicago: University of Chicago Press, 1956), pp. 63–89. So far as I know, the only time the term *polyarchy* was used before was by Hegel, and in a way that seems more in keeping with the actual root of the word. Hegel used it to refer to the *divided* power among the lords in a feudal regime: "Feudal sovereignty is a polyarchy." *Philosophy of History* (New York: Dover Books, 1956), p. 399.

8. Charles McIlwain, in his well-known *Constitutionalism: Ancient and Modern*, has identified modern constitutionalism as having "one essential quality: it is a legal limitation on government; it is the antithesis of arbitrary rule; its opposite is despotic government" (Ithaca: Cornell University, 1947), p. 21. See also Robert Kraynak, "Tocqueville's Constitutionalism," *American Political Science Review* 81, no. 4 (December 1987): 1175–95.

9. This idea of the dual parentage of liberal democracy, though itself not a new theme, has been treated in a most insightful way by Philippe Beneton, *Introduction à la Politique Moderne* (Paris: Pluriel, 1987), pp. 1–21, and by Peter Grag Kilemansegg, in his "concluding comments" to a colloquium, "The Constitution of the United States—American and European Perspectives," held in Charlottesville, Va., 18–22 November 1987.

10. For arguments of the association of the estates with constitutionalism, see, for example, John Locke's *The Second Treatise on Government* and Montesquieu's *Spirit of the Laws*. These authors may in some measure have expressed their argument to fit the only plausible form of constitutional government for the historical epoch in which they lived.

Among those in the United States who at one time or another stressed the importance of estates were John Adams and Gouverneur Morris. There were comments to this effect as well at the Convention. See Gordon Wood, *The Creation of the American Republic*, p. 212. Most Americans hoped to be able to obtain some of the qualities of an upper House by institutional rather than sociological means, i.e., by indirect modes of election and longer terms of office, as distinct from creating a class of nobles.

11. *Federalist 39*, p. 241. Ancient republics were restricted to the free population,

which could be a minority of the populace. There was no principle of inclusiveness. This crucial change to equality as a fundamental principle in modern politics is traced by Harry Jaffa in "Equality, Liberty, Wisdom, Morality and Consent in the Idea of Political Freedom," *Interpretation* 15, no. 1 (January 1987): 3–29.

12. Montesquieu, *Spirit of the Laws* 1, bk. 5, chap. 2, p. 40.

13. Montesquieu, *Spirit of the Laws* 1, bk. 7, chap. 2, p. 96.

14. Jean-Jacques Rousseau, *Gouvernement de Pologne*, in *Du Contrat Social* (Paris: Editions Garnier: 1962), p. 347.

15. For one of the earliest statements in favor of liberal democracy in the seventeenth century, see Benedict Spinoza's *Theologico-Political Treatise*. John Locke's thought can also be interpreted in this sense, though he maintains a monarch.

16. Thomas Jefferson to Major John Cartwright, 24 June 1824, in *Writings of Thomas Jefferson*, 16:45.

17. The first claim is the subject of many of the papers, but above all of *Federalist 10*; the second claim is found in *Federalist 1* and *Federalist 14*.

18. See, in particular, *Federalist* 9 and Hamilton's reference to the "means by which the excellencies of republican government may be retained and its imperfections lessened or avoided" (pp. 72–73). Madison wrote in his essay "Majority Governments" (1833) "If the republican form is, as all of us agree, to be preferred, the final question must be, what is the structure of it that will best guard against precipitate counsels and factious combinations for unjust purposes, without a sacrifice of the fundamental principle of Republicanism" (*James Madison: The Mind of the Founder*, ed. Marvin Meyers [Hanover: University Press of New England, 1981], p. 412).

19. The link between a written constitution and constitutionalism is developed in *Federalist 53*. Madison wrote: "Where no Constitution paramount to the government . . . existed . . . no constitutional security, similar to that established in the United States, was to be attempted" (p. 322).

20. This principle was far from being practiced fully at the time, due to slavery and other forms of servitude and to the unequal status of women.

21. So far as I know, the form of constitutionalism that acknowledges this idea of equality of rights has no single accepted name. Liberalism, however, seems to have this connotation, which is why I have used the term *liberal democracy* as the preferred name for the regime in the United States.

22. Alexis de Tocqueville, *The Old Regime and the French Revolution*, trans. Stuart Gilbert (Garden City, N.Y.: Doubleday, 1955), p. 119 (translation adapted).

23. *Federalist 10*, p. 78.

24. See, for example, Richard Hofstadter, "The Founding Fathers: An Age of Realism" in *The Moral Foundations of the American Republic*, ed. Robert Horwitz, 3d ed. (Charlottesville: University Press of Virginia, 1983); George Will, *Statecraft as Soulcraft* (New York: Simon and Schuster, 1983); and Morris Fiorina, *Congress: Keystone of the Washington Establishment*, 2nd ed. (New Haven: Yale University Press, 1989).

25. *Federalist 55*, p. 346 and *Federalist 68*, p. 414. See David Epstein's excellent *The Political Theory of The Federalist* (Chicago: University of Chicago Press, 1984), and Thomas West, "The Rule of Law in *The Federalist*," in *Saving the Revolution*, ed. Charles Kesler (New York: Free Press, 1987), pp.150–67. Given the authoritative character of *The Federalist* in American politics, it is hardly surprising that scholars have poured over the meaning of a relatively few passages and labored greatly in an attempt to spell out its position.

26. See especially *Federalist 45*: "The powers reserved to the several states will

extend to all the objects which, in the ordinary course of affairs, concern the lives, liberties and properties of the people, and the internal order, improvement, and prosperity of the State" (p. 292).

27. On these questions, Madison and Hamilton had quite different views in later years, and these differences may well have existed even when *The Federalist* was written.

28. Thomas Jefferson, Query 19, in *Notes on Virginia* (New York: Harper and Row, 1964), p. 158.

29. Some of these writers were closer to being pure republicans than liberal democrats, while others seemed confused about their position. For treatments of the theme of republican virtue at the time see the works of Mercy Warren and certain of the antifederalist authors (Richard Henry Lee, John Lansing, Robert Yates and George Bryan).

30. This excepts John Stuart Mill, whose writings on liberal democracy derive largely from Tocqueville.

31. Tocqueville admired *The Federalist* ("a fine book, and though it especially concerns America, it should be familiar to statesmen of all countries"). Still, he considered no single American to be a "great writer on politics," and the notes to *Democracy in America* suggest that Jefferson had nearly as much influence on him as the authors of *The Federalist. Democracy in America*, p. 115.

32. *Democracy in America*, pp. 308, 305. See also p. 287.

33. *Democracy in America*, p. 307: "A great part of the success of democratic government must be attributed to these good American laws, but I do not think they are the main cause. . . . I still have reason for thinking that mores are even more important."

34. Hannah Arendt, *On Revolution* (New York: Viking Press, 1962); and Benjamin Barber, *Strong Democracy* (Berkeley and Los Angeles: University of California Press, 1984), pp. 235–36.

35. I develop these themes at length below in Chapter 2 and Chapter 7.

36. *Democracy in America*, p. 12.

37. See Richard Hofstadter, "The Founding Fathers: An Age of Realism," in *Moral Foundations of the American Republic*, ed. Horowitz, p. 66. This general view is often associated with constitutionalists such as David Hume and Immanuel Kant.

38. Jean-Claude Lamberti, "Adams and Madison, Readers of Montesquieu," a paper presented at the colloquium "The Constitution of the United States—American and European Perspectives," p. 14.

39. Martin Diamond, "Ethics and Politics: The American Way," in *Moral Foundations*, ed. Horowitz, p. 107.

40. For a discussion of the "minimal state" and of the dangers of going beyond it, see Robert Nozick, *Anarchy, State, and Utopia* (New York: Basic Books, 1974).

41. *Federalist 10*, p. 81, and *Federalist 51*, p. 322.

42. Cited in Herbert Storing, *What the Anti-Federalists Were For* (Chicago: University of Chicago Press, 1981), p. 54.

43. The idea that building a compound government requires more political science is a fundamental theme of Montesquieu. "To form a moderate government," he writes, "it is necessary to combine the several powers; to regulate, temper, and set them in motion; to give, as it were, ballast to one, in order to enable it to counterpoise the other. This is a masterpiece of legislation, rarely produced by hazard, and seldom attained by prudence" (*Spirit* 1, bk. 5, chap. 14, p. 62). Tocqueville, referring clearly to this same passage, goes on to argue that the maintenance of such

a government, in its liberal democratic form, requires a continuing participation of political science. "Such a government depends on artificially contrived conventions, and is only suited to a people long accustomed to manage its affairs, and one in which political science has reached into all ranks of the society." *Democracy* 1, pp. 164–65.

44. Charles Lindblom, *Politics and Markets* (New York: Basic Books, 1977), pp. 204, 207.

45. Benjamin Barber, "The Compromised Republic," in *Moral Foundations*, ed. Horowitz, p. 60.

46. *Federalist 1*, p. 33; *Federalist 9*, pp. 72–73; and *Democracy in America*, p. 12.

CHAPTER 2. How Liberal Is Liberal Democracy?

1. Alexis de Tocqueville, *Memoirs, Letters, and Remains of Alexis de Tocqueville*, 2 vols. (Boston: Ticknor and Fields, 1862), 2:38.

2. John Stuart Mill, "M. de Tocqueville on *Democracy in America*," in *The Philosophy of John Stuart Mill*, ed. Morris Cohen (New York: Modern Library, 1961), p. 122.

3. *Democracy in America*, p. 504.

4. Tocqueville did not usually associate his hard despotism in *Democracy in America* with a regime based on ideology, but described it as an extreme individual tyranny that systematically sought to weaken and isolate the individual. Later, in his study of the French revolution, he developed the theme of the use of ideology as a motivating force to mobilize despotic power. See a discussion of this point by François Furet, *Penser la Révolution Française*, p. 211, and Philippe Beneton, *Introduction à la Politique Moderne* (Paris: Pluriel, 1987) p. 239.

5. *Democracy in America*, p. 173

6. Ibid., pp. 19, 311, 315.

7. In the last chapter of volume one, which is also the longest chapter in both volumes, Tocqueville focuses on the United States as a particular case and treats its special problems.

8. In this decade, however, something of a renaissance of interest in Tocqueville has begun to take place, both in the United States and in France. Among some of the most important recent books on Tocqueville are Pierre Manent, *Tocqueville et la Nature de la Démocratie* (Paris: Julliard, 1982); Jean-Claude Lamberti, *Tocqueville et les Deux Démocraties* (Paris: Presses Universitaires de France, 1983); and Roger Boesche, *The Strange Liberalism of Alexis de Tocqueville* (Ithaca: Cornell University Press, 1987).

9. *Democracy in America*, p. 270.

10. Ibid., p. 413.

11. Ibid., pp. 174–75.

12. Ibid., p. 489.

13. Ibid., pp. 481–82: "An abstract word is like a box with a false bottom; you may put in what ideas you please and take them out again unobserved."

14. Ibid., p. 601.

15. Ibid., p. 467.

16. Ibid., p. 703.

17. Ibid., p. xiv.

18. Liberal democracy in this respect is not precisely a *constitution* in the sense

in which that term is used by Plato or Aristotle. A *constitution* for the classics is not a mere descriptive term that refers to any kind of political rule; rather it is a qualitative term referring to a subset of political systems in which a community makes a deliberate effort to mold or form a certain kind of human being. (There are many kinds of rule for Aristotle that are not "constitutions," for example huge empires such as Babylon.)

This concept of *constitution* seems to mark a fundamental difference between classical and modern perspectives; yet when considering liberal democracies as wholes, we find that they exert enormous "deliberate" efforts to guide their citizens and are thus far closer to being "constitutions" in the classical sense than a formal analysis might suggest.

19. *Democracy in America*, pp. 504, 690–95.

20. Tocqueville's concern over the power of the central government as one of the great threats to liberal democracy shows once again how necessary it is to keep the analysis of the specific case of the United States distinct from the analysis of the general regime type. The danger in the United States at the time, according to Tocqueville, was the weakness of the central government: "The federal government is tending to get daily weaker; stage by stage it withdraws from public affairs, continually narrowing its sphere of action" (*Democracy*, p. 394). I discuss the way political science deals with these distinct levels of analysis in chapter three.

21. *Democracy in America*, pp. 674, 679.

22. See Pierre Manent, *Tocqueville et la Nature de la Démocratie*, chap. 8.

23. Tocqueville treats the study of the classics in his chapter "Why the Study of Greek and Latin Literature Is Peculiarly Useful in Democratic Societies," in *Democracy*, pp. 475–77. For the difficulties that face the classics in American universities today, see Allan Bloom, *The Closing of the American Mind* (New York: Simon and Schuster, 1987), and Beneton, *Introduction à la Politique Moderne*, chap 7.

24. *Democracy in America*, p. 496. Tocqueville is speaking here of the writing of history in democratic times. Because the historians whom he is discussing seek to offer systematic explanations, I think it is appropriate to speak here of "social scientists."

25. Ibid., p. 12.

26. Ibid., p. 701.

27. This is in a sense the theme of *Democracy in America* as a whole, but it is treated explicitly in the most important part of the work, volume two, part one.

28. Charles Lindblom, *Politics and Markets* (New York: Basic Books, 1977). Following Marx, Lindblom's own version generally emphasizes the interrelationship of the political and the economic and stresses the primacy of issues of economic equality and alienation.

29. The statement of the need for simple, clear principles for the foundation of modern society is found in Tocqueville's discussion of the complicated character of the American federal system. "Generally speaking," he writes, "it is only simple conceptions that take hold of a people's mind" (p. 164). However, Tocqueville distinguishes between the *basis* of the legal order, which should be clear and simple, and the actual legal order itself, which in some cases can be complicated, as in the United States.

30. Milton Friedman, "Letters to the Editor," *Wall Street Journal*, 29 September 1989.

31. *Democracy in America*, p. 678. See also pp. 671–705. Tocqueville summed up his position as follows: "In most modern nations the sovereign, whatever its origin or constitution or name, has become very nearly all-powerful" (p. 701).

32. This argument is developed in Roger Boesche's *The Strange Liberalism of Alexis de Tocqueville* (Ithaca: Cornell University Press, 1987).

33. *Democracy in America*, p. 670.

34. The indirect and long-term effects of certain measures are often the most important ones. Thus the state can in certain ways encourage or discourage the general conditions that support organized religion (e.g., with tax exemptions) without ever touching directly and obviously on the principle of separation of church and state.

35. *Democracy in America*, p. 12.

36. Some of the terminology I have been using to describe liberalism—for example, the "autonomy" or "de-politicization" of different realms—is drawn from Carl Schmitt, *The Concept of the Political* (New Brunswick: Rutgers University Press, 1976).

CHAPTER 3. Traditional Political Science

1. See Robert Dahl, "The Behavioral Approach in Political Science: Epitaph for a Monument to a Successful Protest" *American Political Science Review* 55, no. 4 (December 1961): 763–72, and Robert Dahl, *Modern Political Analysis*, 4th ed. (Englewood Cliffs, N.J.: Prentice-Hall 1984).

2. Aristotle, *Politics*, 6.1. Aristotle sets out his program for political science at the end of the *Ethics*. Its aim is to study "the sorts of influences that preserve and destroy regimes, and the sorts that preserve and destroy each type" (181b 15–20).

3. The term Aristotle uses is *politea*, which is usually translated as "regime" or "constitution" (the British use the latter term). Montesquieu refers to the fundamental political unit as an "espèce de gouvernement," or more simply a "gouvernement," which I translate here as a "form of government" (*The Spirit of the Laws*, vol. 1, bk. 2, chap. 1). Montesquieu's concept refers to more than formal or legal attributes, but it includes consideration of who rules (what Montesquieu calls the "nature" of each type) and its "principle," that is, "the human passions that set it in motion" (see vol. 1, bk. 2, chap. 1; vol. 1, bk. 3, chap. 1).

4. The definition of political acts is taken from Harold Laswell and Abraham Kaplan, *Power and Society* (New Haven: Yale University Press, 1950). It is cited approvingly and slightly modified by Robert Dahl in his influential *Modern Political Analysis*, pp. 9–11. Dahl goes on to discuss the relevance of this conception to the study of the family and private club.

5. A premise of behavioral research, according to David Easton is that "traditionalists have been reifying institutions." David Easton, *The Political System* (New York: Knopf, 1953), pp. 201–5.

6. See especially Philippe Beneton, *Introduction à la Politique Moderne* (Paris: Pluriel, 1987), pp. 1–21.

7. Tocqueville, *Democracy in America*, p. 402.

8. For Aristotle, "ancient times" in Greece were far less developed technologically and lacked the studies of political science and rhetoric (*Politics*, 3.1, 4.13, and 5.5); Montesquieu sees modern enlightenment and commercial civilization as distinctly different from feudal and ancient times (*Spirit of the Laws*, vol. 1, bk. 10, chap. 3; bk. 15, chap. 3; bk. 20). Tocqueville followed Guizot's famous course on European civilization in Paris in 1829 and 1830.

9. Tocqueville, along with Montesquieu, judged Christian-Enlightenment civi-

lization to be the most powerful and innovative civilization in the world and therefore the one that would determine the next phase of world history. This did not mean that they judged Christian civilization superior in all respects, especially moral, to other civilizations, including the civilization of the "barbarians." See *Democracy in America*, pp. 333, 339, and *Spirit of the Laws*, vol. 1, bk. 21, chap. 21.

10. Montesquieu, "Sur les Causes Qui Peuvent Affecter les Esprits et les Caractères," in *Oeuvres Complètes* (Paris: Seuil, 1964), p. 492. See also *Spirit of the Laws*, vol. 1, bk. 19, chap. 4. The general statements of how these various factors interrelate to one another is what Montesquieu means by laws in the broadest sense.

David Hume adopted this same distinction between physical and moral causes in his essay "Of National Characters," which, along with *The Spirit of the Laws*, helped launch the studies into what we today call "political culture."

11. *Spirit of the Laws*, vol. 1, bk. 5, chap. 14; vol. 1, bk. 19, chap. 3. Following Montesquieu, Tocqueville ascribed a greater weight to the moral causes relative to the physical cause for modern European civilization than for the Native Americans, for the Europeans had developed techniques to tame the physical environment which the Native Americans did not possess.

12. *Democracy in America*, p. 415. Certain broad generalizations about the relative weight of the different elements are nonetheless possible. Tocqueville, as noted, insisted on the primacy of mores, but even this generalization held only after a civilization had developed beyond the stage in which the physical cause exercised the dominant influence.

13. A social state is a synthetic or derivative cause. In Tocqueville's words: "The social state is commonly the result of circumstances, sometimes of laws, but most often a combination of the two. But once it has come into being, it may itself be considered as the prime cause of most of the laws, customs, and ideas which control the nation's behavior" (*Democracy in America*, p. 50).

14. This statement is taken from Tocqueville's notes for a second volume to *The Old Regime and the French Revolution*, which was never written. Tocqueville went on to say that democratic government's "sense is intimately bound to the idea of political liberty. To give the democratic epithet to a government where there is no political liberty is a palpable absurdity." Cited in Raymond Aron, *Main Currents in Sociological Thought*, vol. 1 (New York: Anchor Books, 1965), pp. 240–41.

15. *Democracy in America*, pp. 408–10.

16. *Democracy in America*, p. 277.

17. *Democracy in America*, p. 307. *Spirit of the Laws*, vol. 1, bk. 19, chaps. 4, 5, 10; and Aristotle's *Poetics*, 7.7.

18. *Democracy in America*, p. 382, and *Federalist 39*, p. 240.

19. *Spirit of the Laws*, trans. Thomas Nugent (New York: Hafner Publishing, 1949), vol. 1, bk. 10, chap. 4. Montesquieu's view here may be contrasted with Machiavelli's, according to which any real taking of power, even in domestic politics, is a conquest, leaving open the possibility of laying new foundations. Montesquieu's concept of the general spirit of a people, to which he gives a status or reality of its own in political life, is part of an effort to re-create an autonomous (and more moderate) science of politics, which would be independent of a political science modeled on the physical sciences. The latter led to the idea of reconstituting human society, like so much physical matter, to accord with the will of the scientist-legislator.

20. Tocqueville's statement of the distinctive liberal democratic genius of the American people shows at once the importance and the lack of final determinism of the concept: "If republican principles are to perish in the United States, they

will do so only after long social travail, frequently interrupted and as often resumed; they will have many apparent revivals and will vanish beyond recall only when an entirely new people has taken the place of the one there now. There is no reason to foresee such a revolution, and no symptom indicates its approach" (*Democracy in America*, pp. 397–98).

21. *Spirit of the Laws*, vol. 1, bk. 1, chap. 3. (my translation).

22. The ethical claim is close to the prudential consideration. If one of the ends of politics is life or peace, then there is something to be said for the course of action that entails less disruption and violence, especially where either has little chance of producing a better situation.

23. Montesquieu, *Spirit of the Laws*, vol. 1, bk. 1, chap. 1. Actually, Montesquieu does not use the word *free* in this passage, which in French is: "Il est de leur nature qu'ils agissent par eux-mêmes" (It is their nature that they act by themselves). I will therefore refer to this concept as "self-initiating action."

24. Speech before the Academy of Political Science, 3 April 1852. Alexis de Tocqueville, *Études Économiques, Politiques et Littéraire* (New York: Burt Franklin, 1865), p. 123.

25. It must be said, however, that Montesquieu at times comes close to suggesting a total, autonomous science of development. I refer the reader here to his comment in chapter eighteen of *Consideration on the Causes of the Greatness of the Romans*, that "all accidents are under the control of the [general] causes." The strand of Montesquieu's thought that is deterministic is discussed by Aron, *Major Currents in Sociological Thought*, vol. 1.

26. I am referring here not to the original intention of the communist revolution in Cuba, but for the end on which it settled by the 1970s. The original object of the Cuban communist regime, like the communist regimes in the Soviet Union in the early years and in China up through the 1960s, was to transform the political culture in a way that would create the "new socialist man." This political culture would actively *support* the rule of the party or leader. In all three regimes this effort to remake humanity failed, and in each case the communist regime became content with a passive political culture that merely accepted a dictatorship. See Julie Bunck, "Cultural Change in Cuba." Ph.D. diss., University of Virginia, 1988.

27. Montesquieu, *Spirit of the Laws*, vol. 1, bk. 5, chap. 7; and Aristotle, *Politics*, 5.9.

28. The constitutions of the state governments led to the turbulent "legislative despotisms" discussed by Tocqueville and deplored in *The Federalist*. *Democracy in America*, pp. 151–55.

29. *Democracy in America*, p. 437.

30. This raises the question why we create concepts that designate general ideas. The reason is not only for the purpose of locating or describing actual cases but also to aid us in doing and acting.

31. Tocqueville also discusses, without neatly categorizing, other regime types that he did not consider viable choices for the modern nation-state. These included the small democratic republic (found in the Puritan cities of New England in the colonial period and in ancient Greece); a libertarian-aristocratic order (found among some of the Native American tribes); and the two major regimes of the social state of European "aristocracy" (a feudal monarchy and an absolute monarchy). In regard to the small republic, Tocqueville pointed out that Athens and the other Greek democratic republics were not democratic in the modern sense, as they were not based on the idea of the mass of people being entitled to

citizenship; they did not accept the idea of equality of rights, but only equality among citizens. *Democracy in America*, pp. 475–76.

32. Tocqueville writes: "It is not my aim to describe American mores; just now I am only looking for elements in them which help to support political institutions" (*Democracy in America*, p. 287).

33. Montesquieu, *Spirit of the Laws*, vol. 1, bk. 20, chap. 1; and Tocqueville, *Democracy in America*, pp. 668–74.

34. By speaking here of political science, I do not mean to exclude the individual's experience with political affairs, which when reflected on and applied may embody a good deal of political science. The issue here is whether political science as a systematic study can go beyond—or help inform and correct—the prudence and experience of the statesman.

35. *Federalist* 9, p. 72.

36. *Democracy in America*, p. 245. Under modern conditions, an aristocratic regime either is not viable or else could only be maintained in a way that would make it wholly different (and less desirable) than in an earlier age.

37. *Federalist 10*, p. 84.

38. *Federalist* 9, pp. 72–73.

39. *The Federalist* contained some of the first attempts to spell out the general idea of federalism, even though the authors did not yet use the word *federalism* to describe the innovation.

40. As Martin Heidegger has written of the meaning of the polis before the advent of philosophy, "the Polis is the historical place, the there in which, out of which, and for which history happens. To this place and scene of history belong the gods, the temples, the priests, the festivals, the games, the poets, the thinkers, the ruler, the council of elders, the assembly of the people, the army and the fleet." Heidegger, *An Introduction to Metaphysics* (New Haven: Yale University Press, 1959), p. 152.

41. *Democracy in America*, p. 437. See Aristotle, *The Politics*, 2.8; and *Ethics*, 1104a 6–10; 1180b 12–20.

42. For training students at higher levels of education, it is questionable whether much help is to be had from any body of general educational theory.

43. This question is a title of a chapter by Alasdair MacIntyre in *Against the Self-Images of the Age* (New York: Schocken Books, 1971), pp. 260–80. MacIntyre does not quite argue that such a science is impossible, but he indicates why certain of the scientific approaches today are unhelpful because of their failure to take seriously enough the different "spirits" or cultures of different peoples.

44. Speech of 3 April 1852. In *Études Économiques, Politiques et littéraire*, p. 117.

45. I am speaking here of Hegel's formulation prior to the development of his historicist view of reason working ultimately through history. The evolution of Hegel (and Herder's) view of particularism is treated by Jean Hyppolite, who traces Hegel's development of *sittlichkeit* to Montesquieu's idea of the "general spirit" of a people. See *Introduction à la Philosophie de l'Histoire de Hegel* (Paris: Editions Seuil, 1963), pp. 22–30.

46. "Preface," in *Spirit of the Laws*. For Montesquieu's influence on traditionalism, see chapter 7 below.

47. For a treatment of the development of the "historical school" in the nineteenth century, see Leo Strauss, *Natural Right and History*, chapter 1. Examples of the "hermeneutic approach" can be found in the works of Clifford Geertz, Paul Ricoeur, Alasdair MacIntyre, Charles Taylor, and Hans-Georg Gadamer.

48. *Democracy in America*, pp. 310–311.

49. *Democracy in America*, p. 309. Tocqueville writes: "If geography cannot take the place of laws and mores, can laws and mores take the place of geography?"

50. Montesquieu, *Spirit of the Laws*, vol. 1, bk. 1, chap. 3; and *Democracy in America*, p. 165.

51. *Democracy in America*, p. 315.

52. Montesquieu, *Spirit of the Laws*, vol. 1, bk. 1, chap. 3.

53. *Democracy in America*, pp. 494–95. I would add, however, that while the "hermeneutic" concept may be somewhat less true of the factual situation in the world, it may have an especially salutary role in counteracting the homogenizing mode of thoughts implicit in certain contemporary ideas of social science.

54. From Pericles' Funeral Oration in Thucydides' *The Peloponnesian War*. For a discussion of daring as the special characteristic of the Athenians, see Steven Forde, "Thucydides on the Causes of Athenian Imperialism" *American Political Science Review* 80, no. 2 (June 1986): 433–449.

55. Ernst Troeltsch, "The Ideas of Natural Law and Humanity in World Politics," in Otto Gierke, *Natural Law and the Theory of Society* (Boston: Beacon Press, 1957), p. 204.

56. Ibid., pp. 210–211, 204.

57. Hegel credits Montesquieu for the key insight of having founded a system on the "intuition of individuality and on the character of different peoples." The German concept of *Geist*, with all its connotations, was developed from Montesquieu's idea of "l'esprit générale d'une nation" (the general spirit of a nation). For Tocqueville's preference for diversity, see *Democracy in America*, pp. 315 and 704.

58. Montesquieu, *Spirit of the Laws*, vol. 1, bk. 19, chap. 5.

59. *Federalist 14*, p. 104.

60. *The Essential Comte*, ed. Stanislav Andreski (New York: Barnes and Noble, 1974), pp. 49–53. I have taken some liberty in my presentation of Comte's distinction, but I believe I have stated his essential point.

61. Royer-Collard's comment is cited in Jean-Claude Lamberti's *Tocqueville et les Deux Démocraties* (Paris: Presses Universitaires de France, 1983), p. 171. For the distinction between the comparative and deductive approach in this context, see Lamberti, p. 113, and Leo Strauss, *Natural Right and History*, p. 164.

62. See, for example, *Politics*, 4.13 and 5.5.

63. Usually, maintaining a despotism involves doing the very opposite what one would do to maintain a liberal democracy. At times, even Tocqueville cannot resist giving "advice" to despots: "Despotism sees the isolation of men as the best guarantee of its own permanence" (*Democracy in America*, pp. 509 and 679). Tocqueville's advice here and elsewhere prefigures Hannah Arendt's treatment of modern despotism in *The Origins of Totalitarianism.*

64. *Democracy in America*, p. 314.

CHAPTER 4. Modern Political Science

1. Gabriel Almond, "Separate Tables: Schools and Sects in Political Science," *PS: Political Science and Politics* 21, no. 4 (Fall 1988): 828.

2. For a discussion of these two points, see Stephen Salkever, "Aristotle's Social Science," *Political Theory* 9, no. 4 (November 1981): 1036–61, and David Ricci, *The Tragedy of Political Science* (New Haven: Yale University Press, 1984).

3. The quotes are taken from Weber's famous program for social science, "'Ob-

jectivity' in Social Science and Social Policy," which appeared in "Archiv fur Sozialwissenschaft und Sozialpolitik," in Maurice Natanson, *Philosophy of the Social Sciences* (New York: Random House, 1963), pp. 364, 378.

4. Comte outlined his "positive" method in his "Course in Positive Philosophy" of 1830. Comte insists first on the classification of the various positive sciences, of which *social physics* or *sociology* (Comte invented the term) is one; within each science, we then proceed to "regard all phenomena as subject to invariable natural laws, the discovery of which, and their reduction to the least possible number, is the aim and end of all our efforts" (*The Essential Comte*, ed. Stanislav Andreski [London: Croom Helm, 1974], p. 24).

5. These definitions are taken from Harold Laswell and Abraham Kaplan, *Power and Society* (New Haven: Yale University Press, 1947), p. 240; and Robert Dahl, *Modern Political Analysis*, 4th ed. (Englewood Cliffs, N.J.: Prentice-Hall, 1984), p. 10.

6. According to Weber, "the stimulus to the posing of scientific problems is in actuality always given by practical 'questions.' Hence the very recognition of the existence of a scientific problem coincides, personally, with the possession of specifically oriented motives and values." Natanson, *Philosophy of the Social Sciences*, p. 367.

7. For the use of this term as the identifying concept for the movement, see Robert Dahl, "The Behavioral Approach in Political Science: Epitaph for a Monument to a Successful Protest" *American Political Science Review* 55, no. 4 (December 1961): 763–72.

8. Sidney Verba, "On Revisiting the Civic Culture," in *The Civic Culture Revisited*, ed. Gabriel Almond and Sydney Verba (Boston: Little Brown, 1980), p. 407. This question was the central concern of such leading scientific scholars as Gabriel Almond, Seymour Martin Lipset, and Robert Dahl.

9. Ibid., p. 407.

10. From the time of the establishment of "liberal" or "constitutional" government in the eighteenth century, the question of *scope* of state action has been as important for political science as who rules. This point, so frequently advanced by liberal theorists such as John Stuart Mill, was best articulated by Wilhelm von Humboldt in his *The Limits of State Action:* "In every attempt to frame or reorganize a political constitution, there are two main objects, it seems to me, to be kept distinctly in view . . . first, to determine for the nation in question who shall govern, who shall be governed; . . . and secondly to prescribe the exact sphere to which the government, once constructed, should extend or confine its operations. . . . The inquiry into the proper aims and limits of State agency must be of the highest importance—perhaps greater than any other political question" ([London: Cambridge University Press, 1969], pp. 9–10).

11. *The Nichomachean Ethics* 1181b 16–23. See also *The Politics*, 6.5. The first part of this quotation describes exactly the enterprise of Montesquieu's and Tocqueville's political science.

12. Almond and Verba, *Civic Culture Revisited*, p. 17.

13. These characterizations are cited in Robert Dahl, "The Behavioral Approach in Political Science: Epitaph for a Monument to a Successful Protest" *American Political Science Review* 55, no. 4 (December 1961): 766, 768. The second is taken from David Easton's *The Political System* (p. 203) and the third from David Truman's "The Implications of Political Behavior Research," *Items* (Social Science Research Counsel), December 1951, 137.

14. For the best account of the development of these models, see Lawrence

Joseph, "Democratic Revisionism Revisited," *American Journal of Political Science* 25, no. 1 (February 1981): 160–87. Lawrence is sensitive to the differences among these models, and many analysts have gone too far in collapsing all "pluralists" into one mold.

15. Almond and Verba, *Civic Culture* (Boston: Little Brown, 1965), pp. 352–54.

16. See Gabriel Almond and G. Bingham Powell, *Comparative Politics: A Political Developmental Approach* (Boston: Little Brown, 1966).

17. V. O. Key, *The Responsible Electorate* (Cambridge: Belknap Press), 1966, p. 7.

18. Dahl, "The Behavioral Approach," pp. 766–68. The second quotation is Dahl's citation of David Truman, with whom Dahl "wholeheartedly agrees" on this point.

19. See Brian M. Barry, *Sociologists, Economists, and Democracy* (London: Collier MacMillan, 1970), p. 166.

20. Harold Laswell, "Propaganda," in *Encyclopedia of the Social Sciences* 12, p. 526.

21. See Barry, *Sociologists, Economists, and Democracy*; and Russell Hardin, *Collective Action* (Baltimore: Johns Hopkins University Press, 1982).

22. Aaron Wildavsky, "Choosing Preferences by Constructing Institutions," *American Political Science Review* 81, no. 1 (March 1987): 5–6.

23. Aristotle, *The Politics*, 5.2, and Antonio Gramsci, *Selections from the Prison Notebooks* (New York: International Publishers, 1971), p. 140.

24. Cited in Mancur Olson's "Can Jurisprudence, Economics, and the Other Social Sciences Be Integrated?" A paper presented at the University of Maryland, College Park, Md., December 1987. For the same argument, see James Buchanan and Gordon Tullock, *The Calculus of Consent* (Ann Arbor: University of Michigan Press, 1962).

25. Richard Lipsey and Peter Steiner, *Economics*, 5th ed. (New York: Harper and Row, 1978) p. 152.

26. Ronald Inglehart, "The Renaissance of Political Culture," *American Political Science Review* 82, no. 4 (December 1988): 1203.

27. Morris Fiorina, *Congress: Keystone of the Washington Establishment*, 2nd ed. (New Haven: Yale University Press, 1989), p. 105.

28. See Richard Fenno, "Observation, Context, and Sequence in the Study of Politics," *American Political Science Review* 80, no. 1 (March 1986): 14.

29. The question of distribution is often discussed when economists consider not just overall efficiency but Pareto optimality. It is still fair, nevertheless, to say that economic analysis for the most part equates the most efficient outcome with the best outcome.

30. James Buchanan, *The Economics of Politics* (Lancing, West Sussex: Institute of Economic Affairs, 1978).

31. Almond, "Separate Tables: Schools and Sects in Political Science," 832–33.

32. See, for example, Douglas R. Arnold, *Congress and the Bureaucracy* (New Haven: Yale University Press, 1979).

33. Larry Bartels, *Presidential Primaries and the Dynamics of Public Choice* (Princeton: Princeton University Press, 1988), p. 316.

34. Verba, "On Revisiting the Civic Culture," pp. 408–9.

35. Indeed, the once maligned "classical democratic theory" is sometimes cited as the source of these values. See, for example, the central role ascribed to John Stuart Mill in C. B. Macphearson's *The Life and Time of Liberal Democracy* (London: Oxford University Press, 1977). The sources of these values shall be discussed at greater length in chapter 6.

36. The quotations are taken from Charles Lindblom, "Comment on Manley," *American Political Science Review* 77, no. 2 (June 1983): 384. Lindblom here provides a summary of his own intentions in his recent work, including *Politics and Markets*.

37. See Charles Lindblom, *Politics and Markets* (New York: Basic Books, 1977), and Robert Dahl, "On Removing Certain Impediments to Democracy in the United States," in *The Moral Foundations of the American Republic*, ed. Robert Horwitz (Charlottesville: University Press of Virginia, 1986), p. 248.

38. Walter Dean Burnham, "Revitalization and Decay: Looking toward the Third Century of American Electoral Politics," *Journal of Politics* 38, no. 3 (August 1976): 147.

39. John Manley, "Neo-Pluralism: A Class Analysis of Pluralism I and Pluralism II" *American Political Science Review* 77, no. 2 (June 1983): 369.

40. Charles Lindblom, "Communications to the Editor," *American Political Science Review* 77, no. 2 (June 1983): 384–86.

41. Christian Bay, "Politics and Pseudopolitics: A Critical Evaluation of Some Behavioral Literature," *American Political Science Review* 59, no. 1 (March 1965): 42.

42. Ibid.

43. Many expressed a clear commitment to liberal democracy. Seymour Martin Lipset in 1960 was in no way ashamed to describe it as "the good society itself in operation." *Political Man* (Garden City, N.Y.: Doubleday, 1960), p. 403.

44. See Peter Bachrach and Morton Baratz, "Two Faces of Power," *American Political Science Review* 56, no. 4 (December 1962): 947–52, and Peter Bachrach *The Theory of Democratic Elitism* (Boston: Little Brown, 1967). The "second face of power" refers to the dominance of certain interests in a way that prevents potential challenges to their position from even being considered in the political process.

45. Robert Dahl, *Modern Political Analysis*, 4th ed. (Englewood Cliffs: Prentice Hall, 1984), p. 127.

46. This name I derive from the plea made by Christian Bay to have the profession embark on a new phase of "normative research." Largely shunned at the time, Bay's plea—adopted in essence by many of the very people he criticized—has become an accepted element of by a large part of the contemporary political-science establishment.

47. For the new normativists of the Right, consider those who make the standard of politics the analysis, in virtually every case, of what maximizes individual liberty or market efficiency. This libertarian strain is found in Robert Nozick, *Anarchy, State, and Utopia* (New York: Basic Books, 1974), as well as in some of the rational choice and law and economics literature. The major difference between the Right and the Left as these are expressed in political science today is that the Left often rejects liberal democracy as such, whereas the Right calls for reforming liberal democracy and ridding it of its statist impulses. The Right today, unlike the European Right of a half century ago, does not reject liberal democracy in the name of some other political order.

CHAPTER 5. Reconstructing Political Science

1. For a statement of the new institutionalism, see James March and Johan Olsen, "The New Institutionalism: Organizational Factors in Political Life" (*Amer-*

ican Political Science Review 78, no. 3 [September 1984]: 734–39). This article called for a new departure while ignoring most of the solid institutional work that was already being done. For an approach known as "cultural theory," see Aron Wildavsky's illuminating "Choosing Preferences by Constructing Institutions: A Cultural Theory of Preference Formation" (*American Political Science Review* 81, no. 1 [March 1987]: 3–21), discussed in chapter 4 above. For a survey of modern state theory, see Theda Skocpol's "Bringing the State Back In: Strategies of Analysis in Current Research," in *Bringing the State Back In*, ed. Peter Evans, Dietrich Rueschemeyer, and Theda Skocpol (Cambridge: Cambridge University Press, 1985). Skocpol writes (p. 8): "States conceived as organizations claiming control over territories and people may formulate and pursue goals that are not simply reflective of the demands or interests of social groups, classes, or society." This statement, it is fair to say, would only be illuminating to those who had forgotten what was once well known and fallen victim to dubious recent understandings of the nature of political life.

2. Christian Bay, "Politics and Pseudopolitics: A Critical Evaluation of Some Behavioral Literature" *American Political Science Review* 59, no. 1 (March 1965): 49.

3. For a discussion of this point as the central discovery of political science, see Sheldon Wolin, *Politics and Vision* (Boston: Little Brown, 1960), pp. 33–40.

4. Leo Strauss, *Studies in Platonic Philosophy* (Chicago: University of Chicago Press, 1983), chap. 6.

5. See Mary Nichols, "Education and Political Culture in the Political Thought of Aristotle," *American Political Science Review* 77, no. 4 (December 1983): 1116. Nichols points out how general ideas always risk distorting reality and must continually be elaborated and refined in a process of movement between generals and particulars.

6. Harold Laswell, *The Political Writings of Harold D. Laswell* (New York: Free Press, 1961), p. 513. For an excellent critical discussion of Laswell's work, see Robert Horwitz, "The Master Propagandist," in *The Scientific Study of Politics*, ed. Herbert Storing (New York: Holt Rinehart and Winston, 1962), pp. 226–304.

7. Harry Eckstein, *A Theory of Stable Democracy* (Princeton: Center of International Studies, 1961), p. 21.

8. For an in-depth discussion of this question, see Georg Henrik Von Wright, *Explanation and Understanding* (Ithaca: Cornell University Press, 1971).

CHAPTER 6. The New Normativism

1. Robert Dahl, *Modern Political Analysis*, 4th ed. (Englewood Cliffs, N.J.: Prentice Hall, 1984), pp. 126–27.

2. Benjamin Barber, *Strong Democracy* (Berkeley and Los Angeles: University of California Press, 1984), p. xiv, and "The Compromised Republic," in *The Moral Foundations of the American Republic*, ed. Robert Horwitz, 3d ed. (Charlottesville: University Press of Virginia, 1985), p. 61.

3. See Hannah Arendt, *On Revolution* (Harmondsworth, Eng.: Penguin Books, 1965) and J. G. A. Pocock, *The Machiavellian Moment* (Princeton: Princeton University Press, 1975). For an early elaboration of parallel themes in the literature of American history, see Bernard Bailyn, *The Ideological Origins of the American Revolution* (Cambridge: Harvard University Press, 1967).

4. Robert Shalope, "Republicanism and Early American Historiography," *William and Mary Quarterly*, 3d ser., 39: 335–56. The article is a friendly summary of this whole line of historical research. The republican thesis is discussed—critically—by Thomas Pangle, *The Spirit of Modern Republicanism* (Chicago: University of Chicago Press, 1988).

5. See Gordon Wood, *The Creation of the American Republic* (New York: Norton, 1972). Wood's view on the antifederalists seems to have undergone a striking evolution in his essay "Interests and Disinterestedness in the Making of the Constitution," in *Beyond Confederation*, ed. Richard Beeman, Stephen Botein, and Edward Carter (Chapel Hill: University of North Carolina Press, 1987), pp. 69–109.

6. Gordon Wood. "Hellfire Politics," *New York Review of Books*, 28 February 1985, p. 29.

7. Michael Walzer, *Spheres of Justice* (New York: Basic Books, 1983), p. xiv.

8. Ibid., p. 319.

9. See John Rawls, *A Theory of Justice* (Cambridge: Harvard University Press, 1971), Robert Nozick, *Anarchy, State and Utopia* (New York: Basic Books, 1974), and Ronald Dworkin, *Taking Rights Seriously* (Cambridge: Harvard University Press, 1977).

It should be noted that Rawls and Dworkin have both abandoned a "liberal" foundation in favor of a "communitarian" foundation. The values they derive are admitted now to be merely "our" values—the values of the Anglo-Saxon tradition. See John Rawls, "Justice as Fairness: Political not Metaphysical," *Philosophy and Public Affairs* 14 (1985) and Ronald Dworkin *Law's Empire* (Cambridge: Belknap Press, 1986).

10. One of the major debates in modern contemporary political theory is between these so-called liberals and the communitarians. The communitarians fault the liberals for their ahistorical thought and distinguish themselves from Rawls, Ackerman, and the others by their sensitivity to community and historically derived standards. Yet this entire debate often fails to connect at the political level, for on this level it turns out that greater number of liberals are allied with the greater number of communitarians in their hostility to liberal democracy. The debate virtually ignores the concrete question of regimes, spending its time on the supposedly higher plane of values.

11. Arthur Okun, *Equality and Efficiency: The Big Tradeoff* (Washington, D.C.: Brookings Institution, 1975), pp. 92–106.

12. Jurgen Habermas, "A Review of Gadamer's *Truth and Method*," in *Understanding and Social Inquiry*, ed. Fred R. Dallmayr and Thomas A. McCarthy (Notre Dame: University of Notre Dame Press, 1977), pp. 335–63.

13. Russell L. Hanson, *The Democratic Imagination in America* (Princeton: Princeton University Press), p. 413.

14. The literature on this point is voluminous, and not all of it can be counted as pro-state. Yet this is surely the dominant theme of this literature. As an example, see Phillippe Schmitter and Gerhard Lehmbruch, eds., *Trends towards Capitalist Intermediation* (Beverly Hills, Calif.: Sage Publications, 1979).

15. Walter Dean Burnham, "The Constitution, Capitalism, and the Need for Rationalized Regulation," in *How Capitalist Is the Constitution?* ed. Robert Goldwin and William Schambra (Washington, D.C.: American Enterprise Institute, 1982), p. 103.

16. Walter Dean Burnham, "Elections as Democratic Institutions," in *Elections in America*, ed. Kay Schlozman (Boston: Allen and Unwin, 1987), p. 55. Crisis theory, as I pointed out in chapter 1, is by no means exclusively on the developmental

Left. For a survey and critique of crisis theory on the conservative side, see Claus Offe, "Ungovernability: On the Renaissance of Conservative Theories of Crisis," in *Observations on the Spiritual Situation of the Age*, ed. Jurgen Habermas (Cambridge: MIT Press, 1985), pp. 67–88.

17. This essay first appeared in *Political Science Quarterly* 92, no. 2 (Spring 1977): 1–20. It is reprinted in *The Moral Foundations of the American Republic*, ed. Horwitz, pp. 230–53. Because I shall frequently cite this essay, I shall not supply specific page references.

18. James Madison, *Federalist 10*, in Alexander Hamilton, James Madison, and John Jay, *The Federalist Papers*, intro. Clinton Rossiter (New York: Mentor Books, 1961), p. 84.

19. In Dewey's original version, "ailments" stood in place of "evils." See John Dewey, *The Public and Its Problems* (Chicago: Gateway Books, 1946), p. 146.

20. "Bourgeois capitalism" is the usual Marxist epithet used to describe the American regime; Walter Dean Burnham, one of the political science profession's most well-known electoral analysts, uses the term "Lockean Liberalism," first coined by Louis Hartz; and Benjamin Barber uses "purposelessness" and "privatism" in his essay "The Compromised Republic," in *The Moral Foundations of the American Republic*, ed. Horwitz.

21. Alexander Hamilton, from his speech of 26 June 1787 at the Constitutional Convention, in James Madison's *Notes of Debates in the Federal Convention*, ed. Adrienne Koch (New York: Norton, 1966), p. 196. Madison makes the same point in his famous speech earlier the same day.

22. Andrew Jackson, "Veto of the Bank Bill, 10 July 1832," in *Free Government in the Making*, ed. Alpheus Mason, 3d ed. (New York: Oxford University Press, 1965), p. 451.

23. Charles Beard's thesis was developed in his well-known work *An Economic Interpretation of the Constitution of the United States* (1913; New York: Macmillan, 1954).

24. Octavio Paz, *Tiempo Nublado* (Barcelona: Seix Barral, 1983), p. 47.

25. Alexander Hamilton, "Report on Manufactures, 1791," in *The Works of Alexander Hamilton*, ed. Henry Cabot Lodge, 12 vols. (New York: Putnam's 1904), 4:70–198.

26. Ibid.

27. These terms were taken from the early writings of Marx, especially the *Economic and Philosophic Manuscripts of 1844* and the *German Ideology*. The emphasis on overcoming nature is a theme in Marx's later writings, including the *Communist Manifesto* and *Das Kapital*. If the New Left did not exactly discover the early Marx, it nevertheless was the first to make a fetish of his unpublished manuscripts.

28. Benjamin Barber, "The Compromised Republic," in *The Moral Foundations of the American Republic*, ed. Robert Horwitz, p. 60.

29. Jackson, "Veto of the Bank Bill, 10 July 1832." p. 451.

30. Alexander Hamilton, *Federalist 70*, in *The Federalist Papers*, p. 423.

31. In speaking of private property as a possible right in modern society, nothing so simplistic is intended as saying that there is an absolute natural right to whatever people today may conceive to be property. Clearly, with the exception of the possession of simple physical objects, a pure natural right to property is impossible in modern society, for property in any meaningful sense requires positive law to define and create it. For example, the corporation and the limited part-

nership are forms of business organization that do not exist except by legal construction; the property rights related to them are created by positive law. (By contrast, positive law is not needed to create speech or religious beliefs.)

What the principal of private property as a right refers to, then, is not the direct transference of a natural right into society. Rather, it refers to a claim that government recognize and protect, in ways it deems advisable, what Madison calls "the different and unequal faculties of acquiring property" or the ability to produce wealth. The protection of a right to property, embodied inevitably in property law in its diverse forms, is founded on a recognition of and respect for this natural capacity. Theorists of liberalism have also, of course, been mindful of the social utilities that derive from the protection of property rights. These include promoting economic growth and limiting the scope of direct government control of a large area of social activity, thereby helping to maintain the distinction between the state and civil society.

32. James Madison, *Federalist 37*, in *The Federalist Papers*, p. 227.

CHAPTER 7. Political Science and the Political Culture of Liberal Democracy

1. *Democracy in America*, p. 308.
2. Ibid., pp. 17, 19.
3. Ibid., pp. 301, 429.
4. Ibid., pp. 305, 287; 307, 308.
5. As Tocqueville wrote in a letter to Kergorlay in 1836, "there are three men with whom I commune a little every day; they are Pascal, Montesquieu, and Rousseau." Of these, Montesquieu seems to have been the most influential, and fifteen years later Tocqueville wrote the same friend that he was modeling his next work, *The Old Regime*, on Montesquieu's *Considerations on the Causes of the Grandeur and Decadence of the Romans* (Richard Herr, *Tocqueville and the Old Regime* [Princeton: Princeton University Press, 1962], pp. 48–49).
6. *Democracy in America*, pp. 660, 615.
7. Ibid., pp. 429–33; and *The Old Regime*, pp. 13–169.
8. Edmund Burke, *Reflections on the Revolution in France* (1790; Indianapolis: Liberal Arts Press, 1955), p. 87.
9. The idea of studying Tocqueville's thought as a response to these two schools was suggested by J. P. Mayer in *Alexis de Tocqueville* (New York: Harper, 1960), pp. 111–12. Mayer also noted that the influence of Burke on Tocqueville has never been sufficiently explored. For my treatment of rationalism, I rely heavily on the ideas of Peter Augustine Lawler's "Tocqueville on Democracy and Pantheism" (Paper delivered at a conference on *Democracy in America*, Claremont Institute, Claremont, Calif., 23–26 January 1985). See also Edward Gargan, *De Tocqueville* (New York: Hillary House, 1965); and Pierre Manent, *Tocqueville et la Nature de la Democratie* (Paris: Julliard, 1982).
10. *Democracy in America*, pp. 429–31.
11. Ibid., p. 431; *The Old Regime*, 158–69; 131.
12. *Democracy in America*, p. 438; and *Recollections*, trans. George Lawrence (New York: Anchor Books, 1971), p. 84; *The Old Regime*, pp. 148, 146.
13. *Democracy in America*, p. 429.
14. Although Tocqueville was familiar with the precepts of this school from

French writers such as Joseph de Maistre, he apparently did not trace these ideas to their source until making an in-depth study of Burke's thought during his visit to England in 1833.

15. *Democracy in America*, pp. 235, 17.

16. Cited in Philippe Beneton, *Le Conservatisme* (Paris: Presses Universitaire, 1988), p. 34. The quotation is from Maistre's *Considérations*.

17. *The Old Regime*, p. 154.

18. B. Reardon, *Liberalism and Tradition* (Cambridge: Cambridge University Press, 1975), p. 24.

19. In his correspondence with Gobineau, who contended history was the product of racial characteristics, Tocqueville told his friend, "I believe that [your doctrines] are probably quite false; I know that they are certainly very pernicious." Tocqueville judged an idea by the dual criteria of its "philosophic merits" and "its moral and political effects." See *The European Revolution and Correspondence with Gobineau*, ed. John Lukacs (Gloucester, Mass.: Peter Smith, 1968), pp. 227, 232.

20. *Democracy in America*, p. 705.

21. *The Old Regime*, p. 281.

22. *Democracy in America*, p. 451.

23. Ibid., pp. 705, 496.

24. Alexis de Tocqueville, *Journey to England and Ireland*, trans. George Lawrence and J. P. Mayer (New Haven: Yale University Press, 1958), p. 4.

25. The connection between Montesquieu and Burke has long been noted and is the subject of C. P. Coutney's *Montesquieu and Burke* (Oxford: Basil Blackwell, 1963). Burke considered Montesquieu "the greatest genius which has enlightened this age" (p. ix).

26. For historicist accounts that view a movement or plan for the whole world, see Hegel's *Philosophy of History* and Marx and Engels' *Communist Manifesto*. For the origin of historicist thought in Burke, see Leo Strauss, *Natural Right and History* (Chicago: University of Chicago Press, 1953), pp. 294–321; and Thomas Pangle, *Montesquieu's Philosophy of Liberalism* (Chicago: University of Chicago Press, 1973), pp. 192–93.

27. *Democracy in America*, p. 495.

28. Ibid., p. x.

29. "The laws of the French republic can be, and in many cases should be different from those prevailing in the United States. . . . [L]et us adopt the principles rather than the details of her laws" (*Democracy in America*, p. xiv).

30. *The Old Regime*, p. 21.

31. *Democracy in America*, p. 437; and Gargan, *De Tocqueville*, pp. 42–44.

32. *Democracy in America*, p. 440, 268, 20; see also p. 438.

33. *Democracy in America*, pp. 19–20, 704.

34. *The Old Regime*, p. 147; *Democracy in America*, pp. 97, 723–24. *The Old Regime*, p. 162.

35. *Democracy in America*, pp. 734–35.

36. *Old Regime*, p. 147; see also *Recollections*, pp. 84–85.

37. *Democracy in America*, p. 164.

38. In this section, I borrow freely from the excellent discussion of Tocqueville's thought by François Bourricaud, *Le Bricolage Idéologique: Essai sur les Intellectuals et les Passions Démocratiques* (Paris: Presses Universitaires de France, 1980), pp. 37–69.

39. *Democracy in America*, pp. 183–185.

40. Ibid., pp. 184–85.
41. Ibid., pp. 186, 520.
42. Ibid., p. 185.
43. Tocqueville provides a rough definition of spirit *(l'esprit)* as "certain ways to which all must conform . . . the sum of these common ways is called a spirit; there is the spirit of the bar, the spirit of the court" (p. 185). We are obviously also meant to think of Montesquieu's usage of the term.
44. *Democracy in America*, p. 160.
45. Ibid., p. 267.
46. Ibid., p. 268.
47. Ibid., pp. 268–70.
48. Ibid., p. 268.
49. Ibid., pp. 253–54; 511, 694.
50. Ibid., pp. 442, 304.
51. Ibid., pp. 676, 674.
52. Ibid., p. 62.
53. Ibid., pp. 237–39.
54. Ibid., p. 62.
55. Ibid., pp. 113–14, 152, 164.
56. Ibid., p. 301, 61, 287.
57. Ibid., p. 434.
58. Ibid., p. 435.
59. *The Old Regime*, pp. 158–59; *Democracy*, p. 552, 504. *The Old Regime*, p. 142.
60. *Democracy in America*, p. 443.
61. Ibid., p. 295; *The Old Regime*, pp. 148–57; *Democracy*, p. 535; *The Old Regime*, pp. 11, 157.
62. *Democracy in America*, p. 444.
63. Ibid., pp. 430, 509.
64. Ibid., pp. 236, 510–11, 162, 94.
65. Ibid., p. 43.
66. *Democracy in America*, p. 46. Tocqueville does not fail to note that Winthrop's definition of liberty was given in a speech in which he was defending himself against committing arbitrary acts as a magistrate. Later Tocqueville takes this idea case in part on a religious idea and develops it on more rational, republican lines: "When a man submits to the recognized right of a fellow mortal to give him orders, there is a sense in which he rises above the giver of the commands" (p. 238).
67. *Democracy in America*, pp. 705, 632; *The Old Regime*, p. 169.
68. *Democracy in America*, p. 543.
69. See Daniel Bell, *The Coming of Post-Industrial Society* (New York: Basic Books, 1973); and Barry Bruce-Briggs, ed., *The New Class?* (New York: Basic Books, 1979).
70. See Henry Aaron, *Politics and the Professors* (Washington, D.C.: Brookings Institution, 1978).
71. This line of jurisprudence is associated most closely with the influential thought of Ronald Dworkin. For his most important discussion of rights, see *Taking Rights Seriously* (Cambridge: Harvard University Press, 1977).
72. Frank Fukuyama, "The End of History?" *National Interest*, no. 16 (Summer 1989): 3–18.

CHAPTER 8. The Constitution and Its Critics

1. *Federalist* 9, p. 73.

2. The fall of the Fourth Republic in the spring of 1958 followed a thirty-eight-day ministerial crisis in the winter during which no government could be formed. Finally a weak prime minister was appointed who could do nothing to quell the spreading insurgency in the armed forces. For an account of these events and a discussion of the influence of the American Constitution on the founders of the Fifth Republic, see William Safran, *The French Polity* (New York: David McKay, 1977), pp. 50–59.

3. Lloyd N. Cutler, "To Form a Government," *Foreign Affairs* 59, no. 1 (Fall 1980): 127.

4. Ibid., p. 126.

5. Charles M. Hardin, *Presidential Power and Accountability* (Chicago: University of Chicago Press, 1974), p. 2.

6. Plutarch, *The Lives of the Noble Grecians and Romans*, (New York: Modern Library, n.d.), p. 50.

7. *Federalist 38*, p. 234.

8. Lloyd Cutler, "Political Parties and a Workable Government," in *A Workable Government: The Constitution after Two Hundred Years*, ed. Burke Marshall (New York: Norton, 1987), p. 51.

9. The proposals for straight-ticket voting and congressional participation in Congress are recommended by the committee only as "important enough to deserve further discussion." (See the committee's "Report and Recommendations" January 1987, p. 14). These ideas are supported independently by committee members in their own writings.

10. Most of these regimes have parliamentary governments of one sort or another. One (France) combines presidential and parliamentary features, and America possesses a pure presidential or separation-of-powers system. From this formal perspective, the American system might seem to be the most extreme in that it goes further than any of the others in dividing the executive and legislative powers into two distinct institutions—and, partly as a consequence, in giving greater power to the judicial branch.

11. The statement is by Lord Hailsham; it is cited and discussed in Geoffrey Smith and Nelson W. Polsby, *British Government and Its Discontents* (New York: Basic Books, 1981), pp. 137–39.

12. The American policymaking process since the 1820s has rested on a fine balance in which political parties can be neither too strong nor too weak. If parties were too strong, the division of policymaking authority between the president and Congress might be overcome in practice; if parties were to weak or if they should collapse, an important connective web between the executive and the legislature would be lost. In recent years most observers have argued that parties have become too weak.

14. A judicial determination of the constitutionality of laws was not a part of the classic formulations of the judicial power in Locke and Montesquieu. It obviously required as a prerequisite a written constitution, which was an American innovation. The evidence suggests that judicial review was accepted in some sense by most of the delegates at the Constitutional Convention, well before Hamilton's classic elaboration of the concept in *Federalist 78*. The fact that the judges were assumed to have a power of review was one of the reasons delegates rejected the

proposal at the Convention for a Council of Revision, which would have involved the judges in vetoing laws on the grounds of policy as well as constitutionality. See James Madison's *Notes*, pp. 60–61.

15. For an more extended account of the origins of the executive power, see Gary J. Schmitt, "Executive Privilege: Presidential Power to Withhold Information from Congress," and Robert Scigliano, "The War Powers Resolution and the War Powers," in *The Presidency and the Constitutional Order*, ed. Joseph M. Bessette and Jeffrey Tulis (Baton Rouge: Louisiana State University Press, 1981) and Jeffrey Poelvoorde, "Executive Privilege, Executive Power, and the Constitution." Ph.D. diss., University of Virginia, 1985.

16. For a discussion of the Whig tradition in the colonial and revolutionary period, see Bernard Bailyn, *The Ideological Origins of the American Revolution* (Cambridge: Harvard University Press, 1967).

17. John Locke, *Second Treatise*, sec. 160.

18. Impeachment in the hands of the legislature seems to constitutionalize Locke's extralegal "appeal to heaven" as the way of checking prerogative. In giving the power to remove the president to the legislature, rather than leaving it vaguely with the people, there is a sense in which the American Constitution is based on legislative supremacy. Still, the presidential impeachment process is not a legislative function, but a special process governed directly by the Constitution.

19. *Federalist 37*, p. 228.

20. *Federalist 64*, p. 393.

21. Alexander Hamilton defended the president's prerogative in this area in his Pacificus essays.

22. Both the importance and the limits of Article II, section III need to be stressed. The importance can be seen from the fact that Montesquieu, in his discussion of separation of powers, recommends that the executive be excluded from anything in the policymaking process except a power to reject a legislative proposal. The founders, by giving the president an entrée into the initiating function, went beyond certain views held at the time. The limits can be seen from the fact that the powers in question are discretionary and seemingly rather modest. As they evoked little controversy during the ratification debate, Hamilton wisely does not seek to call attention to them, remarking only in *Federalist* 77 that it would require an "insatiable avidity for censure" to object to them.

23. Arthur Maass, *Congress and the Common Good* (New York: Basic Books, 1983), p. 13.

24. James MacGregor Burns, *Congress on Trial* (New York: Harper and Row), pp. 33–44.

25. Walter Dean Burnham, "The Constitution and the Protection of Capitalism," in *How Capitalistic Is the Constitution*? ed. Robert A. Goldwin and William A. Schambra (Washington, D.C.: American Enterprise Institute, 1982), p. 95; from a slightly different perspective, see the critique of separation of powers in Robert Dahl, "Removing Certain Impediments to Democracy in the United States," in *The Moral Foundations of the American Republic*, ed. Robert Horowitz (Charlottesville: University Press of Virginia, 1977).

26. See *Federalist 46*, pp. 296–97.

27. For a concrete illustration of this point, see Richard Fenno, *Homestyle* (Boston: Little Brown, 1978).

28. James Sundquist, "Needed: A New Political Theory for the New Era of Coalition Government in the United States" (Paper delivered at the Annual Ameri-

can Political Science Association Meeting, Washington, D.C., 1–4 September 1988).

29. James Madison, *Federalist 62*, pp. 380–81. Madison went on: "It will be of little avail to the people that the laws are made by men of their own choice if the laws . . . undergo such incessant changes that no man, who knows what the law is today, can guess what it will be tomorrow."

30. Robert Dahl, *A Preface to Democratic Theory*, pp. 12–13.

31. *The Federalist 47*, p. 301.

32. Hamilton cites this key passage in *Federalist 78*, adding his concurrence, as does Madison in *Federalist 47*, p. 302.

33. William B. Gwyn, "The Separation of Powers and Modern Forms of Democratic Government," in *Separation of Powers—Does It Still Work?* ed. Robert Goldwin and Art Kaufman (Washington: American Enterprise Institute, 1986), pp. 83–84.

34. Anthony King, ed., *The New American Political System* (Washington, D.C.: American Enterprise Institute, 1978).

35. Samuel Beer, *Britain against Itself* (New York: Norton, 1982), pp. 24–33.

Index

Agrarianism: Dahl and, 132–33, 137–38; and immigration, 127; Jefferson and, 127
Almond, Gabriel, 70, 86; *The Civic Culture*, 74, 75, 88
American Revolution and liberal democracy, 11
Anarchy, State, and Utopia (Nozick), 96
Antifederalism: as American tradition, 121–23, 164, 205; and the Constitution, 125, 187; Jackson and, 132–33
Arendt, Hannah, as republican theorist, 115
Aristotle, 34, 41, 42, 59, 74, 82, 96; and general political science, 68–69; *Politics, The*, 68; and regime types, 52, 55; view of social history, 43, 74

Bacon, Francis, 147, 148
Barber, Benjamin, 23; on limits of growth, 131–32; *Strong Democracy*, 115
Bay, Christian, 90, 95
Beard, Charles, 123
Beer, Samuel, 208
Behavioralism: Dahl on, 79; Laswell on, 79–80; and liberal democracy, 75; and political psychology, 79–82; and political science, 71–72, 78–80, 90, 103, 180; and rational choice, 80–81; Truman on, 79
Bentley, Arthur, 79
Bradford, M. E., 116
Bureaucracy and welfare-state capitalism, 129–30
Burke, Edmund, 11; Tocqueville on, 153–54; as traditionalist theorist, 146, 148–49, 151
Burnham, Walter Dean, 89; as theorist of the developmental Left, 118, 200
Burns, James MacGregor, 199
Business corporations and private property, 139–40

Christianity and development of the nation, 43–44, 48, 68
Citizenship: and participation in local government, 161–62; in a republic, 14–16, 18; Tocqueville on, 18
Civic Culture, The (Almond), 74, 75, 88
Collectivism: in American political system, 208–9; and policymaking process, 208
Committee on the Constitutional System and constitutional change, 178–80
Communism, opposition of, to liberal democracy, 174–75
Communitarianism as category of normativism, 116
Community. *See* Local government
Comte, Auguste, 28, 67; and scientific approach to political science, 71
Congress: Keystone of the Washington Establishment (Fiorina), 84
Conservativism and dislike of Tocqueville, 35
Constitutional democracy, establishment of, 8–9
Constitutionalism, 119; and democracy, 177, 178; and democratic republicanism, 11–12, 13, 14–16, 17–18; and equality, 13–14; *The Federalist* and, 12–16, 179; in France, 178, 181; Hobbes and, 189–90; and individual rights, 9–10, 13, 14, 134, 172; Jefferson on,

Constitutionalism *(cont'd)*
11–12; Locke and, 189–90; Montesquieu and, 187, 189–90; nature of, 9–10, 11; and representative government, 12–13; Tocqueville on, 13
Critical theory: as category of normativism, 117; Habermas as proponent of, 117
Cutler, Lloyd, on the Constitution, 178

Dahl, Robert, 92; and agrarianism, 132–33, 137–38; on American democratic evolution, 118–42; analysis of the Constitution, 133–35; on behavioralism, 79; criticisms of proposals by, 123–24, 125–26, 127–30, 132–34, 141–42, 205–6; criticisms of welfare-state capitalism, 128–30; and liberalism, 129–30; and limits of growth, 131–32; on "Madisonian system," 205; on normativism, 114; "On Removing Certain Impediments to Democracy in the United States," 88–89, 118–19, 141; *A Preface to Democratic Theory,* 205–6; and private property, 137–40; as proponent of democracy, 119–20; proposed government reforms, 120–21, 133–36, 139–40, 205; proposed parliamentary system of, 120–21, 133–34; on rational choice, 119; and separation of powers, 205–6; as theorist of procedural democracy, 120; view of American history, 119, 121–22
Democracy: American military establishment and promotion of, 126; compared to republic, 6–8; and constitutionalism, 177, 178; contemporary definition of, 7–8; Dahl as proponent of, 119–20; industrialism and promotion of, 127–28; Madison's definition of, 6–7, 9; nature of, 165; and public opinion, 165; Tocqueville's conditions for in the United States, 143–44, 166–70; Tocqueville's definition of, 44. *See also* Republic
Democracy in America (Tocqueville), 16–17, 26–27, 68, 143, 153; purpose of, 17, 26
Democratic republics: constitutionalism and, 11–12, 13, 14–16, 17–18; nature of, 7, 8–10, 11
Descartes, René, 147, 148
Determinism, historical: Fukuyama and, 175–76; and liberal democracy, 174–75; and political science, 110, 111; traditionalism and, 151–52
Developmental Left: Burnham as theorist of, 118, 200; as category of normativism, 118; Lindblom as theorist of, 118
Diamond, Martin, on liberal democracy, 20
Dworkin, Ronald, 116

Economic behavior: nature of, 84–85, 87; rational choice modeled on, 82–87
Economic development: and liberal democracy, 132; Marx and, 130–31
Economic liberty, nature of, 138–39
Education and liberal democracy, 31–32
"End of History?, The" (Fukuyama), 174–75
Equality: and constitutionalism, 13–14; and political culture, 145; Tocqueville and, 26, 31, 137, 175. *See also* Individual rights
Europe: French Revolution's political effect on, 146–47; liberal democracy in, 27; political culture in, 144; rationalism and traditionalism as philosophical powers in, 144–45, 148

Federalism: as American tradition, 58; contemporary reaction to, 173; modern increase in, 173–74
Federalist, The (Madison and Hamilton), 6, 22, 24, 46, 56, 67, 84, 164, 187; and constitutionalism, 12–16, 179; criticism of, 15; purpose of, 15–16, 17, 164; and separation of powers, 206
Fenno, Richard, 84
Fiorina, Morris: *Congress: Keystone of the Washington Establishment,* 84
Foreign affairs: Congress and, 209–10; and the Constitution, 192; and separation of powers, 191–92, 202
France: abstract nature of the law in, 160, 172; constitutional change in, 178, 181; the press in, 158–59
Free will: rationalism and, 150, 152; Tocqueville and, 152–53; traditionalism and, 151–52
French political philosophy: influence of, on development of rationalism, 144, 146–48; literary character of, 147–48, 155
French Revolution, 61, 113, 167; political effect on Europe, 146–47; Tocqueville and, 146
Fukuyama, Frank: and historical determinism, 175–76; and liberal democ-

racy, 175; "The End of History?" 174–75
Fundamental sovereignty: in American political system, 185, 193; Madison on, 185

Government: belief in legitimacy of, 181; superintendence in, 21–22; Tocqueville and superintendence in, 37–39. *See also* Regimes
Gramsci, Antonio, 82, 92
Great Britain, parliamentary system in, 183–84
Guizot, François, 43
Gwyn, William, 206

Habermas, Jurgen, 117
Hamilton, Alexander: and immigration, 127; and industrialism, 128; on liberal democracy, 22; as political theorist, 6, 11; and separation of powers, 206
Hanson, Russell, 117
Hegel, Georg W. F., 17, 60, 151, 175
Heidegger, Martin, 17, 28
Historicism. *See* Determinism, historical
History: Dahl's view of, 119; Tocqueville's view of, 151–52
Hobbes, Thomas, 15; and constitutionalism, 189–90; as liberal theorist, 116; and separation of powers, 189–90
Hofstadter, Richard, 19
Human nature and liberal democracy, 19–20, 22
Hume, David, 11; as rationalist theorist, 147, 148

Immigration: and agrarianism, 127; Hamilton and, 127
Individualism: and local government, 167–68; and rationalism, 165; and social democracy, 117, 165
Individual rights: constitutionalism and, 9–10, 13, 14, 134, 172; Tocqueville and, 36, 150. *See also* Equality
Industrialism: Hamilton and, 128; Marx and, 128; and promotion of democracy, 127–28; in the United States, 127–28
Inglehart, Robert, 83
Intellectuals: political science and influence of, 170–71; and the press, 171–72; as threat to liberal democracy, 170–71; Tocqueville's opposition to influence of, 152, 154–60, 162–63, 165–66, 173

Jackson, Andrew, and antifederalism, 132–33
Jefferson, Thomas: and agrarianism, 127; on constitutionalism, 11–12; definition of *republic*, 6; *Notes on the State of Virginia*, 16; as political theorist, 11
Judicial activism: and accountability, 210; in American political system, 210
Justice in liberal democracy, 22–23

Kant, Immanuel, 28
Key, V. O.: *The Responsible Electorate*, 76–77

Lamberti, Jean-Claude, on liberal democracy, 19
Laswell, Harold D., 41; on behavioralism, 79–80; on social engineering, 106–7
Law: abstract nature of, in France, 160, 172; change in character of, 172–73; and liberty, 169; organic nature of, in the United States, 160–61, 172; and primary powers, 189–90; and regimes, 177
Liberal democracy, 180; and American Revolution, 11; and behavioralism, 75; communism's opposition to, 174–75; complexity of, 22–23; criticism of, 3–4, 11–12, 23, 89–92; defense of, 91–92; Diamond on, 20; and economic development, 132; and education, 31–32; in Europe, 27; false ideals of, 75; fascism's opposition to, 174; formal principles of, 33–36, 75, 181–82; formal separation of social institutions in, 33–34, 40; Fukuyama and, 175; Hamilton on, 22; and historical determinism, 174–75; and human nature, 19–20, 22; intellectuals as threat to, 170–71; justice in, 22–23; Lamberti on, 19; leftist view of, 5; and liberalism, 115; liberty as goal of, 168, 204–5; and limits of growth, 132; maintenance of, 74–75, 76, 88–89, 90, 93; nature of, 2, 10–12, 19, 22–23, 26–27, 30–31, 55–56, 72–73, 74, 91, 166–67; optimistic future of, 75; and pluralism, 88, 91–92, 99; and policy performance, 88–89; and political culture, 143, 157; and political knowledge, 19–21, 75–76; and political science, 1–2, 16, 23–24, 74, 76, 105–6, 177; and rational choice, 81; and rationalism, 166–67; and religion, 31, 167; and republicanism, 166; rightist

Liberal Democracy *(cont'd)*
view of, 5; scientific approach to, 74–76; and semantic problems, 6–8; and the state, 31, 168; structure of, 5, 6–11, 12, 29, 33–35; superintendence of, 20, 21, 36–39; Tocqueville and, 26–27, 52–53, 143, 157–58, 164, 166; Tocqueville and difficulty of maintaining, 30–32; Tocqueville on, 17–18, 24; and traditionalism, 166–67; Verba on, 72–73, 88

Liberalism: as category of normativism, 116–17; contemporary definition of, 116–17; Dahl and, 129–30; Hobbes as theorist of, 116; and liberal democracy, 115; Locke as theorist of, 115, 116; republicanism opposed to, 115

Libertarianism, 116

Liberty: as goal of liberal democracy, 168, 204–5; and the law, 169; and local government, 168; protection of, in American political system, 204–6; Tocqueville's definition of, 168–69

Limited government and Tocqueville, 35–36

Limits of growth: Barber on, 131–32; Dahl and, 131–32; and liberal democracy, 132

Lindblom, Charles, 23, 34, 89; *Politics and Markets*, 88; as theorist of the developmental Left, 118

Local government: balanced against central government, 163, 173–74; citizen participation in, 161–62; and individualism, 167–68; and liberty, 168; and rationalism, 162, 163, 167–68; Tocqueville on, 161–64, 167–68

Locke, John, 15, 178; and constitutionalism, 189–90; as liberal theorist, 115, 116; and private property, 140

Maass, Arthur, on presidential system, 196

Madison, James: on the Constitution, 179; definition of democracy, 6–7, 9; definition of republic, 6–7; on fundamental sovereignty, 185; as political theorist, 6, 11, 22, 120, 142; and regime types, 105–6; on separation of powers, 187, 190, 206

"Madisonian system," 14–15, 199–200; Dahl on, 205

Maistre, Joseph de, as traditionalist theorist, 149

Manley, John, 89

Marshall, Alfred, 83, 84

Marx, Karl, 17, 28, 122, 140, 151, 152; and economic development, 130–31; and industrialism, 128

Marxism, 118, 119; view of social institutions, 34

Merriam, Charles, 41

Military establishment, American: and promotion of democracy, 126; and world-power status, 125–26

Mill, John Stuart: and regime types, 105–6; on Tocqueville, 26

Montesquieu, Charles de, 11, 19, 34, 41, 59, 96; and constitutionalism, 187, 189–90; and general political science, 53–54, 61, 68–69, 112; and genius of the nation, 46–47, 66; and idea of the "general spirit," 151; influence of, on Tocqueville, 68, 144; and regime types, 52–53, 64; on the republic, 9–10; and separation of powers, 189–90, 191, 206; *The Spirit of the Laws*, 68; view of social history, 43–44, 156

Nation: genius of the, 45–47, 49–50; nature of the, 44–45; political science in the, 57–58, 62–67; and regime types, 57–58, 62–65, 177

Neustadt, Richard, on separation of powers, 188

Nietzsche, Friedrich, 17, 152

Normativism: as approach in political science, 3–4, 24, 70, 73, 92–93, 95–99, 103, 106; communitarianism as category of, 116; critical theory as category of, 117; Dahl on, 114; developmental Left as category of, 118; and history of political science, 115–16; liberalism as category of, 116–17; nature of, 95–96, 115–16; republicanism as category of, 114–16; resurgent in political science, 114–15; and standards of value, 96–97, 114, 117

Notes on the State of Virginia (Jefferson), 16

Nozick, Robert, 21, 116; *Anarchy, State, and Utopia*, 96; as libertarian theorist, 116

Okun, Arthur, 117

"On Removing Certain Impediments to Democracy in the United States" (Dahl), 88–89, 118–19, 141

Parliamentary system: American political system compared to, 200–206; capacity for change in, 203–4; defects of, 183–84; elements of, 182–83, 202;

in Great Britain, 183–84; national variations in, 183; and political parties, 182; proposals for, in the United States, 178–80, 183; separation of powers in, 205–6
Philosophe rationalism. *See* Rationalism (school of philosophy)
Plato, 41, 42; *The Republic*, 179
Pluralism and liberal democracy, 88, 91–92, 99
Pocock, J.G.A., as republican theorist, 115
Policy issues: nature of, 97–98, 101; and regimes, 96–99, 101–2, 201
Policymaking process: in American political system, 192–95, 200–201, 207; collectivism and, 208; and the Constitution, 192–95; elements of, 192; fragmentation of, 207–8; nature of, 195; and presidential system, 193, 200–201; proposed changes in, 209–10; and separation of powers, 192–93, 194, 200–201
Policy performance: and liberal democracy, 88–89; nature of, 101; and regimes, 101–2
Political culture: differences among nations, 144–45, 180–81; and equality, 145; in Europe, 144; and liberal democracy, 143, 157; nature of, 143, 145, 157; and regime types, 145–46; sources of, 144–45; Tocqueville and, 143–45, 176; in the United States, 144, 180–81, 201
Political institutions: definition of, 198; limitations of, 197–98
Political knowledge: and liberal democracy, 19–21, 75–76; nature of, 77, 110; Tocqueville on, 18, 154
Political parties: and the Constitution, 180, 197; and parliamentary system, 182; and separation of powers, 199–200
Political power, 48–49, 197, 199; and regime types, 49–51; Tocqueville and, 49, 51
Political psychology: and behavioralism, 79–82; nature of, 80
Political science (as a discipline): as alternative to rationalism and traditionalism, 145–46; and analysis of regimes, 96–97, 100, 102, 103–6, 109–10; and behavioralism, 71–72, 78–80, 90, 103, 180; and change in orientation, 89, 108–9; and changes in regimes, 111–13; conservatism of, 99–100; general and particular in, 58–61; and historical determinism, 110, 111; historical development of, 41–42, 59–61, 67–69, 72–74, 81–82, 94–95, 175; humanistic approach to, 71–72, 74, 78, 87–92; and influence of intellectuals, 170–71; and knowledge of place, 42–51, 62, 109–10, 112; and liberal democracy, 1–2, 16, 23–24, 74, 76, 105–6, 177; limitations on, 71; in the nation, 57–58, 62–67; nature of, 1–3, 32–33, 41–42, 53, 145; normative approach to, 3–4, 24, 70, 73, 92–93, 95–99, 103, 106; normativism and history of, 115–16; normativism resurgent in, 114–15; and positivism, 95, 113; practical application of, 106–8, 111–13; psychological assumptions of, 81–82; purpose of, 2–3, 24–25, 37–38, 39–40, 47, 72–74, 94, 176; question of activism by, 3–4, 5, 24, 106–7; rational-choice approach to, 70, 78–87, 93; and rationalism, 112–13; realism in, 99; scientific approach to, 3, 15, 24–25, 60, 67–78, 71–72, 74–78, 92–93, 94, 103–7, 119–20; self-consciousness of, 2–3, 75–77; self-examination by, 70–71; significance of research in, 78; and social institutions, 73–74, 108; superintendence function of, 37–38, 39–40; terminology in, 110; Tocqueville and metaphysics of, 59; Tocqueville and purpose of, 29–30, 40, 175–76; Tocqueville on, 154–55; Tocqueville's influence on, 28; training in, 71–73, 77, 78–79, 107; Weber and scientific approach to, 71
Political science, general, 52–56, 60–61, 65; Montesquieu and, 53–54, 61, 68–69, 112; nature of, 54–55, 62, 66–67, 109–10, 111–13, 153–54; objections to, 60–61; Tocqueville and, 53–54, 56, 68–69, 112–13, 153–54, 156–57; and traditionalism, 152–53
Politics and Markets (Lindblom), 88
Politics, The (Aristotle), 68
Populism: and American Whigs, 188; and modern reform movement, 207; Tocqueville opposition to, 161
Positivism and political science, 95, 113
Preface to Democratic Theory, A (Dahl), 205–6
Presidential system: capacity for change in, 203; criticism of, 184, 188–89, 196, 209; elements of, 182–83; Maass on, 196; and policymaking process, 193, 200–201

Press, the: change in character of, 171; in France, 158–59; and intellectuals, 171–72; and public opinion, 171–72; rationalism and, 158; Tocqueville and power of, 158–59; in the United States, 159, 171–72
Primary powers: constitutional allocation of, 185–88, 190, 191–92, 193; definition of, 185; federalist and Whig views of, 188, 191; and law, 189–90. *See also* Separation of powers
Private property, 117, 122; and business corporations, 139–40; Dahl and, 137–40; Locke and, 140
Procedural democracy: and American democratic traditions, 124; Dahl as theorist of, 120; maintenance of, 133; nature of, 120–23; socialist elements of, 120–22
Public opinion: and democracy, 165; formation of, 164–66; and the press, 171–72; and rationalism, 164–65; Tocqueville and, 163, 164–66

Rational choice: and behavioralism, 80–81; Dahl on, 119; empirical basis of, 86–87; and liberal democracy, 81; modeled on economic behavior, 82–87; nature of, 79, 83–84; in political science, 70, 78–87, 93; "soft" variant of, 86–87
Rationalism (school of philosophy): change in orientation of, 148; development of, 147; and free will, 150, 152; French influence on development of, 146–48; generalization in, 147–48; Hume as theorist of, 147, 148; and individualism, 165; and liberal democracy, 166–67; limitations of, 166–69; and local government, 162, 163, 167–68; nature of, 154–55; and political science, 112–13; political science as alternative to, 145–46; as power in Europe, 144–45; and the press, 158; and public opinion, 164–65; and religion, 147; Tocqueville and consequences of, 149–50, 155; Tocqueville on, 146, 147–48, 149–50, 156; traditionalism as reaction to, 146, 148–49, 156
Rawls, John, 116; as social democratic theorist, 116; *A Theory of Justice*, 96
Realism in political science, 99
Reform movement, modern: in American political system, 207–8; and Congress, 207–8; and populism, 207
Regimes: changes in, 50–51, 97, 102–3, 111–13, 140, 141, 152–53; disequilibrium in, 50–51; elements of, 177, 180; and law, 177; maintenance of, 96–97, 98–99, 100, 103–5; nation and, 57–58, 62–65, 177; nature of, 97, 103–4, 181; and policy issues, 96–99, 101–2, 201; and policy performance, 101–2; political analysis of, 96–97, 100, 102, 103–6, 109–10; political culture and types of, 145–46; political power and forms of, 49–51; and standards of value, 96–98; types of, 49–51, 52–53, 55–56, 57–58, 73–74, 76, 101, 104–6, 145, 175. *See also* Government
Religion: and liberal democracy, 31, 167; and rationalism, 147; Tocqueville on, 166–67; and traditionalism, 149
Representative government: balances in, 12–13, 19; constitutionalism and, 12–13; nature of, 12–13; state of, in the United States, 135–36; Tocqueville supports, 161
Republic: citizenship in a, 14–16, 18; compared to democracy, 6–8; contemporary definition of, 6–7; Jefferson's definition of, 6; Madison's definition of, 6–7; Montesquieu on the, 9–10; virtue and the, 10, 14, 18. *See also* Democracy
Republic, The (Plato), 179
Republicanism: Arendt as theorist of, 115; and liberal democracy, 166; nature of, 114–16; opposition of, to liberalism, 115; Pocock as theorist of, 115; and standards of value, 115–16
Responsible Electorate, The (Key), 76–77
Rousseau, Jean-Jacques, 11, 28, 115

Separation of powers: in American political system, 177, 184, 196–97, 200–201, 205–6; and the Constitution, 185–89, 191–92; criticism of, 195–96, 199–200, 210; Dahl and, 205–6; doctrine of, 185, 186–87, 189–91; in *The Federalist*, 206; and foreign affairs, 191–92, 202; Hamilton and, 206; Hobbes and, 189–90; Madison on, 187, 190, 206; Montesquieu and, 189–90, 191, 206; Neustadt on, 188; in parliamentary systems, 205–6; and policymaking process, 192–93, 194, 200–201; and political parties, 199–200; reasoning behind, 186–87; Sundquist on, 204
Shalhope, Robert, on virtue, 115
Smith, Adam, 15, 140

Social democracy, 116, 118; and individualism, 117, 165; Rawls as theorist of, 117
Social engineering, 129–30; Laswell on, 106–7
Social institutions: formally separated in liberal democracy, 33–34, 40; Marxist view of, 34; and political science, 73–74, 108; and the state, 21; state and separation of, 37; Tocqueville and separation of, 34–35, 36–39, 63, 157; traditionalist view of, 149
Socialism, 118; change in orientation of, 130–31; and dislike of Tocqueville, 35; and procedural democracy, 120–22
Spheres of Justice (Walzer), 116
Spirit of the Laws, The (Montesquieu), 68
State: liberal democracy and the, 31, 168; and separation of social institutions, 37; social institutions and the, 21
Strong Democracy (Barber), 115
Sundquist, James, on separation of powers, 204
Superintendence: as function of political science, 37–38, 39–40; in government, 21–22; of liberal democracy, 20, 21, 36–39

Theory of Justice, A (Rawls), 96
Tocqueville, Alexis de, 41, 42, 96; and balance between central and local government, 163, 173; on Burke, 153–54; on citizenship, 18; and conditions for democracy in the United States, 143–44, 166–70; and consequences of rationalism, 149–50; and consequences of traditionalism, 149–50; conservative dislike of, 35; on constitutionalism, 13; definition of democracy, 44; definition of liberty, 168–69; *Democracy in America*, 16–17, 26–27, 68, 143, 153; and difficulty of maintaining liberal democracy, 30–32; and equality, 26, 31, 137, 175; errors of, 29; and free will, 152–53; and French Revolution, 146; and generalization, 157–58; and general political science, 53–54, 56, 68–69, 112–13, 153–54, 156–57; and individual rights, 36, 150; influence of, on political science, 28; on the legal profession, 160–61; and liberal democracy, 26–27, 52–53, 143, 157–58, 164, 166; on liberal democracy, 16–17, 24; and limited government, 35–36; on local government, 161–64; and metaphysics of political science, 59; Mill on, 26; Montesquieu's influence on, 68, 144; and natural right, 162–63; opposition of, to intellectuals' influence, 152, 154–60, 162–63, 165–66, 173; opposition of, to populism, 161; and political culture, 143–45, 176; on political knowledge, 18, 154; and political power, 49, 51; on political science, 154–55; as political theorist, 26–29; and power of the press, 158–59; and public opinion, 163, 164–66; purpose of, in visiting the United States, 26–27, 52, 143; and purpose of political science, 29–30, 40, 175–76; on rationalism, 146, 147–48, 149–50, 156; and regime types, 52–53, 63–64, 105–6; on religion, 166–67; and separation of social institutions, 34–35, 36–39, 63, 157; socialist dislike of, 35; and superintendence in government, 37–39; supports local government, 161–63, 167–68; supports representative democracy, 161; on traditionalism, 148–53; on truth, 155–56; view of history, 151–52; view of social history, 43–45, 156
Traditionalism (school of philosophy): Burke as theorist of, 146, 148–49, 151; and free will, 151–52; and general political science, 152–53; and historical determinism, 151–52; and idea of the "general spirit," 151; and liberal democracy, 166–67; Maistre as theorist of, 149; Montesquieu as theorist of, 148, 151; nature of, 148–49, 150–51; political science as alternative to, 145–46; as power in Europe, 144–45; as reaction to rationalism, 146, 148–49, 156; and religion, 149; Tocqueville and consequences of, 149–50, 155; Tocqueville on, 148–53; view of social institutions, 149
Troeltsch, Ernst, 65
Truman, David, on behavioralism, 79

United States: antifederalism as tradition in, 121–23, 164, 205; Dahl on democratic evolution in, 118–42; development of welfare-state capitalism in, 119, 126–32; federalism as tradition in, 58; growth of, as intellectual center, 169–71; industrialism in, 127–28; military establishment and world-power status, 125–26; organic nature of the law in, 160–61, 172; political culture in, 144, 180–81, 201; the

United States *(cont'd)*
press in, 159, 171–72; procedural democracy and democratic traditions in, 124; proposals for parliamentary system in, 178–80, 183; state of representative democracy in, 135–36; Tocqueville's conditions for democracy in, 143–44, 166–70; Tocqueville's purpose in visiting, 26–27, 52, 143; and world-power status, 119, 125–26
United States Congress, 84–86, 180; and foreign affairs, 209–10; and modern reform movement, 207–8
United States Constitution, 115, 164, 172; and allocation of primary powers, 185–88, 190, 191–92, 193; and antifederalism, 125, 187; antimajoritarian elements of, 133–35; and Committee on the Constitutional System, 178–80; criticism of, 178–80, 184, 187, 195–97; Cutler on, 178; Dahl's analysis of, 133–35; and foreign affairs, 192; and formal separation of powers, 185–89, 191–92; limitations of proposed changes in, 199–200; Madison on, 179; and policymaking process, 192–95; and political parties, 180, 197; proposed changes in, 177, 180, 181, 196–200; and proposed "zero-based" reforms, 178–80, 183, 200; Wilson as critic of, 177, 195
United States political system: accountability in, 203, 210; capacity for change in, 203–4; collectivism in, 208–9; compared to parliamentary system, 200–206; efficiency of, 202–3; fundamental changes in, 207–10; and fundamental sovereignty, 185, 193; judicial activism in, 210; modern reform movement in, 207–8; nature of, 200–206; and policymaking process, 192–95, 200–201, 207; possible superiority of, 182; protection of liberty in, 204–6; and separation of powers, 177, 184, 196–97, 200–201, 205–6; structure of, 184–95, 196–97; Whiggism in, 209–10

Value: normativism and standards of, 96–97, 114, 117; republicanism and standards of, 115–16
Verba, Sidney, on liberal democracy, 72–73, 88
Virtue: and the republic, 10, 14, 18; Shalhope on, 115

Walzer, Michael: *Spheres of Justice,* 116
Weber, Max, 28; and scientific approach to political science, 71
Welfare-state capitalism: and bureaucracy, 129–30; Dahl's criticisms of, 128–30; development of, in the United States, 119, 126–32; purpose of, 129
Whiggism in American political system, 209–10
Wildavsky, Aaron, 82
Wilson, Woodrow, as critic of the Constitution, 177, 195
Wood, Gordon, 115

"Zero-based" reforms, proposed for the Constitution, 178–80, 183, 200

Designed by Patricia Crowder.

Composed by Brushwood Graphics, Inc., in Aster text and Serifa display.
Printed by Bookcrafters, Inc., on 50-lb. Booktext Natural.

Lightning Source UK Ltd.
Milton Keynes UK
UKHW011831200123
415700UK00001B/26

9 780801 845116